D1478979

TEMPERAMENT: EARLY DEVELOPING PERSONALITY TRAITS

TEMPERAMENT: EARLY DEVELOPING PERSONALITY TRAITS

ARNOLD H. BUSS
University of Texas

ROBERT PLOMIN
University of Colorado

LAWRENCE ERLBAUM ASSOCIATES, PUBLISHERS
1984   Hillsdale, New Jersey   London

Lawrence Erlbaum Associates, Inc., Publishers
365 Broadway
Hillsdale, New Jersey 07642

Library of Congress Cataloging in Publication Data

Buss, Arnold Herbert, 1924-
Temperament: early developing personality traits.

Bibliography: p.
Includes indexes.
1. Temperament. 2. Personality in children.
3. Arousal (Physiology) 4. Emotions. I. Plomin,
Robert, 1948-   . II. Title.
BF798.B868 1984   155.4'13   84-13636
ISBN 0-89859-415-4

Printed in the United States of America
10 9 8 7 6 5 4 3 2 1

Contents

1 Introduction

The modern history of temperament dates back only three decades to the book *Personality and Temperament* by Diamond (1957). Unlike the other personality texts of that era, it emphasized the constitutional origins of personality:

> A crucial problem in the study of personality is to determine what are the most fundamental respects in which individuals differ from each other. All attempts to do this on the basis of observation of adult human behavior, no matter how sophisticated in either a statistical or a clinical sense, have the common failing that they are unable to distinguish between the essential foundations of individuality and its cultural elaboration. (pp. 3–4)

These essential foundations would not be restricted to humans, for "The human being, whatever else he may be, is first of all an animal, and must be understood as such" (p. 4).

Diamond went on to describe four temperaments shared by all primates and to some extent, by social mammals: fearfulness, aggressiveness, affiliativeness, and impulsiveness. He conducted no research on human behavior, however, nor did he provide any instruments to assess his temperaments. Furthermore, the 1950s were marked by a deep and pervasive environmentalism which, in this country at least, rejected the possibility of built-in tendencies and the relevance of animal behavior for the understanding of human personality. In this atmosphere, Diamond's contribution was ignored and subsequently has rarely been mentioned.

From a different perspective, pediatric researchers of three decades ago were rebelling against the psychoanalytic approach and the environmentalism that dominated child development. Their new approach highlighted the 1960s, especially two books by Thomas, Chess, and their colleagues (1963, 1968). These investigators sought the personality traits that were both related to problems of early childhood and likely to lead to later problems or adjustment. They delineated nine temperaments in young children and assessed these temperaments by interviewing parents; the interviews were later complemented by parental questionnaires. The pediatric approach has generated an outpouring of research, and it currently dominates the area of temperament.

1

In parallel with the first two developments, behavioral genetics emerged as a strong trend in the 1960s. Following the lead of Diamond and earlier behavioral genetics research, we published a theory of temperament in 1975. This was a return to the personality approach to temperament, again with an emphasis on tendencies that have an evolutionary heritage. We provided measures of the temperaments, demonstrated their heritability, and suggested their course of development.

Thus the recent history of temperament is highlighted by four books: Diamond's in the 1950s, that of Thomas, Chess and their colleagues in the 1960s, and our book and another by Thomas and Chess in the 1970s. Meanwhile, developmental psychology surged forward and became a major force in psychology. The most recent manifestation of this trend has been a focus on infancy. During the past few years, infancy researchers have been investigating individual differences in infancy and calling these personality traits temperaments. Their articles and book chapters signal the era of the 1980s.

The present era is marked by three major perspectives of temperament: pediatrics, individual differences in infants, and inherited personality traits that appear early in life. Whatever the diversity of these perspectives, they converge on personality traits that develop early in life, hence the title of this book. Tendencies that start in infancy, whether personality or other tendencies, are thought to be *constitutional* in origin. This broad term comprises inheritance, prenatal events, and postnatal events. Though such breadth is convenient, its vagueness poses problems for its scientific usefulness and this merits discussion. This we have done in Chapter 2, which also outlines temperament in our mammalian and primate ancestors. Presumably, temperament evolved in our forebears and was maintained during the evolution of the human species, for it is difficult to believe that most constitutional tendencies are uniquely human.

Approaches to temperament other than our own may be divided into two groups. The first consists of the pediatric approach of Thomas, Chess, and their colleagues (1963, 1968, 1977) and that of Brazelton (1973). The theory of Thomas and Chess has led to more published research than any other perspective and therefore warrants a chapter of its own, with the brief addition of Brazelton's work at the end of Chapter 3.

The second group of approaches to temperament derives from an interest in individual differences among infants. Infants differ in many ways, but one of the most striking dimensions of variation is *arousal*. Even neonates vary in their sleep-wakefulness cycle, their alertness when awake, and their level of distress when they are hungry or uncomfortable. Arousal, especially emotional arousal, tends to consist of diffuse behavioral reactions which require little from the young organism in the way of learning or skill. Such diffuse reactions occur early and therefore may be regarded as constitutional in origin. Any investigator who observes infants even briefly will see that they vary considerably in their emotional reactions. It is therefore no surprise that students of individual differences among infants tend to focus on arousal. Their focus is not always the same, but there is sufficient overlap for them to be included in the chapter on arousal. Before discussing their individual contributions, however, some background on arousal is necessary. Therefore, Chapter 4 begins with a section on the concept of arousal, and the three approaches to arousal in infants are then reviewed. All of these approaches justify their use of the term *temperament* by referring to Allport's definition:

> *Temperament refers to the characteristic phenomena of an individual's emotional nature, including his susceptibility to emotional stimulation, his customary strength and speed of response, the quality of his prevailing mood, and all the peculiarities of fluctuation and intensity of mood, these phenomena being regarded as dependent upon constitutional make-up and therefore largely hereditary in origin* (1961, p. 34).

As may be seen, this definition is sufficiently broad to support views of temperament as emotional in nature or as originating constitutionally or genetically.

The remainder of the book deals with our approach to temperament. Though we have retained much of the theory stated in our 1975 book, there are changes. Our approach to activity temperament is the same, but there are theoretical additions to the temperaments of emotionality and sociability. Chapter 5 starts with a background exposition of emotions, placing high and low arousal emotions in the context of an evolutionary scheme. Most of the chapter consists of elaborations of our previous theory of emotionality as a temperament. Sociability is discussed in Chapter 6, which begins with the motives and rewards of social interaction and then relates them to the temperament of sociability. Older children and adults seek others for slightly different reasons than do infants, which leads us to theorize about the developmental course of sociability. This temperament can easily be confused with shyness and also with extraversion; the necessary distinctions complete the chapter.

Previously, we offered five criteria of temperament, the crucial one being inheritance. We have retained inheritance as crucial and added presence early in life as an ancillary part of the definition. These issues are discussed in Chapter 7, along with our reasons for dropping impulsivity as a temperament. In this chapter, we also elaborate our ideas about how emotionality, activity, and sociability can affect the environment or modify its impact. Also included are details of new measuring instruments for the three temperaments.

A fundamental assumption in our theory is that some personality traits are inherited. It does *not* follow from this assumption that all or even most personality traits are inherited. Nor does it follow that the inherited tendencies are immutable, for they can certainly be modified by environmental influences. We do assume, however, that like any well-entrenched disposition, temperaments will resist modification, and no one should expect dramatic changes. Nor should anyone be surprised that heredity can account for only a portion of the variance of temperaments, which means that environment must play an important role. We raise these issues because inheritance seems to be a controversial topic, about which there may be more heat than light. Thus as a prelude to presenting data on our temperaments, we offer some essentials of behavioral genetics in Chapter 8. Here we discuss not only genes and behavior but also stability during development, gene-environmental interaction and correlation, whether some personality dispositions are more heritable than others, and also the components of the environment.

With this background, we review behavioral genetics data on our three temperaments: emotionality, activity, and sociability (Chapter 9). Though these three temperaments are not fixed and constant, they may be expected to display reasonable stability throughout childhood. Furthermore, though temperaments are susceptible to environmental influence, they may be difficult to modify. Data bearing on these two issues, continuity during development and the environment's impact, are presented in Chapter 10.

We conclude in Chapter 11 by reviewing the salient aspects of our theory and showing how it differs from other approaches to temperament. We see temperaments as one class of personality traits, which means that issues currently being debated in the area of personality, especially breadth and stability of traits need to be discussed. Finally, we speculate about future directions for the study of temperaments.

2 Evolution and Development

Temperament researchers typically come from the disciplines of pediatrics, personality, or infancy research. Though these various perspectives have led to diverse conceptualizations of temperament, they do converge on the assumption that temperament involves *early-developing personality traits*. *Traits* are individual differences that are relatively enduring across time and situations. *Personality* is meant to exclude other traits such as physical and physiological characteristics and, by convention, intelligence.

The focus on infancy and childhood assumes that biological influences are more important in traits that develop early than in traits that emerge later in development. Some scientists hesitate to cope with the issue of etiology, but the clear implication is that these early-developing traits are biological in origin. *Biological* in this sense is loosely defined to include prenatal and perinatal events—usually referred to as *constitutional*—as well as physiological factors and genetics.

EVOLUTION AND EARLY DEVELOPING TRAITS

We assume that the personality traits that appear in infancy derive from millions of years of evolutionary processes. If this were true, humans would be likely to share these traits with other animals, especially those closest in the evolutionary line that led to humans. Clearly, no theory of temperament will stand or fall on whether human personality traits may also be observed in other species. The presence of such traits in other species, however, is consistent with the idea that these early-developing traits have an evolutionary heritage.

Two preliminary issues should be mentioned. Unlike comparative psychologists (e.g., Diamond, 1957), we are concerned with individual differences within a species rather than modal personality types that characterize a species. A second issue relates to evolutionary processes that can account for the appearance of similar traits across species. To argue that traits are adaptive usually connotes directional selection—that more is better. This creates a problem in that directional selection reduces

5

genetic variability within a species. Thus, a trait tightly linked to reproductive fitness would cease to exist as an individual differences trait because no variability within the species would be tolerated by natural selection.

However, population geneticists no longer focus on directional selection exclusively and have come to recognize the importance of other types of selection which, unlike directional selection, serve to maintain genetic variability (Plomin, 1981). Such *stabilizing selection* seems more relevant to temperament than does directional selection. Consider sociability, for example. Though the human animal is indeed highly social, directional selection for high sociability could lead to individuals unable to act alone. It would be more adaptive to select for a *range* of sociability, some individuals being more sociable than others. Stabilizing selection of this sort, which conserves genetic variability within the species, is reflected in heritable traits. Obvious examples are variations in height and intelligence. If stabilizing selection has been important in our evolutionary past, traits seen in humans are likely to occur in other primates and even in other mammals.

Primates

The similarity between humans and chimpanzees in social and emotional behavior was observed decades ago by Robert Yerkes, a pioneer primatologist: "Long and intimate acquaintance with the animals enables one to recognize and distinguish expressions of shyness, timidity, fear, terror; of suspicion, distrust, resentment, antagonism, anger, rage; of interest, curiosity, excitement, elation, contentment, pleasure; of confidence, friendliness, familiarity, sympathy, affection; of disappointment, discouragement, loneliness, melancholy, and depression" (1943, p. 29). As a species, chimpanzees might share all these tendencies with humans and still not be characterized by the same set of *individual differences*. Yerkes suggests that they do have similar personality traits and may be different from each other as we are:

> Individuality expresses itself entertainingly, and also expressively, in temperament or disposition. This is well illustrated by the following contrasts. Wendy is willful, obstinate, unpredictable, courageous, rash, determined, persistent, unaffectionate. . . . . Bill, one of the first chimpanzees I came to know intimately, may be fairly described as her opposite. He was notably good-natured, even-tempered, buoyant, suggestible, cooperative, friendly and adaptable, dependable, cautious, and, for a male, quite timid, conservative, observant, alert, gentle, and affectionate. (p. 33)

These observations of personality traits are entirely consistent with the accounts of the Gardners (1969) and the Kelloggs (1933) with home-reared chimpanzees and of Jane Goodall (1971) who could easily recognize chimpanzees in the wild not only by appearance but also by personality traits.

More recently, chimpanzees were closely observed in a situation midway between captivity and the free-ranging situation of the wild (de Waal, 1982). After several years of watching these animals, the ethologists could easily characterize their individuality. The fastest and brightest chimpanzee in the group is Nikki: "His boundless energy and boisterous, provocative behavior has had the effect of a catalyst. Bit by bit he has disrupted the structure of the group. On cold days Nikki keeps the others warm with his constant activity and on hot days he disturbs their sleep" (p. 70). Yeroen is described as slow-moving, crafty, and calculating, as well as someone who could not be trusted. Dandy is something of a clown, but his guile and trickery may have been responsible for several attempted escapes. Franje is timid and fearful; she attempts to avoid any confrontation or danger and is always the first to give the alarm.

These observations of chimpanzees have been complemented by systematic observations of rhesus monkeys over periods as long as 4 years (Stevenson-Hinde, Stillwell-Barnes, & Zung, 1980). Observers rated each member of a colony of monkeys for a number of personality traits. The ratings were collated, correlated, and subjected to a principal components analysis, which yielded three components: (1) fearful, tense, subordinate versus aggressive, effective, confident; (2) slow, equable versus active, excitable; and (3) solitary versus sociable. These three bipolar dimensions, which seem to involve fearfulness, activity, and sociability, do not offer an exhaustive description of the personality traits of the monkeys, but they do provide dimensions directly comparable to those seen in human children.

These data are consistent with earlier findings on rhesus monkeys who were deprived of their mothers but allowed to play with peers (Chamove, Eysenck, & Harlow, 1972). Observations of the monkeys' play were correlated, and three factors emerged from the correlation matrix: fearfulness, hostility, and affiliativeness. Parenthetically, the first two are represented in our temperament of emotionality, and affiliativeness is synonymous with our temperament of sociability.

This research suggests that temperaments exist in primates, but little is known of the origins of such individual differences in primates, though recent research by Suomi (1982) suggests some genetic influence on fearfulness in rhesus monkeys. Much more is known about individual differences and their etiology in other mammals, especially dogs and rodents.

Fearfulness in Dogs

Dogs tend not to be studied by behavioral genetic researchers because they are slow breeders and no truly inbred strains are available. However, their familiarity and human-like social behavior make research with dogs worth mentioning. Some very old accounts of behavioral differences among breeds of dogs have been recorded (Scott & Fuller, 1965). For example, in 1576, the earliest English book on dogs classified breeds primarily on the basis of what they were bred for: terriers that would creep into burrows to drive out small animals, and spaniels that would creep up on birds and then spring to frighten the birds into a hunter's net. With the advent of the shotgun, spaniels were bred to point rather than to crouch, though cocker spaniels still crouch when frightened. The author of a 1686 book expressed particular interest in the temperament of dog breeds. For example, "*Spaniels* by *Nature* are very loving, surpassing all other Creatures, for in *Heat* and *Cold, Wet* and *Dry, Day* and *Night,* they will not forsake their *Master*" (cited by Scott & Fuller, 1965, p. 47).

Studies of dogs in the 1940s found significant breed and hybrid differences using laboratory measures of behavior (Fuller & Thompson, 1960). The most important study of temperament in dogs, conducted by Scott and Fuller (1965), focused on emotional behavior and socialization. During the 20-year study, five purebreds—basenji, beagle, cocker spaniel, Shetland sheepdog, and wirehaired fox terrier—were tested on an extensive battery of tests during the first year of life under standard environmental conditions. The well-known differences among the breeds reflect their breeding history. Spaniels are people-oriented and nonaggressive; terriers are more aggressive; basenjis are fearful of people until a few months old, at which time they can be rapidly tamed; and Shetland sheep dogs are quite responsive to people and to training throughout development.

Scott and Fuller (1965) assessed fearfulness in a variety of conditions including a threatening approach and electric shock while the dogs were restrained in a Pavlov stand:

> A few subjects reacted so violently to simple restriction of movement that testing had to be discontinued or carried out in a modified form. Even more common were dogs which slumped down in the harness and were so inhibited throughout that little differentiation of reactivity was detectable from episode to episode. These two types corresponded to Pavlov's (1928) "excitable" and "inhibited" animals which he tested under similar conditions. Between these two classes, there was an enormous range of variability. (p. 195)

To a large extent, fearfulness was strain specific. Most of 13 physiological and behavioral measures yielded significant breed differences, which accounted for 22% to 41% of the variance. In general, Shetland sheep dogs and cocker spaniels were less fearful at all ages than the other breeds.

There were also developmental trends. Basenjis and beagles became more fearful during the first year, cocker spaniels and fox terriers became less fearful, and Shetland sheep dogs remained at a low level of fearfulness throughout the first year. The authors suggest that dogs tend to converge on their breed norms during the first year.

This study also provides some dramatic examples of genotype-environment interaction, specifically of breed with trainability. Thus cocker spaniels and sheep dogs are less fearful in most training situations than the other breeds. Scott and Fuller (1965) summarize their research on fearfulness by noting, "All this strongly supports the conclusion that heredity greatly affects the expression of emotional behavior and also that differences in emotional behavior form a prominent part of the characteristic behavior of breeds and individuals" (p. 204).

Fearfulness in Mice and Rats

Some of the earliest research on temperament focused on activity and fearfulness in rats and mice (Fuller & Thompson, 1960). This research documents not only the existence of temperamental characteristics in other mammalian species but also genetic origin of these traits. For example, activity in running wheels was the target of a successful selection experiment 50 years ago (Rundquist, 1933). In the same decade, Hall (1938) conducted a selection study of high and low fearfulness in rats in an open-field apparatus. Nocturnal mammals such as rats and mice defecate, urinate, and "freeze" in a large, brightly lit, open-field arena, and these measures are used to infer fearfulness. Hall selected rats for the number of days out of 12 in which defecation or urination occurred. He obtained a threefold average increase in fearfulness. Selection for decreased fearfulness was not successful beyond the first selected generation, perhaps because a "floor" was reached for the fearfulness score. Another study of fearfulness in rats selected for both activity and defecation (Broadhurst, 1958, 1960) and replicated Hall's results. Broadhurst (1975) also generated two lines of rats, called the Maudsley Reactive and Maudsley Nonreactive lines, which are widely used in research on emotionality.

The longest behavioral selection study of mammals, involving 30 generations of selection, focused on open-field activity in mice (DeFries, Gervais, & Thomas, 1978). Selection was so successful that eventually there was no overlap between the two lines of mice. Comparisons among inbred strains of mice have also demonstrated genetic involvement in individual differences in fearfulness. One of the first large-scale investigations compared 14 inbred strains of mice on a defecation measure and found greater than eightfold differences among the inbred strains (Thompson, 1953).

*   *   *   *

In summary, personality traits commonly observed to develop early in human life are also found in other primates and even in nonprimate mammals. Genetic influences on the development of these individual differences have been documented. These results are consistent with the view that such early-developing personality traits have a biological origin that stretches back into our evolutionary past.

CULTURE AND EARLY DEVELOPING TRAITS

If early-appearing personality traits are part of our evolutionary heritage, we might expect such traits to be present in all cultures. Though cultures differ in their socialization practices, such socialization comes into play primarily *after* infancy. Thus the traits common to all cultures are likely to be found early in life.

As in cross-species comparisons, the focus is on individual differences within cultures, not with average differences among cultures. Much of the anthropological literature, beginning with Margaret Mead's study, *Coming of Age in Samoa* (1949), emphasized average differences among cultures, such differences presumably demonstrating the importance of nurture over nature in the origin of personality. Such average differences among cultures have few implications for the origin of individual differences within cultures. Perhaps one reason for the sharp disagreements among cultural anthropologists—for example, Derek Freeman's book (1983) which reverses Mead's interpretations of Samoan culture—is that individual differences within a culture make it difficult to discover the typical personality of a culture.

This focus on modal personality resulted in the neglect of individual differences in personality in different cultures until the recent wave of interest in temperament. Though average differences among cultures have been found, similar early-developing individual differences (personality traits) have emerged in all countries studied to date, including Finland (Huttunen & Nyman, 1982), India (Malhotra, Randhawa, & Malhotra, 1983), the Netherlands (Leenders, 1981), Norway (Torgersen, 1982), Puerto Ricans in New York (Thomas & Chess, 1977), Sweden (Persson-Blennow, & McNeil, 1980), Taiwan (Hsu, Stigler, Hong, Soong, & Liang, in press), and three East African tribes (DeVries & Sameroff, reported in Thomas & Chess, 1977), in addition to English-speaking countries.

Thus, similar dimensions of early-developing personality traits appear in all cultures studied. These findings are consistent with the hypothesis that evolution has shaped these traits but of course do not constitute proof.

CONSTITUTION AND EARLY ENVIRONMENT

There are individual differences in personality-relevant behavior soon after birth. On the first day of life, babies differ considerably in the intensity and amount of crying, and such differences are stable during the first few days (Korner, Hutchinson, Koperski, Kraemer, & Schneider, 1981), though neonatal variability may not predict later behavior (Sameroff, Krafchuk, & Bakow, 1978). Thomas and Chess suggest that "temperamental individuality is well established by the time the infant is two to three months old. The origins of temperament must therefore be sought in the factors reviewed in this chapter: genetic, prenatal, and early postnatal parental influences" (1977, pp. 152–153).

Though such early personality traits might be inherited, let us assume for the moment that inheritance is an insufficient explanation. We cannot invoke the usual environmental or experiental causes as an explanation because the traits occur too early in life. We are forced by this logic to seek chemical or biological causes that occur during embryonic or fetal development (prenatal) or around the period of birth (perinatal). Early postnatal experiences are also sometimes included in definitions of *constitution*.

A variety of *prenatal* influences on the offspring are well documented in the medical literature. In addition to a wide range of abnormalities caused by chemical or physical anomalies, well known to physicians, the general public has been alerted to the damage to fetuses caused by the tranquilizer thalidomide and by the mother's smoking or drinking. These facts tell us that the prenatal environment can be an important cause of *biological abnormality* in the offspring. Biological variations in health—the intactness of the organism—comprise one kind of individual differences. They must be distinguished from differences in *personality traits among biologically normal individuals*. If this distinction were not maintained, those who studied temperament in children would be forced to include in their purview a large list of biological abnormalities.

In contrast to the abundant literature on prenatal causes of biological abnormality, there is a sparse literature on prenatal causes of personality trait differences among normal children (Kopp & Parmelee, 1979). So far as we know, the only trait for which such causes have been established is intelligence. Twins and babies born prematurely are known to have a lower IQ than the average of the population. However, the Collaborative Perinatal Project, which includes over 26,000 children, suggests that the combination of prenatal/perinatal factors explains less than 4% of the variance of IQ by 4 years of age (Broman, Nichols, & Kennedy, 1975). Though twins tend to be born premature and with low birth weights, twin decrements in verbal performance disappear by school age (Wilson,

1978). The current view is that prenatal and perinatal factors have few long-term effects unless the child's environment continues to be adverse (Sameroff & Chandler, 1975).

Surprisingly little work has been done on prenatal and perinatal antecedents of temperaments. Carey, Lipton, and Meyers (1974) studied the effect of maternal pregnancy anxiety on children's "difficult temperament." Adoptive mothers of 41 adopted children rated the children's temperament. Presumably, the biological mothers who relinquished the children for adoption had been anxious during an unwanted pregnancy, and their anxiety might somehow cause their children to be difficult. However, the adoptive mothers of these children rated them as no more difficult than a sample of 200 control infants who were rated by their natural mothers. Within the sample of adopted infants, however, infants whose biological mothers had been especially anxious were more likely to be rated as difficult by their adoptive mothers; thus, the explanation might also be genetic. Some other suggestive evidence along these lines has been reported (Thomas & Chess, 1977). Birth complications and prematurity appear unrelated to temperament (Hertzig, 1974; Torgersen, 1973). Even a sample of mentally retarded infants did not differ in temperament from normal samples (Thomas & Chess, 1977). Results such as these led Thomas and Chess to conclude: "Other prenatal and perinatal traumata, such as obstetrical and birth difficulties or perinatal brain damage, do not appear to significantly influence temperamental characteristic" (p. 141).

During the past decade or so, a few obstetricians have claimed that the usual delivery of newborn infants in hospitals causes psychological trauma and perhaps even a drop in intelligence. Quiet, dark surroundings are said to be best when the baby is born, and it should never be spanked to induce breathing. Research has begun to test these speculations, but even if true, they would not establish that method of birth has any long-term impact on the offspring.

There are *perinatal* events of considerable importance, but they are the well-documented impacts of insufficient or excessive oxygen, problems attending breech birth, Caesarian sections, and so on. Such events can cause biological abnormalities, but again there is no evidence that they influence the development of personality traits in normal children. Klaus and Kennell (1977), in their influential book *Maternal-Infant Bonding,* state that the "original mother-infant bond is the wellspring for all the infant's subsequent attachments and is the formative relationship in the course of which the child develops a sense of himself" (p. 1), and that "we strongly believe that an essential principle of attachment is that there is a *sensitive period* in the first minutes and hours after an infant's birth which is optimal for the parent-infant attachment" (pp. 65–66). Though Klaus and Kennell present some evidence to support their claim, the evidence can also be interpreted so as not to support their claim (Chess & Thomas, 1982).

The absence of current evidence does not deny that prenatal or perinatal events *might* influence personality development. Such vague possibilities, however, offer no scientific basis for invoking the earliest environment as an important source of variation in personality traits.

In the absence of evidence, why do some scientists speculate about prenatal and perinatal influences on personality traits? There appear to be three reasons. First, some scientists prefer to use the term *constitutional* to include all events prior to early infancy: genetic, prenatal, and perinatal. They suggest that there is simply not enough evidence to indicate which of these three causes, or their combinations, account for early-appearing personality traits.

Second, some scientists expand the term *constitutional* to include any aspect of one's physical make-up, often interpreting physical correlates of behavior as causal. After Galen's humoral theory of temperament, the major constitutional theory was Sheldon's (1942), which related body types to temperament. Even if there were better evidence for Sheldon's theory than now exists, it could not be assumed that body type causes temperamental differences among children. The effect of body type on temperament would be more likely to be mediated environmentally, perhaps in the way people react to children with different body builds.

Modern research emphasizes physiological and neural correlates rather than anatomical factors. For example, research on fearfulness in animals, reviewed earlier, has included diverse studies of physiological, hormonal, and pharmacological correlates of fearfulness (Fuller & Thompson, 1978). Research on temperament in humans may move in this direction as well, with signs of the shift already in the literature (e.g., Garcia-Coll, Kagan & Reznick, 1983; Tennes, Downey & Vernadakis, 1977). For this reason, lessons learned from the animal research are timely. Thus, researchers first guessed that fearfulness was related to endocrine gland activity, but little evidence accrued to support this hypothesis. It seems to be an emerging principle that there is no direct, simple relationship between behavior and hormones, enzymes, or neurotransmitters; current thinking focuses on neural sensitivity to these physiological factors. Most human researchers now know better than to seek any simple physiological correlate of temperament. Moreover, we cannot assume that such correlates are causal, that biological characters are any more heritable than behavioral ones, or that biological correlates are linked genetically to behavior (see Plomin & Deitrich, 1982, for further discussion).

A third reason for invoking prenatal and perinatal causes is that for some scientists, genetic causation is anathema. The presence of personality traits early in infancy cannot be explained by the usual environmental influences—parents, peers, socializing agents, everyday experience—which poses a problem for those who insist on environmental causation. A last resort is available, however, in the environment preceding early infancy: the perinatal and prenatal periods. If these early environments could be shown to influence personality, the extreme environmental position would be tenable and there could be a continuing denial of genetic causation. Given these strong reasons for invoking early environment as a cause, it is easy to see how the position can be maintained in the absence of evidence.

CONTINUITY AND CHANGE

Scientists' views on the issue of change and continuity of temperament depend upon their perspective. Infancy researchers tend to ignore the later developmental course of temperament. The personality researchers who seek the developmental origins of personality traits expect consistencies between temperaments in early childhood and adult personality traits. Pediatric researchers are less interested in the continuity of traits throughout development than in prediction of clinically relevant outcomes from early temperament. Thus, temperament researchers take different positions on the issue of continuity, though most would probably expect greater stability for temperamental characteristics than for other personality traits.

Favoring continuity rather than change derives from temperament's early appearance and biological foundations. However, neither early appearance nor biological etiology necessarily implies stability. For example, crying appears early in life but shows little rank-order stability past infancy. Biological influences are sources of change as well as continuity in development, as discussed in Chapter 8.

What do the data suggest concerning continuity/discontinuity? It is useful to put temperament in the perspective of other characteristics. Height is stable from the first year of life, yielding correlations greater than .70 with adult height. Infant and adult weight correlate about .50. For both height and weight, stability correlations do not change substantially during infancy and early childhood. A different pattern of stability is shown by IQ. Though IQ sources are reliable in infancy, long-term stability of infant scores is negligible. Stability increases sharply after infancy, reaching levels of stability similar to height by the early school years.

Temperaments display yet another pattern. Data from the New York Longitudinal Study (Thomas & Chess, 1977) show median year-to-year correlations of about .30, with no increase from 1 to 5 years of age. Longer intervals produce lower correlations: From the first to the fifth year of life, the median correlation was .10. Activity and adaptability (related to shyness and sociability) tend to be modestly more stable than other traits. Similar results have been found by other investigators (Huttunen & Nyman, 1982; McDevitt, 1976; McDevitt & Carey, 1978, 1981). Later in childhood, temperament appears to become more stable (Buss & Plomin, 1975). For example, over a 4.4-year span from 3–7 years to 8–12 years, a median correlation of .42, with a range from .40 to .59, was obtained for a parental rating instrument assessing several temperamental dimensions (Hegvik, McDevitt, & Carey, 1981).

Some temperaments may show stability, others not. How might we select those likely to be stable? One possibility is early-developing traits that have already been identified in adults. Surely no one would be surprised if personality traits found in adulthood could be traced back to origins in early childhood. Also, one might expect that early-developing traits of genetic origin would be likely to persist. In brief, the observed instability of most of the currently identified temperaments may be due to faulty selection of the traits designated as temperaments. Perhaps if personality traits were selected with the above two characteristics in mind, greater stability would be found.

Nonetheless, temperament is unlikely to be constant during development. The dramatic cognitive, social, and emotional changes wrought during the transition from infancy to early childhood surely affect temperament. At the least, such changes may affect the behavioral expression of temperament, which will require the search for heterotypic continuity rather than homotypic continuity (Kagan, 1971). Developmental changes in the biological and environmental factors might also affect the organization of temperament during the transition from infancy to childhood.

In summary, temperaments may be expected to display both continuity and change over the course of development. Though at first glance this statement might seem contradictory and difficult to test, it is neither. The events of childhood are likely to modify the personality tendencies that have been built in, and therefore temperaments must undergo change. Like other strong dispositions, however, temperaments resist change and therefore manifest at least some stability over time. Correlations over time are elevated by the inherited nature of temperaments but diminished by the environmental events that modify temperaments. Thus we should expect stability correlations that are neither near 1.00 nor near 0. Instead, we should expect stability coefficients in the .30 to .50 range. Whether they are in the upper or lower limit of this range may well depend on appropriate selection of temperaments and adequate measurement of them. The identification of particular temperaments and their assessment vary considerably from one theoretical approach to the next, as we shall see in the next two chapters.

3 The Pediatric Approach

This perspective has been favored by those involved in the mental and physical health of children. It originated with dissatisfaction several decades ago with the prevailing theories that were strongly environmental, strongly psychoanalytic, or both:

> Like innumerable other parents, we are struck by the clearly evident individual differences in our children, even in the first few weeks of life. . . . As clinicians, we were repeatedly impressed by our inability to make a direct correlation between environmental influences, such as parental attitudes and practices, and the child's psychological development. . . . As mental health professionals, we became increasingly concerned at the dominant professional ideology of the time, in which the causation of all child psychopathology, from simple behavior problems to juvenile delinquency to schizophrenia itself, was at the doorstep of the mother. . . . We ourselves have called this ideology the "Mal de Mere" syndrome. . . . Finally, a review of the literature revealed that there was considerable skepticism of this exclusively environmentalist view. (Thomas & Chess, 1977, pp. 3–6)

Thomas, Chess, and their colleagues formulated the dominant approach to temperament and began a long-term study, the New York Longitudinal Study (NYLS).

The NYLS began in 1956 and has now followed 133 individuals from 84 families, predominantly college-educated New York families, from 3 months of age to adulthood. Most parents were interviewed four times during the first year and twice a year until adolescence, with a follow-up in adulthood (18–22 years). Later assessments of the children include home and school observations, teacher interviews, and standardized cognitive and achievement tests. This mountain of facts has recently been preserved on microfilm and inventoried by the Lerners of the Pennsylvania State University, who solicit collaboration from other researchers interested in exploiting this unique data set (Lerner & Lerner, 1983). In addition to the core sample of 133 middle-class children and their families, the NYLS also includes longitudinal temperament data from a working-class sample of 97 Puerto Rican children and their families and a largely middle-class sample of 52 mentally retarded children and their families.

Four books present the results of this 30-year study (Thomas & Chess, 1977, 1980; Thomas, Chess, & Birch, 1968; and Thomas, Chess, Birch, Hertzig, & Korn, 1963), and another book is forthcoming on the adult follow-up study. In this chapter we describe and evaluate the NYLS conceptualizations and how they are operationalized in measuring instruments. Accounts of research are limited to these goals, for it would be beyond the bounds of this book to review the enormous body of research accumulated by the NYLS project.

DESCRIPTION OF THE MEASURES

Their approach begins with nine dimensions of temperament formulated by Thomas et al. (1963) in this way:

> A content analysis was therefore performed on the interview protocols of the first twenty-two children studied. In the course of this analysis the protocol data were distributed against a wide variety of formal behavioral attributes. It was found that nine categories of functioning could be scored continuously throughout the protocols. Further, the distributions of scores in each of these categories were sufficiently wide to permit differentiation among individuals within each category. Although various amounts of data were available for additional categories of functioning, their distribution failed to satisfy either the requirement of ubiquitousness (being scorable and present in all protocols), or of sufficient variability to permit interindividual comparison. (p. 40)

The nine categories, as adapted from Thomas et al. (1963) are:

1. *Activity Level*—the extent to which a motor component exists during bathing, eating, playing, dressing, and handling; information on the sleep-wake cycle, reaching, crawling, and walking. Example: "Dressing him becomes a battle because he squirms so."
2. *Rhythmicity*—the predictability in time of such functions such as sleep-wake cycle, hunger, feeding, and elimination. Example: "Child falls asleep at approximately the same time each night."
3. *Approach or Withdrawal*—the nature of the response of a new stimulus (food, toy, or person). Example: "Child loves new toys."
4. *Adaptability*—change in response to new or altered situations (not initial response as in Approach/Withdrawal). Example: "He used to spit out cereal whenever I gave it to him, but now he takes it fairly well."
5. *Intensity of Reaction*—the energy level of response. Example of high intensity of reaction: "Whenever she hears music she begins to laugh and to jump up and down in time to it."

6. *Threshold of Responsiveness*—the intensity level of stimulation needed to evoke a response. Example of high threshold: "I can never tell if he's wet unless I feel him."
7. *Quality of Mood*—the amount of pleasant, joyful, and friendly behavior, as contrasted with unpleasant, crying, and unfriendly behavior. Example of positive mood: "If he's not laughing and smiling, I know he's getting sick."
8. *Distractability*—the effectiveness of extraneous stimuli in interfering with the ongoing behavior. Example: "Stops crying when picked up."
9. *Attention Span and Persistence*—persistence refers to the continuation of an activity in the face of obstacles. Example of attention span: "Child will look at books for half an hour." Example of persistence: "Child attempts to continue activities after parent says no."

The NYLS approach to temperament may have prevailed because it offered the first modern approach, longitudinal data, and measuring instruments. The original NYLS interviews were unstructured in the sense that no probes were used to assess specific situations. Rather, parents were simply asked to describe recent events, a procedure that provides a rich but unsystematic store of information. Investigators in England (Graham, Rutter, & George, 1973—see Appendix C in Thomas & Chess, 1977) have developed a standardized interview based on the NYLS conceptualization of temperament, which includes an initial probe question for each behavioral or situational category. The interviewer continues to elicit sufficient information about specific details of each probe until an adequate rating can be made.

A major stimulus for use of the NYLS conceptualization of temperament has been the availability of the parental rating questionnaires created by William Carey and his colleagues. Carey, a practicing pediatrician, wanted a quick temperament profile of his clients and therefore constructed parental rating items to measure each of the nine NYLS dimensions in infants from 4 to 8 months of age. In 1970, Carey published the Infant Temperament Questionnaire (ITQ), which has been revised by Carey and McDevitt (1978). The revised 95-item ITQ can be scored to yield values on the nine NYLS dimensions, as well as for *Easy, Difficult, Slow-to-Warm-Up,* and *Intermediate* patterns of temperament. For example, an infant is classified as difficult if the score for intensity is above the mean for the standardization sample; if at least three of the scale scores for rhythmicity, approach/withdrawal, adaptability, and quality of mood are below the mean; and if two of these five scores are at least one standard deviation from the mean. Global ratings are also obtained for each of the dimensions and for the difficult syndrome.

Carey and his colleagues have devised similar instruments for 1- to 3-year-olds, the Toddler Temperament Scale (Fullard, McDevitt, & Carey, 1978); for 3- to 7-year-olds, the Behavioral Style Questionnaire (McDevitt & Carey, 1978); and for 8- to 12-year-olds, the Middle Childhood Temperament Questionnaire (Hegvik, McDevitt, & Carey, 1982). Like the ITQ, each of these questionnaires has approximately 100 items, takes about 30 minutes to administer, and has high test-retest reliability and internal consistency (items that did not correlate substantially with the appropriate scale were dropped).

An NYLS-based self-report and rating instrument with the same factor structure in early childhood, middle-to-late childhood, and early adulthood has been generated by Richard Lerner and his colleagues at Pennsylvania State University (Lerner, Palermo, Spiro, & Nesselroade, 1982). The result is the Dimensions of Temperament Survey (DOTS), a 34-item, true-false questionnaire. An advantage of the DOTS is that both self-report and rating versions are available; parents can rate children and themselves, and these ratings can be compared to the children's self-reports. Other NYLS-related parental rating scales have been produced by Persson-Blennow & McNeil (1980), and McNeil & Persson-Blennow (1982). There is also a parental rating measure of difficultness with corresponding home observation measures (Bates, Freeland, & Lounsbury, 1979).

In addition to these widely used parental rating questionnaires, a 64-item Teacher Temperament Questionnaire (TTQ) constructed by Thomas and Chess (1977) measures all NYLS dimensions in children from 3 to 7 years of age. Barbara Keogh (1982) abbreviated and revised the TTQ to measure higher-order factors.

EVALUATION OF THE MEASURES

Dimensionality

The nine dimensions of temperament derive from an intuitive content analysis of two-dozen protocols obtained from the parents of children. Are there nine distinct temperaments? The answer obviously must come from factor analyses of the NYLS instruments. The NYLS group has been unfortunately silent here, and the factor analytic research has been done by others.

Rowe and Plomin (1977) paraphrased the interview protocols contained in the Appendix of the initial NYLS book (Thomas et al. 1963). For example, Threshold of Responsiveness includes "No startle reaction to noises; no reaction to lights" (p. 111); this became the questionnaire item,

"Child dislikes bright lights and loud noises." Each item was rated on a 5-point scale by mothers of 182 children who ranged in age from 2 to 6 years.

The 54-item scale yielded seven rotated factors, each of which had at least three items with factor loadings more than .40. Of the nine NYLS dimensions, only Attention Span/Persistence emerged as a clear, unequivocal factor. The Distractibility dimension appeared only as a means of calming children by engaging their attention elsewhere than themselves, which means that the factor is best regarded as Soothability. Of the items on the Rhythmicity dimension, only sleep items loaded on a narrow Sleep factor, which did not include the remaining Rhythmicity items pertaining to feeding and bowel movements. None of the other NYLS dimensions emerged as a factor, though the factors that did emerge were of interest. Various items from Approach/Withdrawal, Adaptability, and Threshold of Responsiveness clustered on a factor best labeled Sociability. "Child cries loudly and long when frightened" and similar items from the Approach/Withdrawal, Intensity of Reaction, Threshold of Responsiveness, and Quality of Mood dimensions loaded on an Emotionality factor. Items from Approach/Withdrawal, Adaptability, and Threshold of Responsiveness assembled as a narrow factor, Reactions to Foods, a typical item of which was "Child has strong likes and dislikes in food." Parts of the NYLS scales of Intensity of Reaction, Quality of Mood, Distractibility, and Attention Span/Persistence aggregated as a factor called Stubbornness, the highest loading item of which was "Child doesn't take No for an answer."

To recapitulate, this study yielded seven factors—Attention Span/Persistence, Sociability, Reactivity, Sleep Rhythmicity, Soothability, Reaction to Foods, and Stubbornness, only the first of which matches a NYLS dimension. Similar findings have been reported by Lerner and his colleagues (1982), who discovered that the Dimensions of Temperament Survey (DOTS) consisted of five factors. Their Activity factor appears at first glance to be similar to the Activity dimension of the NYLS, but the items were limited to activity during sleep (I move a great deal in my sleep). In the absence of items referring to activity during wakefulness, this factor cannot be considered to be a general measure of activity. The second factor, Rhythmicity, is also narrow: Half of the items involve sleep, and the other half involve eating (e.g., I eat about the same amount at breakfast from day to day; I eat about the same amount at supper from day to day; My appetite seems to stay the same day after day).

The third factor is an impulsivity-like factor, similar to the one found by Rowe and Plomin (1977), containing items from the NYLS dmensions of Attention Span/Persistence and Distractibility. The fourth DOTS factor, labeled Adaptability/Approach-Withdrawal, is viewed as a combination of these two NYLS dimensions. The item content, however, suggests that this is a Sociability factor (e.g., It takes me a long time to get used to new people; In meeting a new person I tend to move toward him or her).

The last factor, Reactivity, is also similar to a factor in the analysis by Rowe and Plomin. It includes items from the NYLS categories of Activity, Intensity, and Threshold of Responsiveness. The DOTS Reactivity factor is evenly split between Emotionality items (I react intensely when hurt; When I react to something, my reaction is intense) and Activity items (I can't sit still for long; I never seem to slow down).

Thus, two different approaches find scant factor analytic support for the nine NYLS dimensions. Further disconfirmation of the NYLS dimensions comes from the work of Rothbart (1981), who devised an infant temperament measure (discussed in next chapter) based in part on the NYLS conceptualization. Though she did not employ factor analysis, item-scale correlations were examined as a criterion for selecting items. Only an Activity scale replicated the NYLS conceptualization, a result similar to that of Lerner et al. (1982). As in the Rowe and Plomin analysis, a satisfactory Soothability scale was developed. The rest of Rothbart's scales assess specific behaviors such as smiling, duration of orienting, fear, and distress to limitations.

Though the results of these three studies are similar, they provide only indirect tests of the dimensionality of the NYLS. A more direct test would be a factor analysis of one of the Carey parental rating questionnaires, which are widely used to measure the nine NYLS traits. One study in Sweden using the Infant Temperament Questionnaire for infants in the first year of life mentioned in passing "it was also clear that factor analytically derived dimensions were not close replicates of the nine NYLS dimensions, which the item pool was designed to measure" (Bohlin, Hagekull, & Lindhagen, 1981, p. 85). Similarly, in a conference report of a factor analysis using the revised ITQ items in the first year of life, only one of the nine NYLS dimensions emerged (Seifer, 1983). We are aware of no other published factor analysis of a Carey questionnaire nor any mention of factor analyses past infancy, but we have analyzed the McDevitt and Carey (1978) Behavioral Style Questionnaire (BSQ) using data from the Colorado Adoption Project (Plomin & DeFries, 1983). For 200 4-year-old adopted and nonadopted children, we factor analyzed a slightly abbreviated version of the BSQ (82 of the 100 items). The BSQ includes from 9 to 13 items per scale, and we deleted 1 to 3 items per scale (items 22 and 68–84). Mothers' ratings on the BSQ were submitted to factor analysis, using standard options such as principal components for an initial solution and Varimax rotation of principal components with eigenvalues greater than 1.0.

There were 25 factors with eigenvalues greater than 1.0; selected for rotation, they account for 75% of the total variance of the BSQ items. Table 3.1 lists BSQ items that load above .40 on each of the first nine

TABLE 3.1
Exploratory Factor Analysis Of Behavioral Style Questionnaire

Loading	Item
	I. Sociability/Shyness
− .87	31. The child is outgoing with strangers.
.83	98. The child tends to hold back in new situations.
.82	86. The child avoids new guests or visitors.
− .70	29. The child smiles or laughs when he/she meets new visitors at home.
− .69	43. The child approaches children his/her age that he/she doesn't know.
.69	50. The child holds back until sure of himself/herself.
.65	55. The child has difficulty getting used to new situations.
.61	8. The child needs a period of adjustment to get used to changes in school or at home.
− .56	61. The child adjusts easily to changes in his/her routine.
.43	10. The child is slow to adjust to changes in household rules.
	II. Reaction to Discipline
− .76	56. The child will avoid misbehavior if punished firmly once or twice.
.71	17. The child does not acknowledge a call to come in if involved in something.
.68	65. The child repeats behavior for which he/she has previously been punished.
.56	2. The child seems not to hear when involved in a favorite activity.
− .49	3. The child can be coaxed out of a forbidden activity.
.44	10. The child is slow to adjust to changes in household rules.
.44	32. The child fidgets when he/she has to stay still.
− .41	26. The child sits quietly while waiting.
	III. Distractibility
.81	85. The child responds to sounds or noises unrelated to his/her activity.
.73	57. The child is sensitive to noises (telephone, doorbell) and looks up right away.
.70	66. The child looks up from playing when the telephone rings.
.59	51. The child looks up when someone walks past the doorway.
.47	89. The child interrupts an activity to listen to conversation around him/her.
.43	95. The child wants to leave the table during meals to answer the doorbell or phone.
41	37. Unusual noises (sirens, thunder, etc.) interrupt the child's behavior.
	IV. Persistence
.67	40. The child becomes engrossed in an interesting activity for one half hour or more.
− .58	39. The child loses interest in a new toy or game the same day.
.48	35. The child practices an activity until he/she masters it.
− .47	87. The child fidgets when a story is being read to him/her.
.42	44. The child plays quietly with his/her toys and games.

V. Doublet

.93	54. The child accepts new food within one or two tries.
.85	67. The child is willing to try new foods.

VI. Emotionality—Distress

.80	41. The child cries intensely when hurt.
.70	88. The child becomes upset or cries over minor falls or bumps.
.42	64. The child cries or whines when frustrated.
.40	53. The child reacts strongly (cries or complains) to a disappointment or failure.

VII. Doublet

.85	36. The child eats about the same amount at supper from day to day.
.65	62. The child eats about the same amount at breakfast from day to day.

VIII. Emotionality—Anger

.75	97. The child frowns when asked to do a chore by the parent.
.50	96. The child complains of events in school or with playmates that day.
.42	34. The child is annoyed at interrupting play to comply with a parental request.

IX. Doublet

.93	23. The child falls asleep as soon as he/she is put to bed.
.71	47. The child is sleepy at his/her bed-time.

factors. Our discussion would be the same if we included additional factors, but there are nine factors in Table 3.1 because the NYLS emphasizes nine dimensions and because the tenth factor consisted of only a single item with a high loading and subsequent factors consisted primarily of doublets.

The first factor comprises mainly sociability and shyness items, hence its name. Though most of these items are meant to be included in the NYLS Approach/Withdrawal dimension, the flavor of the factor is clearly approach/withdrawal to *people,* not approach/withdrawal in nonsocial contexts.

A problem with several of the other factors of the BSQ items is that item *doublets* appear to be responsible for their appearance, the clearest examples being Factors V, VII, and IX. For example, the correlation between two items such as "The child eats about the same amount at supper from day to day" and "The child eats about the same amount at breakfast from day to day" will yield a separate cluster in a factor analysis of heterogeneous items. Doublets such as these occur because of semantic similarity, not because the items tap a general dimension of temperament. For example, a tight factor will emerge from items such as "Child eats ice-cream cones quickly," and "Child prefers to gulp down ice-cream treats rather than savoring the taste slowly." However, a "speed-of-eating-ice-cream" factor is obviously a trivial aspect of behavior. This problem makes it difficult to interpret Factor II, which consists primarily of two correlated doublets, items 56 and 65 and items 17 and 2.

The items in Factor III make it easy to name this factor Distractibility. Every item deals with reaction to noise, however, which poses a problem of interpretation. We cannot say whether this factor represents a narrow component of distractibility or merely the clustering of items dealing with response to noise. The remaining three factors contain relatively homogeneous items, rendering it a simple matter to label the clusters Persistence, Distress, and Anger.

What do these findings tell us about the dimensionality of the NYLS system? Distractibility is clearly confirmed, as is the persistence component of Attention Span/Persistence, but it strains credulity to equate Approach/Withdrawal with the obtained Sociability/Shyness factor. This means that only two of the NYLS dimensions appear in a factor analysis of one of the most frequently used measures of the NYLS temperaments.

We had also planned to conduct a more elegant test of the hypothesis that the structure of the BSQ reflects the hypothesized nine NYLS traits. Using maximum likelihood confirmatory factor analysis (e.g., Hertzog, 1984), one can determine the fit between the observed covariance structure among the BSQ items and the hypothesized nine temperaments of NYLS. The hypothesized structure is determined by the placement of the BSQ items on the nine NYLS dimensions. The fit between the observed covariance structure of the BSQ and the NYLS conceptualization is so poor, however, that a confirmatory factor analysis is not warranted.

In summary, the results of these various factor analyses converge on this conclusion: There is no empirical basis for the nine distinct temperaments formulated by the NYLS group. Though two of the proposed temperaments receive some confirmation from factor analyses, the other seven contain item contents that spread out over several factors. Unless one is willing to ignore standard psychometric criteria, it is clear that the nine NYLS temperaments must be restructured. Furthermore, these disconfirming factor analyses call into question the theoretical assumptions underlying the NYLS approach.

CONCEPTUAL ISSUES

Easy-Difficult

The nine temperaments of NYLS were combined to yield three types of children: easy, difficult, and slow-to-warm-up. These types were subsequently replaced by a dimension, ranging from easy to difficult, which is defined by five of the temperaments. It was assumed that children toward the difficult end of the dimension would subsequently develop behavior problems.

The easy-difficult dimension has been confirmed by a large body of research, for it is congruent with the way most parents evaluate their children: as easy to handle or as causing problems for the parents. Concerning whether easy-difficult predicts later behavioral problems, the evidence is predominantly negative. Scores on the easy-difficult composite of five temperaments in infancy (1 and 2 years of age) correlated .08 with home adjustment at 3 years, − .01 with home adjustment at 5 years, − .04 with school adjustment at 5 years, − .01 with early adult adaptation, and .00 with adult adaptation (Thomas & Chess, 1982). Easy-difficult scores at 4 and 5 years of age correlated significantly with early adult adaptation. This positive finding is problematical, however, because the more difficult children at 4 and 5 years of age were also found to be significantly *better* adjusted in childhood by one method and significantly *worse* adjusted by another method.

Daniels and Plomin (1983) found that Difficult Temperament at 12 and 24 months of age related primarily to parental ratings of Emotionality, which supports Bates' (1980) contention that Difficult Temperament is little more than crying and fussing: "it seems certain, no matter who is defining difficultness . . . that the central feature of the perception of an infant as difficult appears to be frequent fussing and crying" (p. 308). This interpretation might explain why Difficult Temperament in infancy does not predict later behavioral problems: Longitudinal studies find that crying and fussing in infancy do not predict later behavioral problems. After infancy, Difficult Temperament—defined on the basis of what parents find difficult in infants—becomes predictive of behavioral problems simply because children who cry and fuss like infants when they are preschoolers are more likely to present problems.

Though the easy-difficult dimension makes sense in everyday terms, it poses conceptual problems. There is more than one way for a child to be easy and many ways for a child to be difficult. Thus children can be difficult because they are excessively active and therefore irritate those who would prefer them to be less restless, because they demand excessive attention, because they do not heed adults and cannot be disciplined, or because they are excessively emotional and cry easily.

A related problem concerns the child's familial and social environment: For whom is the child being easy or difficult? Some parents can tolerate excesses of the behavior of their children, but others cannot; some parents demand good, quiet, and responsible children, whereas other parents do not emphasize discipline and self-control. Clearly, the personality and childrearing approach of parents and other caretakers are major determinants of whether the child is judged as easy or difficult.

The course of development poses another problem for the easy-difficult concept. Children who are difficult because they are too active or too unrestrained early in life may pose no problems later in childhood because either they begin to mature and can exercise more self-control or the social environment opens up and becomes less restrictive. Children who are easy early in life may appear so because they are relatively inactive and docile, whereas later in life they might appear difficult because of their laziness and lack of initiative. In brief, the NYLS concept of easy-difficult needs to specify the different ways a child might be easy or difficult, the relationship of the demands of the social environment to the child's being easy or difficult, and the changing criteria or judgments of easy or difficult during the course of development. The last two issues bear on the related concept of goodness of fit.

Goodness of Fit

To their credit, Thomas and Chess (1980) have moved beyond easy-difficult to the idea of a fit between organism and environment:

> Goodness of fit results when the properties of the environment and its expectations and demands are in accord with the organism's own capacities, motivations, and style of behaving. When this *consonance* between organism and environment is present, optimal development in a progressive direction is possible. Conversely, poorness of fit involves discrepancies and dissonances between environmental opportunities and demands and the capacities and characteristics of the organism, so that distorted development and maladaptive functioning occur. (p. 90)

The idea of stresses and strains resulting from a poor fit between temperament and environment is an appealing way of thinking about possible outcomes of temperament. However, few data have as yet been collected to support the hypothesis. Thomas and Chess (1982) provide examples of the phenomenon at the group level: High activity was stressful in the NYLS Puerto Rican sample but not in the main NYLS sample, presumably because of differences in the amount of living space and availability of safe play areas for the two groups. Another example at the level of average group differences is that night awakening was found to be less stressful for Kokwet families in Kenya than for parents in the United States (Super & Harkness, 1981).

Scholom, Zucker, and Stollak (1979) studied teacher-rated adjustment in relation to the fit between parental and infant temperament, but there were only weak relationships. Moreover, the significant results were odd: The greater the temperament match between fathers and sons, the *poorer* the adjustment of the boys as rated by their teachers. For girls, the match between parent and daughter temperaments was not related to school adjustment.

A program of research by the Lerners (Lerner, in press; Lerner & Lerner, 1983; Lerner, Lerner, & Zabski, in press) has also applied the goodness of fit model to school adjustment and achievement. Their strategy is to examine congruence between children's self-reported temperament and temperament expectations of teachers and peers. The DOTS self-report questionnaire was completed by eighth-grade students in one study (Lerner, 1983) and fourth-grade students in another (Lerner et al., in press). Teacher and peer expectations for temperament were assessed using a modification of the DOTS. Dependent measures included teacher ratings of adjustment and achievement, grades, and objective achievement data.

Teachers were consistent in their expectations for temperament. Not surprisingly, they wanted their students to be Easy: low in Activity, high in Attention Span and Adaptability, high in Rhythmicity, and low in Reactivity. Each child's temperament score was subtracted from the teacher's temperament expectation score, and two groups were formed: children whose self-reported temperament met or exceeded the teachers' expectations, and children who fell below expectations. Some support was found for the hypothesis that children whose temperament met teachers' expectations for Reactivity, Attention Span, and Adaptability performed better at school. The subtraction scores for Reactivity were related to teacher ratings of adjustment and ability, as well as to objective performance differences, in the predicted direction: Children who were less reactive performed better. Attention Span was related to teacher ratings but not to objective performance. No relationship was found for Adaptability.

However, this research does not bear on the main issue of goodness of fit between temperament and environment. All teachers' expectations for temperament tended to be similar, which means that the difference between children's temperament scores and their teachers' expectations— the basic measure of goodness of fit—merely subtracted a constant from the children's temperament scores. Thus, this analysis assessed only the simple relationship between temperament and school performance: Children who were above or below their teacher's expectations for Attention Span, for example, were simply children high or low in Attention Span, respectively. Though certain dimensions of temperament were related to school performance, this was not a test of goodness of fit. Other investigators of the relationship between temperament and school adjustment have found only modest correlations, though these other studies have used parental ratings of temperament rather than self-reports of the children as in the Lerners' work. For example, Carey, Fox, and McDevitt (1977) found that of the nine NYLS dimensions rated by parents of school age children, only Adaptability was significantly correlated with school adjustment (r = .35). Paradoxically, in the same study children categorized as easy in infancy were significantly *less* adjusted as compared to other temperament types.

Goodness of fit is an interaction in the statistical sense. Suppose that, as in the Scholom et al. study (1979), the goal was to evaluate the fit between temperament and an environmental measure, say parental personality, in terms of its effect on school adjustment. The goodness of fit model proposes that the prediction of adjustment is possible only from joint information about temperament and environment (parental personality in this case), independent of the main effects of temperament and environment. Interactions indicate conditional relationships between temperament and environment on the one hand and adjustment on the other: Temperament predicts adjustment only as a function of the environment. In this example, the conditional relationship is the agreement between temperament and parental personality as they predict adjustment jointly. This interaction is independent of the main effects of temperament and environment in that it does not matter whether temperament is directly related to adjustment or the environmental measure directly predicts adjustment. Goodness of fit evaluates the interaction between temperament and environment and asks whether the joint product, or interaction, of temperament and environment adds to the predictability of the dependent variable.

Interactionism

The NYLS group has been careful not to implicate any particular origin of temperaments, but in some of their writings they appear to favor the approach we have labeled *constitutional:* "This review of the available data suggests an appreciable, but by no means exclusive, genetic role in the determination of temperamental individuality in the young infant. . . . Temperamental individuality is well established by the time the infant is two to three months old. The origins of temperament must therefore be sought in the factors reviewed in this chapter: genetic, prenatal, and early postnatal parental influences" (Thomas & Chess, 1977, pp. 152–153).

This quotation would appear to be a straightforward espousal of very early determinants of temperament, to the virtual exclusion of later environmental influences. In other writings, however, the NYLS group has downplayed genetic or constitutional origins of temperament and opted for an approach called *interactionist:* "Behavioral phenomena are considered to be the expression of a continuous organism-environment interaction from the very first manifestations in the life of the individual" (Thomas, Birch, Chess, & Robbins, 1961, p. 723). Surely, no one will disagree with this truism, but it is not particularly informative. Nor do Thomas and Chess (1980) advance knowledge or understanding when they suggest that development is a "fluid dynamic process which may reinforce, modify, or change specific psychological patterns at all ages" (p. 80) or when they invoke the phrase "dialectical interpenetration of opposites" (p. 250).

Behavioral geneticists and personality researchers do not deny the impact of environment, and many investigators who study the development of personality concede that there is some genetic input. In this sense, most researchers are interactionists, seeking to discover how genes and environment determine how personality traits develop, especially traits that appear early. What is needed is not a declaration of interactionism but specific models about the ways heredity and environment interact and the ways that children interact with their social environment. Tentative models of heredity and environment are described in Chapter 8, and child-social environment models are scattered throughout Chapters 6 to 10.

Style

If temperaments are not constitutional or genetic in origin—and the NYLS group appears to have retreated from that position—what distinguishes temperaments from other personality traits? One possibility is style, which the NYLS group insists is the way to define temperament: "Temperament can be equated with the term *behavioral style*. Each refers to the *how* rather than the *what* (abilities and content) or the *why* (motivation) of behavior" (Thomas & Chess, 1977, p. 9). Their definition of style as the how of behavior in contrast to the what or why appears to be entirely reasonable, but does this definition fit their nine temperaments?

Activity level and possibly Rhythmicity might involve the how of behavior, but the other seven temperaments appear to be defined by particular *contents* of behavior. Thus Approach/Withdrawal involves the directional component of behavior, Adaptability appears to be habituation to novelty, Intensity of Reaction is defined by the amplitude of the reaction and Threshold of Responsiveness by the amplitude of the evoking stimulus, Quality of Mood includes emotional reactions, and Distractibility and Attention Span/Persistence deal with instrumental behavior and inhibitory control of attentional processes. In brief, most of the NYLS temperaments are not stylistic aspects of behavior. If the NYLS temperaments cannot be defined as behavioral styles, how are they different from other personality traits in children? We see no clear conceptual option, and perhaps the answer lies in the intuitive way in which these nine dimensions were selected in the beginning.

Overall Evaluation of NYLS

The NYLS formulation may be divided into five separate aspects: the nine temperaments, the easy-difficult dichotomy, goodness of fit, interactionism, and style. Having already commented on these issues, we shall be brief.

When theorists posit a specific number of traits in their theoretical conception, an empirical test requires factor analysis or another quantitative analysis for discovering just how many clusters or dimensions are present. Factor analyses of the NYLS items have confirmed only two of their nine temperaments, and items from the remaining seven temperaments tend to be scattered over various other factors. Thus, there is currently no empirical basis for retaining the nine original NYLS temperaments.

Five of the original nine NYLS temperaments were used to assign infants to a place on the easy-difficult dimension. Such assignment is not especially predictive of later behavioral problems. The idea of children being difficult is not specific to the NYLS temperaments, and merely asking parents if their children are difficult would yield the same results. The issue is not empirical but conceptual: The NYLS group has not specified the different ways in which a child might be difficult. Furthermore, the criteria for labeling a child difficult in infancy will almost surely change in later childhood, and the NYLS group has not dealt with this problem.

The concept of goodness of fit is a theoretical advance in that it takes into account not only the child's temperament but the social environment. This concept requires research designs that include statistical interaction, and so far the NYLS group has not used such designs. Furthermore, it remains to be seen whether their temperaments are the best personality traits to use in determining goodness of fit, especially in older children.

The NYLS group is currently dedicated to an interactionism of determinants of personality, which not only includes many influences on personality but suggests that the action of these determinants is "dynamic" and "dialectical." No one denies the influence of multiple determinants, but unless the way they interact is specified in detail, there is no way of testing the conception.

Finally, the NYLS group have defined temperament in terms of *style:* the how of behavior. Style would appear to be too broad a concept to be useful in the study of temperament. Suppose two children aggress, but one shouts insults and the other uses physical violence. Should we say that they differ in aggressive style? Even if we were to accept the NYLS definition of style as sufficiently specific, most of their temperaments do not fit the definition; quality of mood is an obvious example.

We have found much to criticize in the NYLS system. None of this critique, however, can detract from their pioneering efforts, which have spawned a generation of research on temperament.

INDIVIDUAL DIFFERENCES IN NEONATES

Though not considered in the mainstream of temperament research, T. Berry Brazelton has studied individual differences in the behavior of neonates. His concepts and methods have proceeded in much the same way as the NYLS. The Neonatal Behavior Assessment Scale (NBAS; Brazelton, 1973) served to promulgate the approach, just as the Carey parental rating scales have enhanced the NYLS approach to temperament. Though the NBAS measures physical status, several behaviors are also assessed, including alertness, irritability, and quieting (Strauss & Rourke, 1978); these are similar to temperamental characteristics studied in older children.

Temperament researchers have shown little interest in neonatal assessment. The NYLS group first interviewed parents when the children were older than 3 months of age because of their suspicion that behavioral differences among neonates were not stable. Their hunch appears to be correct. In a monograph edited by Sameroff (1978) evaluating the NBAS, NBAS scores were found to lack day-to-day reliability: The average correlations are about .30. Moreover, NBAS scores are only marginally related to infant behavior at 4 months (Sameroff, Krafchuk, & Bakow, 1978).

Parental ratings of temperament in later infancy and childhood are considerably more reliable, with median correlations of about .80. Observational measures of temperament in infancy and childhood are a more appropriate comparison to the NBAS; these show lower reliability (about .50) than the parental ratings, though these are still substantially higher than the NBAS reliability. However, if aggregating neonatal data improves their reliability, as shown by Kaye (1978), the stability and predictiveness of the NBAS scores might be similar to those of other attempts to measure infant temperament using observational techniques. Furthermore, a recent report suggests relationships between NBAS scores *after* the first 2 days of life and parental ratings of infant temperament at 4 months of age (Sullivan, Pannabecker, & Horowitz, 1982).

4 Arousal

Arousal seems intuitively to be linked to the biological aspect of personality, but there are more specific reasons for the association. Arousal involves diffuse behavior that is not focused in any particular direction, behavior that usually implicates the entire organism. The slow-moving, cyclic variations in sleep-wakefulness and menstrual cycles are obviously tied to biological processes. The diurnal variations that become aversive in *jet lag* also serve to remind us of the biological substrate on which behavior rests. And the diffuse excitement that occurs in certain emotional states can be traced to activation of the autonomic nervous system. In brief, behavior involving arousal appears to be diffuse and linked closely with neural activation, and it is often cyclic.

Arousal is not a single dimension: "I think the experiments show that electroencephalographic, autonomic, motor, and other behavioral systems are imperfectly coupled, complexly interacting systems. Indeed, I think the evidence shows that electrocortical arousal, autonomic arousal, and behavioral arousal, may be considered to be *different forms* of arousal, each complex in itself" (Lacey, 1967, p. 15). Lacey does say that there are conditions, mainly great excitement, under which all three kinds of arousal occur simultaneously, but otherwise they should be regarded as disparate. His view prevails in the field today, and most psychologists find it useful to distinguish among the three kinds of arousal.

THREE KINDS OF AROUSAL

Behavioral Arousal

In everyday life we are most familiar with behavioral arousal, which varies along a continuum from deep NREM sleep to great excitement. Its most obvious aspect is activity. In deep sleep there is little movement—only the occasional twisting and turning of the body and, rarely, sleepwalking or sleeptalking. During the first stage of wakefulness (drowsiness) there is more activity, but movements are sluggish and energy expenditure is small. Activity is moderate during ordinary wakefulness, as we go about the business of dealing with the environment, and it peaks during great excitement or in heavy exercise or work. Thus the higher the level of arousal, the greater the motor activity.

If activity is regarded as the output aspect of arousal, sensitivity to stimuli may be regarded as the input aspect. In deep sleep individuals are not unconscious, for they can be wakened, but the need for alarm clocks is sufficient evidence that sensitivity to stimuli is minimal. People are somewhat more alert when drowsy and most alert when in a state of ordinary wakefulness. In great excitement, however, attention is narrowed and people tend to miss much of what is happening.

Autonomic Arousal

Widespread bodily arousal, involving respiration, heart rate, blood flow, sweating, and the starting or stopping of digestive processes, is mediated by the autonomic nervous system. Of its two well-known divisions, the parasympathetic division is more or less synonymous with *tonic* autonomic arousal; it is involved in the low arousal, routine vegetative functioning necessary to maintain life. The sympathetic division, which is more or less synonymous with *phasic* autonomic arousal, is involved in the high arousal necessary for dealing with emergencies. High arousal is especially necessary in the face of threat, when the organism reacts with a fight-or-flight reaction that requires massive physical exertion.

Stated simply, the two divisions of the autonomic nervous system work together, sometimes in opposition and sometimes in sequence. Most of the time, when the body is carrying out its routine maintenance functions, the parasympathetic dominates slightly. When an emergency occurs or when there is simply a massive output of energy, the sympathetic tends to dominate. Emergency actions, however, must be shortlived, for the body cannot continuously be in a state of emergency. There are homeostatic mechanisms that return the body to its normal resting state, and in this optimal condition the slight dominance of the parasympathetic is restored.

Brain Arousal

During wakefulness the brain is stimulated by a variety of inputs from the environment which are largely absent during sleep. Large, slow brain waves are associated with low brain arousal, but the pattern of great excitement is small, fast, irregular EEGs. These brain waves are recorded predominantly from the cerebral cortex, which can be stimulated by a variety of neural structures; the major one is the reticular formation. Reduced to its simplest terms, the extent to which the cortex is aroused depends on how much input it receives from the reticular formation, which itself receives stimulation. This stimulation can arise from the senses, which pass on inputs from the environment; from the cortex itself, which can stimulate the reticular formation with exciting thoughts; and from the limbic system, which conveys the arousal involved in motivation and emotion. The key, however, is the reticular formation, which is believed to regulate the amount of neural input coming from the senses or neural structures and going to the cortex (Lindsley, 1961). Presumably, the reticular formation selectively allows certain kinds of inputs to reach the cortex, especially those involving novel stimuli, while stopping the flow of inputs involving habitual and repetitive stimuli (Lindsley, 1957).

Individual Differences

Behavioral Arousal. Individual differences in behavioral arousal have been studied mainly in dogs. Pavlov (1927) distinguished two extreme types of dogs, excitable and inhibited. The excitable dogs were lively and alert, sniffing at all possible odors, ears pricking to any sound, and eyes moving to see anything that moved. The inhibited dogs were quiet, almost sleepy, easy to handle, and docile in adapting to the conditioning procedure.

This distinction was pursued by James (1941), who provided details on dogs of contrasting breeds. His excitable dogs were hyperactive, often moving about with no particular direction or goal and displaying excessive energy. They reacted violently to restraint and did not settle down while conditioning was attempted. The lethargic dogs tended to be passive and quiet. They were easy to handle and adapted well to the conditioning procedure. Random activity, which was low at the start, dropped out completely in the experimental situation. These descriptions roughly match such common breeds of dogs as basset hounds (lethargic) and wirehaired terriers (excitable). Though it may be possible to train dogs to become excitable or lethargic, no one has yet demonstrated how this might be done, and so far, such differences have been produced through breeding.

Individual differences in behavioral arousal in humans have rarely been studied. The exceptions are studies by Thayer (1967, 1978a, 1978b), who used a checklist of adjectives denoting variations in activation and found four factors (1967). A later study (1978a) revealed that these factors were correlated in patterns that suggested two bipolar factors. One bipolar factor involves more or less energy: lively, active, full-of-pep, and vigorous versus sleepy, tired, and drowsy. The other bipolar factor concerns more or less tension: jittery, clutched up, fearful, and tense versus quiet, calm, and placid. This tension factor appears to describe the behavioral aspects of autonomic arousal. Consistent with this idea, the high end (clutched up and jittery) correlates significantly with elevations of pulse rate and respiration rate (Clements, Hafer, & Vermillion, 1976). Thus the self-reports of human subjects reveal two independent dimensions of individual differences in arousal. One appears to be unequivocally behavioral arousal (energy and vigor), and the other seems to be what has here been labeled autonomic (tense and distressed).

Autonomic Arousal. Individual differences in *autonomic* arousal have been studied mainly by Wenger and his colleagues (Wenger, 1941; Wenger, Coleman, Cullen, & Engel, 1961; Wenger, Engels, & Clemens, 1957); most of the research was summarized in a later paper (Wenger, 1966). Wenger sought to distinguish between people with excessive sympathetic activity and those with excessive parasympathetic activity, but he could not measure each division's arousal separately. His solution was statistical: "Since most of the autonomic functions that have been measured are innervated by both the sympathetic nervous system and the parasympathetic nervous system, it is to be expected that only one autonomic score is to be found and that measurements of it for a particular individual will show only his position in relation to the rest of the individuals on whom the study was based. It will show how much he deviates from the mean score for the group and the direction of the deviation" (Wenger, Jones, & Jones, 1956, p. 266).

When children and Air Force men were tested, normal distributions were found. Among the adults, roughly one third had a clear imbalance tilted toward either the sympathetic or parasympathetic end. Injection of adrenaline tilts the balance toward the sympathetic side, as expected. Graduate students tested the day before an important oral examination (and therefore fearful) tend to have sympathetic dominance in comparison to tests conducted a month later. Neurotics, who are presumably high in anxiety, tend to have sympathetic dominance. Children rated as emotional tend to have a sympathetic dominance. Sympathetic or parasympathetic dominance tends to be stable over a period of several years, and there is evidence suggestive of an inherited component (Jost & Sontag, 1944).

Despite this research, which started several decades ago, there has been little follow-up by other investigators, with the possible exception of the research by Thayer (1967, 1978a, 1978b) and by Clements et al. (1976) which dealt with the general concept of activation rather than specifically autonomic arousal. This omission is unfortunate, especially in light of the conclusion of a recent book on psychophysiology (Andreassi, 1980) that the idea of parasympathetic versus sympathetic dominance is a useful way to approach individual differences in autonomic functioning. Wenger and his colleagues provided initial evidence that fear situations can induce sympathetic dominance and that fearful people are likely to have sympathetic dominance. Further research might link sympathetic dominance to a temperament such as emotionality.

A final point about autonomic arousal concerns the possible heterogeneity of the various measures that comprise such arousal. Lacey (1956, 1967) has argued that there is too much response specificity among the various measures of autonomic arousal to combine them into a single score. However, his suggestion is denied by research showing that all the various indices of autonomic arousal tend to covary with increasing arousal (Eason & Dudley, 1971).

Brain Arousal. Individual differences in brain arousal are postulated by Fiske and Maddi (1961; also Maddi, 1972) as part of their activation model of personality. For them, "activation is a neuropsychological concept, referring on the psychological side to the common core of meaning of such terms as alertness, attentiveness, tension, and subjective excitement, and on the neural side to the state of excitation in a postulated center of the brain" (Maddi, 1972, p. 170). The neural focus of activation is believed to be the reticular formation. Individual differences are assumed to exist in the optimal level of activation in the reticular formation.

Long before American personality theorists mentioned individual differences in brain arousal, European researchers focused on them. As mentioned earlier, Pavlov (1927) distinguished two temperamental extremes of dogs on the basis of their behavioral arousal: those with weak nervous systems and those with strong nervous systems. This dichotomy spawned a half-century of research on brain arousal in the Soviet Union, Europe, England, and even the United States. Pavlov wrote about excitation and inhibition of the brain as if he had observed cortical activity, but his theory was based on what Hebb (1955) has called the "conceptual nervous system." Nonetheless, subsequent research has extended the study of Pavlov's concept of strong and weak nervous systems to electrophysiology, including average evoked potentials, their Russian analogue, photic driving, as well as neurotransmitters including the endorphins.

Though scarcely known to Westerners, there has been extensive research on neurological models of personality in the Soviet Union and Poland during the past 30 years. The theorizing of Teplov (1956) and Nebylitsyn (1956, 1966) influenced Soviet psychology in continuing the search for biological correlates of Pavlov's typology. Unlike Western psychologists, who focus on complex behavior and try to work back toward physiology, Soviet psychologists generally begin with physiology, often electrophysiology, and work toward more complex behavior.

A direct descendant of Pavlov's approach is the work of Jan Strelau in Poland who uses conditioning techniques to study the balance between excitation and inhibition. Strelau's theory involves the autonomic nervous system and the hormonal system as well as the brain, and his recent work emphasizes optimal levels of arousal rather than the balance between excitation and inhibition. After 25 years, his theory is finally becoming known in the West with the recent inclusion of his work in edited volumes in English (e.g., Strelau, 1983a) and with a book that summarizes his work (Strelau, 1983b). Unlike most Soviet researchers, Strelau has developed a questionnaire, the Strelau Temperament Inventory; he reports that the Pavlovian constructs measured by the questionnaire correlate highly with psychophysiological indices.

Another important Soviet researcher is Vladimer Rusalov (1979) of Moscow, whose work, not yet available in English, focuses on EEG and average evoked potentials in humans and their relationship to temperament. In the past decade, several twin studies in the Soviet Union have related EEG properties to temperament, and systematic research on this topic continues in the Moscow laboratory of Ravich-Scherbo (e.g., Meshkova & Ravich-Scherbo, 1981). Soviet twin researchers contend that the genetic contribution to temperament decreases with age.

This review of Eastern research on the brain arousal correlates of personality is merely a sketch. A recent review by Mangan (1982) describes this research in more detail and indicates the current state of flux of Eastern research.

Western researchers are more familiar with the work of Eysenck (1967) on extraversion-introversion and Zuckerman (1969) on sensation-seeking. In the West, the original neurological theories of Eysenck, Zuckerman, and Fiske and Maddi's (1961) activation model of personality were simple extensions of neural theories of optimal level of arousal such as those of Hebb (1955) and Lindsley (1961). However, as early as 1964, Jeffrey Gray (1983) showed that Western thoughts about optimal levels of arousal are closely related to Pavlov's concept of nervous system strength. These neural theories hypothesized that individual differences in optimal levels of arousal were caused by differences in sensitivity or in the balance of excitation and inhibition in the reticular formation. Thus, persons with low optimal levels of arousal ("weak nervous systems," introverts, non-sensation-seekers) are easily aroused and find low levels of stimulation pleasant but high levels unpleasant. High optimal levels of arousal ("strong nervous systems," extraverts, sensation-seekers) cause people to be easily aroused and to find low levels of stimulation boring but high levels pleasantly exciting. For a detailed discussion of research and theory on optimal level of arousal, see Zuckerman (1979).

Unlike most Soviet researchers, Eysenck did not rely on electrophysiology. Instead, he used drug manipulations and perceptual and learning measures to study Pavlovian excitation/inhibitory balance presumed to operate via the reticular formation. In the 1970s, Gray (1971, 1972) began to consider the reward and punishment areas in the limbic system as an additional site for individual differences in brain arousal. The limbic system rather than the reticular formation is now generally viewed as the neural focus of activity relevant to extraversion and sensation seeking (Zuckerman, Ballenger, Jimerson, Murphy, & Post, 1983), though the welter of data from new techniques leaves conflicting results and hypotheses. Though theories of brain activation following Pavlov's conception of strength of the nervous system dominate research on the biological correlates of personality, these theories have little to say about development, particularly in early childhood, which is critical to our definition of temperament.

Temperament and Arousal

In conceptualizing individual differences in early childhood and in operationalizing these conceptions, researchers have focused mainly on behavioral and autonomic arousal. Three formulations of temperament appear to have arousal as the centerpiece of either the theorizing or the measures of behavior.

TEMPERAMENT AS AFFECT

Goldsmith and Campos (1982a, 1982b) construe temperament in terms of emotional behavior, which is one aspect of Allport's definition of temperament (1961). They define emotions as, "feeling states with their associated central nervous system states which serve both to *motivate* the individual, and, unless blocked from behavioral expression, to *communicate* socially significant information to others in the environment" (1982a, p. 177). Neither in this quotation nor anywhere else in their statement of theory do they specify which behaviors are to be included as emotional. A subsequent paper by Goldsmith (1982), however, offers five dimensions of temperament:

1. Motoric Activity—locomotion, trunk and limb movements, and toy manipulations;
2. Anger—distress, "anger" facial expression, flushed face, and muscle tension;

3. Fearfulness—distress, pre-cry face, behavioral avoidance, and "fear" facial expression;
4. Pleasure/Joy—smiling, laughter, and "positive vocalization";
5. Interest/Persistence—attention span (sustained looking), distractibility, and "interest" facial expression.

In measuring temperaments, they insist on studying only individual differences in the intensive and temporal aspects of behavior. Intensity includes both the amplitude of response (more or less anger, for example) and the threshold of response (the measurement of which is not specified). The temporal aspects include three borrowed from Rothbart and Derryberry (1981): time between stimulus and response, time taken for the response to reach its maximum intensity, and recovery time (presumably, total duration of response would also be counted).

To the question of why they confine their study of temperament to infancy, Goldsmith and Campos answer, "the infant is less susceptible to a number of socializing influences which can later mask underlying temperament" (1982, p. 174). It follows that they assume a biological origin for temperaments, but they refrain from speculating about how temperaments originate, while admitting the possibility of genetic influences.

Comment

A basic assumption of this approach is that temperament refers to the emotional aspects of behavior. The only way we can decide what Goldsmith and Campos mean by emotion is to examine how they operationalize the term, and this has been done in Goldsmith's (1982) list of five dimensions of temperament. Three elements on the list—anger, fearfulness, and pleasure/joy—are obviously emotions. There may be a serious problem of distinguishing fear from anger early in infancy, and it would appear that joy at seeing a loved one would be qualitatively different from the pleasure of playing with a toy, but these are minor issues. In terms of these three emotions, the twin results from this research suggest moderate heritability for fear and anger but not for pleasure/joy: "The results for both assessment strategies showed that individual differences in negative emotions (fear, anger) are moderately heritable. Hedonically positive emotions (pleasure, interest) evinced primarily shared environmental effects" (Goldsmith, 1983, pp. 73–74).

The major issue concerns the two remaining elements on the list: motoric activity and interest/persistence. Goldsmith and Campos (1982) see activity as "general arousal expressed via the motor system" (p. 181), a phrase that is broad enough to include many different aspects of behavior. Motor activity cannot be considered to be emotional in nature and therefore does not belong on a list of dimensions of temperament limited to emotion. Similarly, interest/persistence would seem to be a cognitive aspect of behavior, involving curiosity and the maintenance of attention; it does not belong on a list of dimensions of temperament defined as emotional. If interest/persistence and activity are examples of affect, it is hard to see which behaviors would not also be examples of affect. The theory would be clearer if it stated what is meant by *emotional* and operationalized the concept accordingly.

An insistence on the intensive and temporal aspects of behavior is entirely reasonable, but these aspects can be measured when assessing any kind of behavior, temperamental or otherwise. So far as we know, there are only three fundamental aspects of responses: amplitude or intensity, frequency or rate, and temporal characteristics (latency and duration). The problem with using these as criteria for defining temperament is that they define *all* responses.

In this approach is there any difference between temperament and personality? Goldsmith and Campos state that there is no clear distinction between the two but add that personality is marked by increasing importance of "social relations with others besides the primary caretaker(s) and the emerging concept of self" (1982, p. 179). Does this mean that temperament necessarily involves social relations with the primary caretaker? Does it mean that temperament comprises the foundation on which other aspects of personality are built? These questions are left unanswered, and we are forced to conclude that personality and temperament cannot be distinguished in this approach.

If we had to summarize this approach briefly, it would be: personality traits in infants, some emotional and some not, the causes and later developmental course being left unspecified. In reflecting on their definition of temperament, we find it difficult to distinguish temperament from other individual differences. In fairness to Goldsmith and Campos, they are aware that their formulation "does not qualify as a true theory of temperament" (1982, p. 1874). Rather it appears to be their approach to studying particular individual differences in infants, which might yield interesting developmental data.

REACTIVITY AND SELF-REGULATION

The approach of Rothbart and Derryberry (1981) attempts to link temperament to the way the nervous system functions. To this end, they have chosen as central concepts *reactivity* and *self-regulation,* which are properties of both the nervous system and behavior (in this instance, temperamental behavior). So far, they have dealt only with infant behavior, though their approach is similar to the theory proposed by Strelau (1965, 1983b) for adults.

The concept of reactivity appears to be defined by three response characteristics. The first is *threshold,* which reflects the infant's sensitivity to stimuli. It is well known that infants vary considerably in their responsivity, some reacting to the slightest noise or movement and others not reacting until the stimulation is stronger.

The second response characteristic is *intensity,* which refers to the strength of the infant's reaction. When upset some infants howl, whereas others merely whimper. Such reactions tend to rise to a peak and then subside as the infant becomes soothed. This *temporal* aspect of intensity is the third response characteristic.

Thus responses are initiated, rise to a peak of intensity, and then subside and disappear. Reactivity, however, is not the sole determinant of such response characteristics; the concept of self-regulation is also involved "to increase, decrease, maintain, and restructure the patterning of reactivity in either an anticipating or correctional manner" (Rothbart & Derryberry, 1981, pp. 51–52). Self-regulation is managed through three behavioral processes.

The first is *approach or avoidance,* concepts already discussed in the last chapter. The second is *attention:* the infant can increase arousal by attending to stimuli or decrease arousal by directing attention away from the eliciting stimulus. The third is *self-stimulation* or *self-soothing,* which are self-explanatory. Thus self-regulation can be achieved by motor behavior (approach/avoidance), by cognitive behavior (attention), or by self-reactions. What is being regulated is the infant's level of behavioral or neural arousal, hence the inclusion of this approach in our chapter on arousal.

These concepts must of course be operationalized, but the only instances we discovered were the Infant Behavior Questionnaire and related observations of infants at home. There are four dimensions: activity level, smiling and laughter, fear, and distress to limitations. The last three obviously refer to emotional behavior and involve the phasic behavior that is the focus of this approach. Thus distress, fear, and laughter all have a threshold, a rise in intensity, and a subsidence. Activity level, however, refers to an average energy output over time (minutes, hours, days) and therefore involves few of the response characteristics central to this approach. We do not understand why activity level is included with the other dimensions, which involve one or another emotional response.

The issue leads to the broader question of how temperaments are different from other behaviors. All phasic behavior is characterized by variations in threshold and the temporal aspects of intensity, whether the response is fear or looking through a telescope. All such behaviors involve reactivity and self-regulation. Rothbart and Derryberry do not make it easier to differentiate temperaments from other behaviors by linking reactivity with both behavioral and physiological systems and by linking self-regulation to both behavioral and neural processes. Most behaviors involve these systems and processes, and they have specified no particular physiological or neural measures that serve to operationalize their concepts.

They have also made it difficult to test their hypotheses about reactive and self-regulatory processes by intertwining them: "In an approach emphasizing the on-going, simultaneously interacting, nature of reactive and self-regulatory processes, the two are virtually inseparable. Self-regulating processes come into play at the earliest phase of the processing sequence, influencing the resultant reactivity at every level" (pp. 54–55).

If temperaments are not distinguishable from other behavior by their underlying processes, perhaps they differ in their origins. In this approach, temperaments are clearly labeled as *constitutional* in origin. At first glance, this would seem to offer a basis for distinguishing temperaments from other behaviors of nonconstitutional origin. Rothbart and Derryberry, however, define constitutional as "the relatively enduring biological makeup of the organism influenced over time by heredity, maturation, and experience" (1981, p. 40). In our view, most personality dispositions originate in some combination of heredity, maturation, and experience. We are therefore forced to conclude that this approach does not distinguish temperaments from other dispositions, and we remain puzzled why some behaviors are selected for study and others omitted.

Finally, if Rothbart and Derryberry are offering a theory of temperament, we must reluctantly conclude that its assumptions, operationalization, and hypotheses are not spelled out in sufficient detail. If they are merely discussing the background of their particular preferences for studying individual differences and have no theoretical aspirations, any evaluation must await the outcome of their research enterprise.

TEMPERAMENT AS "BEHAVIORAL INHIBITION"

It may appear strange to have a section on behavioral inhibition in a chapter on arousal. The reason for its inclusion will become clear as we examine the work of Kagan and his colleagues (Garcia Coll, Kagan, & Reznick, in press; Kagan, 1982b). How they operationalize their construct is of prime importance, so we shall start with this issue.

In the Garcia Coll et al. research (in press) 21- and 22-month-old infants were selected on the basis of extremes of the approach/withdrawal dimension that is part of the Toddler Temperament Scale (Fullard et al., 1978). The infants were brought to the laboratory and observed in a variety of social situations, including unfamiliar adults and unfamiliar objects. In coding the infants' behavior, the emphasis was on inhibition, fear, and withdrawal, as exemplified by crying, fretting, expressions of distress, clinging to the mother, and inhibition of play. Heart rate was also recorded.

A composite of all the behavioral observations correlated between .50 and .60 with parental ratings of the child's approach/withdrawal on the Toddler Temperament Scale. In addition, children who cried, clung more, and inhibited play tended to have a higher and more stable heart rate than children who were relaxed and uninhibited in play. Many of these children were observed interacting with peers 10 months later, and their prior laboratory behavior correlated .66 with the later peer behavior. In brief, parents' reports of temperament are related to the emotional behavior of their infants in the laboratory, and the laboratory behavior predicts later peer interaction. A cautionary note, however: These correlations were calculated by selecting only extreme subjects, leaving out the middle range, a procedure that leads to inflated correlation coefficients.

Garcia Coll et al. (in press) have clearly demonstrated the value of the temperament variable they call *behavioral inhibition*. We suggest, however, that this term may be misleading. The infants are not inhibiting behavior in the usual sense of this term: delaying response, resisting temptation, taking one's time in solving a problem (an issue extensively investigated previously by Kagan). Instead, the children are inhibiting their play behavior because they are fearful or distressed in a novel situation. Consider the examples offered by these investigators of the behavior they coded: sobbing, vocalizing distress, and clinging to the mother. These are all behavioral indicators of an aroused, distressed, and fearful child, and therefore we prefer to call the temperament they are assessing *emotionality*.

The way Garcia Coll et al. (in press) relate their work to that of others demonstrates that their concept is really emotionality. The approach/withdrawal dimension of the Toddler Temperament Scale (Fullard et al. 1978) consists largely of being afraid or not being afraid of novel social contexts. They also cite our earlier work (Buss & Plomin, 1975), in which the only relevant temperament would be emotionality. They refer to behavioral genetics research on emotionality and shyness (Plomin & Rowe, 1979) and to racial/ethnic differences in emotionality on the second day of life (Freedman, 1974). They also mention individual differences in introversion/extraversion, probably because so much of the behavior of infants is assessed in a social context. We maintain, however, that a distressed, fearful infant is not being given the opportunity to display any tendency to be more or less sociable; only placid children who are not upset are likely to engage in social interaction, especially when novelty is involved. In such situations only a single variable is needed: fearfulness. Fearful children will not interact, and children who are not afraid are likely to interact. In summary, we suggest that both scientific communication and conceptual clarity would be facilitated by calling the temperament under consideration *emotionality*.

Like some other investigators of individual differences in infancy, Kagan and his colleagues have not explicitly stated the origin of their temperament or its developmental course. The rationale for calling it a temperament resides in Allport's definition of temperament, which mentions the emotional aspects of behavior. Thus, Kagan and his colleagues have no specific theory of temperament, but do offer a distinctive perspective on early-appearing personality traits and their physiological correlates. The approach must be regarded as promising, for the empirical findings are good.

AROUSAL AND TEMPERAMENT

This chapter began by differentiating among brain, behavioral, and autonomic arousal. European researchers and a handful of American investigators have studied and theorized about temperament and brain arousal. They have paid scant attention, however, to temperament in young children or to the development of temperament. Most American students of temperament, on the contrary, have emphasized temperament and arousal in infants and children. One of our own temperaments, emotionality, is defined in terms of autonomic and (to a lesser extent) behavioral arousal. The exposition of our theory of emotionality in the next chapter should offer a comparison of how we and others approach temperament in terms of arousal.

5 Emotionality

Previous chapters have included general issues about temperament and others' approaches to temperament. The remainder of the book deals with our revised theory of temperament and relevant research. We begin with emotionality, which appears in one form or another in all approaches to temperament.

Virtually all discussions of emotion include three different components: expressions, feelings, and arousal. The expressive component deals mainly with the facial reactions that signal the presence of emotions. Though there is disagreement about how many different emotions can be discerned through observation of facial expressions, there is a consensus that fear, anger, elation, and depression can be distinguished (Ekman & Friesen, 1975; Izard, 1982; and Plutchik, 1980). Expressiveness, however, is not at issue in the present context, and we shall not pursue it.

The experiential or feeling component has been used to define emotions, but there are two problems with this approach. First, though we can subjectively separate such emotions as fear, anger, elation, and depression, we have considerably more trouble in distinguishing between anger and hatred, elation and love, shame and guilt, and so on. The problem is that the inner feelings are vague and subject to various personal interpretations and therefore offer a poor basis on which to evaluate emotions. Second, making experience the crucial aspect of emotion denies that animals have emotions, for we have no way of discovering their experience of emotion. Beyond these issues, Brady (1970) has suggested a good reason for distinguishing between feelings and emotions:

> Emotional behavior seems most usefully considered as part of a broad class of affective interactions, the primary consequences of which appears to change the organism's relationship to its external environment. Feelings or affective behavior, on the other hand, can be distinguished as a generic class of interactions, the principal effects of which are localized within the reacting organism rather than in the exteroceptive environment. Many different subclasses of feelings may be identified within this broad affective category, but emotional behavior seems uniquely definable in terms of a change or perturbation, characteristically abrupt and episodic, in the ongoing interaction between organism and environment. (p. 70)

Extrapolating from Brady's distinction, we suggest that what he calls emotional behavior involves arousal, but feelings do not.

The third component, arousal, is central to the present discussion. Which emotions involve arousal? An answer to this question requires a *baseline* of arousal for nonemotional behavior. It is well known that when people peer through a telescope or try to solve a mathematics problem, they are at least mildly aroused (Lacey, 1956). When a stimulus commands attention, the result is an orienting reflex, which is accompanied by an increase in muscle tone and skin conductance, changes in heart rate and blood pressure, and brain waves that are faster and of lower voltage (Lynn, 1966). Thus in the absence of emotion—an orienting response being perceptual or cognitive but certainly not affectively toned—there is some autonomic and brain arousal. If emotion involves an aroused state, it must be judged against the baseline of arousal that occurs in nonemotional states. Furthermore, behavioral and autonomic arousal are central, for these are the kinds of arousal associated with emotion (see Chapter 4).

Given this baseline of arousal as the basis of comparison, there appear to be only three emotions that involve arousal beyond that seen in the orienting response: fear, anger, and sexual arousal. This short list omits some of our most basic emotions: elation, depression, and love. When elated, people sometimes jump with joy, but it is the exercise of jumping that involves behavioral arousal, not the emotion itself; and there is no particular autonomic arousal in elation. Depression is of course a *low* arousal state. Love involves no particular behavioral or autonomic arousal unless it is accompanied by sexual arousal; the love of parents and the love of friends are low-arousal states. To this list of low-arousal emotions we can add admiration and contempt, pride and shame, hope and despair. They may be regarded as feelings in the sense meant by Brady (1970). As such, they involve not arousal but one or more of several bipolar dimensions: approach-withdrawal, acceptance-rejection, and pleasure-dysphoria. The various feelings have been classified along these lines in Table 5.1.

So far there is a short list of high-arousal emotions and a longer list of low-arousal emotions. This distinction has evolutionary and adaptive significance. Fear, anger, and sexual arousal are present in all mammals, and all three are strongly adaptive. Fear and anger are involved in the preparation of the organism to deal with threat: fear is preparation for flight, and anger is preparation for fight. They share an intense physiological build-up for massive action, a build-up mediated mainly by the sympathetic nervous system. The massive action of fight or flight has an obvious survival value. Sexual arousal is of course part of the physiological build-up for the sexual behavior necessary for reproduction. The initial phase of the arousal involves the parasympathetic division, which mediates tumescence; the later phases involve the sympathetic division

TABLE 5.1
Dichotomies of Low-Arousal Emotions (Feelings)

Dichotomy	Positive Pole	Negative Pole
Approach-Withdrawal	delight	disgust
	admiration	contempt
Acceptance-Rejection	love	hate
	pride	shame
Pleasure-Unpleasure	elation	depression
	hope	despair

(Masters & Johnson, 1966). Thus the three high-arousal emotions are crucial for survival of the individual (fear and rage) or survival of the species (sexual arousal), and they are present in all mammals.

Three of the low-arousal emotions—love, elation, and depression—seem to be present only in social mammals. Love may be considered as a basic unifying element among animals and humans. It starts with the mother-infant bond, which helps guarantee the care and social stimulation required by the infant and marks the beginning of all social relationships for the infant. Affection binds individuals together into nuclear families, kinship groups, or groups of individuals unrelated by blood ties. The deprivation of mother-infant affectional ties has been shown to induce profound grief at first and great elation when a pair is reunited (Kaufman & Rosenblum, 1967). In developmental terms, primordial elation and depression seem to be, respectively, the result of receiving affection or being denied it. Later in development, these two affects can be conditioned to other events, many of them nonsocial. Elation also appears to be the consequence of frisky play of the young, the adaptive aspects of which are well known. Thus the low-arousal emotions of love, elation, and grief occur only in social mammals, and these emotions are either adaptive or the consequences of adaptations.

The remainder of the low-arousal emotions—admiration, contempt, and so on, which comprise much of Table 5.1—confer no special adaptive advantage. Rather, they appear to be consequences of advanced cognitions of the kind found principally in *humans*. Pride and shame, for instance, are exclusively human. Though there are some researchers who claim them for other mammals as well, we suggest that such claims are based on anthropomorphism, for other animals lack the necessary advanced self known to be present in humans (Buss, 1980, Chapter 1).

The various kinds of emotions are summarized in Table 5.2. The sensory emotion of disgust occurs in all mammals. Primordial disgust, shared by all mammals is a reaction to a bad smell (skunks, for example), though in humans this reaction can be conditioned to a variety of aversive events—the sight of a dismembered body, for instance. The *autonomic* emotions of fear, anger, and sexual arousal are also present in all mammals, and their adaptiveness is well known. Social mammals have the previously mentioned emotions but also the *social affects* of love, elation, and depression, which are highly adaptive for animals whose existence depends on social bonding and group attachment. The *cognitive* emotions of admiration-contempt, hope-despair, and pride-shame have no particular adaptive value; their presence is merely a consequence of advanced cognitions that lead to an advanced sense of self (pride and shame) or to an elaboration of sensory, autonomic, or social emotions. Thus admiration might be elaborated from affection; contempt, from disgust or anger. Hope is obviously a product of the more primitive elation; despair is an elaboration of grief.

INHERITANCE

We have distinguished between low-arousal and high-arousal emotions. The high-arousal emotions included fear, anger, and sexual arousal; the low-arousal emotions included love, elation, depression, and a variety of cognitively toned emotions such as pride and contempt. There are undoubtedly individual differences in all these emotions, regardless of their arousal level. Which of these emotions is likely to involve individual differences that have an inherited component? The cognitively toned emotions—admiration and shame, for example—would appear to be largely shaped by the experiences of everyday life, and there is no particular reason for assuming that individual differences in them are inherited.

Individual differences in love, elation, and depression might have an inherited component, which means that they are potentially tempera-

TABLE 5.2
Evolution and Four Kinds of Emotions

	Sensory	*Autonomic*	*Social*	*Cognitive*
Mammals	disgust surprise	fear anger sexual arousal		
Social Mammals	disgust surprise	fear anger sexual arousal	love elation grief	
Humans	disgust surprise	fear anger sexual arousal	love-hate elation-grief	admiration-contempt hope-despair pride-shame

ments. Concerning individual differences in the tendency to be affectionate, insofar as there is an inherited component we suggest that it derives from sociability. Sociable people want the company of others and are strongly rewarded by it (by definition), and therefore, other things equal, they are likely to be more affectionate than unsociable people. Any inherited individual differences in affection, then, may be attributed to the temperament of sociability.

Individual differences in elation and depression may have an inherited component, if only by extrapolation from the abnormal range of these emotions. An inherited component has been established in both manic-depression psychosis and psychotic depression (Plomin, DeFries, & McClearn, 1980), but we shall not consider any psychological abnormality as a temperament; we include only individual differences in the normal range of personality. There may be inherited dispositions to be elated or dysphoric, but we suggest that, like the disposition to be more or less affectionate, such individual differences may be attributed to one or more of our temperaments. The elation-depression dimension appears to consist of two components. One is activity level. We are lively and energetic when elated, and dull and lethargic when depressed; one of the therapies for depression is activity therapy—getting the patient moving and involved in tasks. The second component of the elation-depression dimension is positive or negative affect. We speculate that the primordial feeling of dysphoria derives from being neglected or rejected by others. Sociable people have a greater need for others, and their higher level of motivation demands that they continue to seek social contacts when they are deprived of them. Unsociable people, needing people less, are more likely to give up the task of seeking others when they are needed. Depressed people, almost by definition, tend to surrender to their fate and find life too hopeless to continue struggling; such a feeling, we suggest, is more likely in unsociable people. Sociable people, being more motivated to seek others, will tend not to give up and will continue striving for the interaction and acceptance they seek. In brief, the temperaments of activity level and sociability, taken together, may suffice to account for any individual differences in the normal range of elation-depression that have an inherited component.

There remain the three high-arousal emotions of fear, rage, and sexual arousal. Though there are undoubtedly individual differences in sexual arousal, they have rarely been studied in humans. We are not referring to surveys of sexual practices or of frequency of sexual outlets but to the physiological arousal that has been studied by Masters and Johnson (1966). In contrast to the arousal of fear and anger, the arousal involves both the sympathetic and parasympathetic divisions of the autonomic nervous system. Individual differences in physiological sexual arousal have been established, but it is not known whether there is a genetic component. Thus, there is no empirical basis for including sexual arousal as a temperament.

EMOTIONALITY AS DISTRESS

We consider distress to be primordial emotionality. As used here, this term means not only being upset but also being in a state of high autonomic arousal. In everyday usage, distress is a broad term that includes not only such high-arousal states as pain and acute frustration but also low-arousal states such as bereavement. We exclude grief because it involves only low arousal. Underlying this usage is the assumption that what is inherited is the tendency to become aroused (autonomically) easily and intensely.

Distress can be observed in infants from the first day of life. They crinkle their face as if to cry, though no tears come forth. The face reddens, breath comes in gasps, and wailing commences. Some arch their back and make small thrashing movements. Such infants are obviously uncomfortable, and their distress is usually assuaged by picking them up, cradling them, and sometimes feeding them.

If distress can be observed so early in life, it follows from our approach that individual differences should also be apparent. They are. Lipton and his colleagues (Lipton & Steinschneider, 1964; Lipton, Steinschneider, & Richmond, 1961) recorded a variety of measures in neonates (heart rate, blood pressure, and so on) and found marked variations from one child to the next. The best behavioral measure of distress in infants is the presence of crying: the wailing complaint of an upset child, whether or not accompanied by tears. There are marked individual differences in crying on the first day of life (Korner, Hutchinson, Koperski, Kraemer, Schneider, 1981). Furthermore, these individual differences do not immediately disappear, for there is considerable reliability over the first 3 days of life: first-day versus third-day crying yielded a correlation of .80.

DIFFERENTIATION OF FEAR AND ANGER

We follow Bridges (1932) in assuming that distress, the most primitive negative emotion, differentiates during infancy into fear and anger. Bridges' observations were made in a foundling home, and the number of infants observed at that age was small, but she attempted to base her identification of various emotions on the infants' behavior rather than on her own intuitions or on analogy to adult reactions. Unlike Bridges, we assume that fear differentiates earlier than anger. Individual differences among infants are so marked, however, that it is difficult to assign an age in months at which fear and anger first appear. For our purposes such a precise estimate is unimportant. What is important is that during the first few months of life, all an observer can notice is distress. Some parents and some researchers may claim to see fear or anger during the first several months of an infant's life, but they may be seeing a distressed infant and labeling it as either fearful or angry.

When fear and anger do appear, they can be differentiated by the direction of behavior. (Later in childhood, fear, anger, and other emotions can also be distinguished by their particular facial expressions, but not early in infancy). Fear is accompanied by a shrinking from the aversive stimulus, an attempt to escape from the threat. At 2 to 3 months, infants have sufficient muscular control and coordination to turn the head or twist the body in an attempt to recoil from a fear stimulus. There are also the usual signs of distress: crying, screaming, and thrashing. What marks fear as different from distress, however, is the instrumental attempt at flight from the threatening stimulus.

Anger first appears some time later, probably during the sixth month. The aversive stimuli that elicit anger are not threatening but annoying or frustrating to infants: "Anger is expressed more in protesting shouts, pushing and kicking, but less in tearful screaming" (Bridges, 1932, p. 332). Whereas a fearful infant cowers and shrinks from a threatening stimulus, an angry infant attacks, pushes away, or complains loudly about a noxious stimulus. Fearful infants are insecure and need to be soothed; angry infants are negativistic and intemperate, and need to be distracted. The point to be emphasized here is that fear and anger involve opposite directions of behavior: escape or avoidance in fear, and attack or negativism in anger.

Though Bridges' paper has been the standard reference since 1932, the foundation she built for understanding the ontogenesis of emotion might be shaky for reasons mentioned above, such as her foundling sample, their hospital environment, and the unsystematic conditions for observations. Nonetheless, Sroufe's (1979) recent attempt to modernize Bridge's work has largely confirmed her conclusions. Sroufe's scheme shows wariness appearing at about 4 months, followed by anger at 7 months.

Both fear and anger involve more instrumentality of behavior than is observed in mere distress, which consists merely of uncoordinated kicking, squirming, and screaming. Fear requires only a small increase in instrumentality, for it requires little coordination and motor control to freeze, recoil, or twist away from the feared object. Attacking or pushing away an aversive stimulus requires more coordination and control, and thus anger involves more behavioral instrumentality. For this reason anger tends to appear later in infancy, once the infant has achieved a measure of skill in motor acts.

The greater instrumentality of anger over fear has an implication for their relationship to distress. Undifferentiated emotionality (distress) involves no particular instrumentality; it consists simply of being aroused and upset, accompanied usually by complaints about this aversive state. The differentiation of fear is only a small step, often involving only freezing or shrinking. It follows that fear is closer to distress than is anger. In psychometric terms, this means that there should be more overlap between fearfulness items and distress items than between anger items and distress items.

Another implication of the difference in instrumentality concerns conditioning. Classical conditioning tends to be somewhat passive, the organism responding (often emotionally) after learning to respond to a stimulus that was previously neutral. The fear response tends to be somewhat passive and is therefore more likely to be susceptible to classical conditioning. The anger response is more active and instrumental and is therefore more susceptible to instrumental conditioning, which is response learning. None of this implies that anger and fear are linked specifically to a single kind of learning. There can be instrumental conditioning in fear, the organism learning different kinds of escape responses. And there can be classical conditioning of anger responses, the organism learning that previously neutral stimuli incite anger—reflexive rage when the flag is desecrated, for example. The point being made is that there is a tilt or susceptibility toward one or another kind of learning: New stimuli are more likely to be linked to fear (classical conditioning), and new responses are more likely to be linked to anger (instrumental conditioning).

Physiology

For some time there has been a belief that anger and fear can be distinguished physiologically. If in children there were two entirely different patterns of physiological reactivity, one for fear and one for rage, our assumption of a single inherited tendency (distress) would be challenged. The available evidence involves only adult subjects, in whom different patterns might have been acquired, but the data do bear indirectly on our theory.

The experiments most cited to support distinct physiological patterns are those of Ax (1953) and J. Schachter (1957). Both experiments used the same procedures, and there was also overlap in subjects' data. Subjects were angered by being harassed by an experimental aide, and they were also scared by the threat of being exposed to severe electric shock. Six of the 14 recorded physiological measures were significantly different when subjects were angered than when they were frightened. To evaluate these findings, we must examine the experiments in more detail.

Here is how Ax (1953) angered the subjects:

> At the beginning of the anger stimulus, the operator entered the room stating that he must check the wiring because some calibration might be off. The experimenter objected but agreed to go into the other room and operate the polygraph. The operator shut off the music, criticized the nurse, and told the subject sarcastically that it would have helped to be on time. He checked the electrodes, roughly adjusted the subject, and criticized him for moving, non-cooperation, and other behavior. After five minutes of abuse, the operator left. (p. 435)

Though the subject was provoked by jostling and insults, at no time was he treated so badly as to become enraged. Contrast the mildness of the anger manipulation with severity of the fear manipulation:

> The fear stimulus consisted of a gradually intermittent shock stimulus to the little finger which never reached an intensity sufficient to cause pain. When the subject reported the sensation, the experimenter expressed surprise, checked the wiring, pressed a key which caused sparks to jump near the subject, then exclaimed with alarm that this was a dangerous high voltage short circuit. The experimenter created an atmosphere of alarm and confusion. After five minutes from the time the subject reported the shock, the experimenter removed the shock wire, assuring the subject that all danger was past. (p. 435)

This realistically dangerous situation effectively frightened the subjects, one of whom reported saying his prayers. A comparison of the fear manipulation with the anger manipulation reveals that the fear induction was more intense, which contaminates the comparison of physiological arousal for the two emotions: any differences in arousal might be due to greater fear than anger.

Concerning the data, neither Ax nor Schachter found mean differences between fear and anger for systolic blood pressure, diastolic blood pressure, or heart rate. Furthermore, Ax found much larger changes in heart rate in both fear and anger than did Schachter, which raises a serious problem of the reliability of the physiological measures.

Ax selected only the measures that significantly differentiated fear from anger, and for each measure he correlated the changes in fear with those in anger. The correlations ranged from .26 to .77, with a mean of .53. Thus, on the very measures that specifically distinguished fear from anger in this study, the correlations between fear and anger ranged from moderate to high. And, given the reliability of measurement, the average correlation of these measures between fear and anger (.53) suggests that physiological reactivity in these two emotions is closely related. Such a relationship could occur even if the intensities of the emotions were different, as suggested earlier; only mean changes would be affected by differences in intensity of arousal between anger and fear.

In attempting to understand their data, Ax and others have suggested that anger mimics the action of noradrenaline and fear mimics the action of adrenaline (both substances are neural transmitters). Close examination of their data in Buss (1961, pp. 94–97) reveals that they do not conform to the physiological patterns hypothesized for these two neural transmitter substances. In addition, there is a serious question of whether there is a meaningful distinction between physiological arousal that occurs as a result of an excess of noradrenaline versus an excess of adrenaline (Frankenhaeuser, 1971).

In brief, there is little basis at present for distinguishing *physiologically* between fear and anger. Even if minor differences were found, however, they would not negate our hypothesis, for both fear and anger involve a physiological arousal preparatory for massive action in the face of threat. Whether the response to threat is flight or fight, massive action is needed, the preparation for which involves widespread changes in the distribution of blood and the utilization of energy. In physiological terms, it would hardly be adaptive to have an entirely different physiological pattern of arousal in fear than in anger. The sympathetic division of the autonomic nervous system is involved in both fear and anger; given the chain of sympathetic ganglia, it is difficult to envision the kinds of differential patterns that Ax and others have suggested. Thus, our reading of the physiological evidence suggests that it is consistent with our hypothesis that what is inherited in emotionality is the tendency to become physiologically aroused (sympathetic reactivity) regardless of whether the particular emotion is distress, fear, or anger.

THEORY OF EMOTIONALITY

We can now present our approach to emotionality temperament in its entirety. Emotionality equals distress, the tendency to become upset easily and intensely. Compared to unemotional people, emotional people become more distressed when confronted with emotion-laden stimuli—the stresses of everyday life—and they react with higher levels of emotional arousal. It follows that they should be harder to soothe, an expectation that is borne out in children: emotionality correlates $-.42$ with soothability (Rowe & Plomin, 1977). We assume that underlying this arousal is an overactive sympathetic division of the autonomic nervous system.

The primordial distress differentiates during the first year of life into fear and anger. Fear occurs first, presumably because it involves less coordination and instrumentality to recoil and retreat than to attack. Thus anger may require a few weeks more of the maturation process. With continued development, emotionality appears more and more as either fear or rage, less and less as undifferentiated distress. Distress, however, does not disappear entirely and may be seen in adults, usually as the emotion reaction typically described as frustration. Many people become distressed when they must wait for an event to happen, even when the event is not aversive and therefore is anticipated with neither fear nor anger. Calamities can cause distress; typical examples are discovering that one's car has been wrecked, though no one is at fault; or an election outcome that one regards as disastrous. And aversive biological states can cause considerable distress; many people get extremely upset when they suffer pain, hunger, or thirst, but none of these conditions usually causes anger or fear. All these situations share a common inability to cope with the problem by means of running away or of attacking, and so neither fear nor anger is an appropriate emotion. This lack of instrumentality is directly analogous to the situation of the infant, who has no means of dealing with aversiveness and who therefore responds with undifferentiated distress.

Fear is closer to distress in its relative lack of differentiation and lesser need for instrumentality; anger differs more from distress in these attributes. It follows that fear should be more correlated with distress than is anger. It also follows that, other things equal, distress is more likely to differentiate in the direction of fear than in the direction of anger: Given that an infant is emotional, it is more likely to develop into a fearful child or adult than an angry one.

Other things are often not equal, and there are variables that tilt emotionality toward fear or toward anger. The first concerns other temperaments and traits. A child who is high in activity is more likely to take vigorous action in response to threat and therefore to manifest more anger than fear. Similarly, a child high in the trait of excitement seeking will not shrink from the challenge of fighting, whereas a child low in excitement seeking is unlikely to be aroused by challenge and will therefore be less rewarded and less likely to engage in angry aggression. The other variables that tilt children toward fear or anger involve the events of development.

Development

When infants are upset, they let everyone know it by whimpering and howling; as parents know, some infants tend to cry loudly and often. During the first year of life, parents deal with their infants' complaints first by soothing them and later by soothing or ignoring them. Starting some time in the second year of life, however, most parents are less tolerant of their infants' crying. As children mature, they are expected to become less distressed and to voice their complaints less frequently and with lower volume. Young children are allowed to express fear, but with increasing maturity, they are gradually denied expression of distress or rage. Parents tend to react by either ignoring or punishing such outbursts, and most children gradually diminish the frequency and intensity of their outbursts either by discovering instrumental means of dealing with emotional situations or by suppressing expression of their distress.

Thus as children mature, there is a normative diminution of the negative emotions, fostered by the socialization practices of parents and other caretakers and by the unwillingness of peers to put up with outbursts. Controlling and minimizing expressions of distress, fear, and rage are especially difficult for children high in the temperament of emotionality. They tend to have more frequent and more intense emotional reactions, by definition, and therefore have more negative behavior that needs to be controlled. Metaphorically, they have a larger engine, which requires stronger brakes.

By the second half of the first year of life, distress has differentiated into fear and anger. Children are especially susceptible to the classical conditioning of fear, attaching it to a variety of events and objects that do not innately induce fear. The frequency and intensity of such fear conditioning should be enhanced by the temperament of emotionality; consequently, emotional children should develop more fears than unemotional children. There are no longitudinal data that might test this prediction, but there are findings from research on the common fears of twins (Rose, Miller, & Pogue-Geile, 1981). Comparison of identical twins with fraternal twins revealed an inherited component for fear of spiders and snakes, public speaking, and negative social evaluation. Not all strong fears had a heritable component, however; identical twins and fraternal twins did not differ on fear of illness or death, others' illness or death, or fear of water. These behavioral genetics findings—that several common fears have an inherited basis—are in accord with our hypothesis that children high in the temperament of emotionality are likely to develop severe fears.

Early in childhood, sometimes even in infancy, children have been labeled as *easy* or *difficult* (Thomas & Chess, 1977). We suggest that the major reason for any child's receiving one of these labels is its emotionality. Children low in emotionality get upset less, have fewer temper tantrums, and tend not to whine and cry in fear; children high in emotionality are at the opposite pole. The term *difficult* may conceal important differences, for in terms of emotionality, children can be difficult in two different ways. One way is to be timid, anxious, and whiny. Such children tend to remain excessively dependent on their caretakers, demanding of help and soothing, and hard to soothe because of the intensity of their distress. Daniels, Plomin and Greenhalgh (1983) have shown that difficult temperament correlates .45 with emotionality (distress) and $-.35$ with soothability which lends support to the view of difficult children as easily distressed and difficult to soothe.

The other kind of difficult child is aggressive, hostile, argumentative, and negativistic. Like the fearful child, the angry child is hard to deal with because of its intense and frequent emotional reactions—usually temper tantrums, a major share of which may be attributed to the temperament of emotionality.

When children are first identified as difficult early in infancy, the reason may be their undifferentiated tendency to become distressed. When they are labeled as difficult later in childhood, however, it is likely that they will be described as *either* fearful or angry, but not both. Thus the later description may not exactly match the earlier one, the earlier distress having given way to either fear or anger. When the later problem is anger, the descriptions may even be regarded as a mismatch, when in reality the later anger is merely a specific form of the earlier, less differentiated distress.

Concerning these *difficult* children, they are likely to tilt toward one or the other side of the dominance-submission polarity later in childhood and in adolescence. Fearful children may be expected to become submissive because they tend to recoil and retreat in the face of threat. Angry children, other things equal, may be expected to become dominant because they tend to react angrily to threat and resort quickly to angry expression, one result of which can be dominance over peers.

Gender Roles.   Among older children, boys tend to express more anger than girls, and girls tend to express more fear than boys. These facts have been well documented (Buss & Plomin, 1975; Maccoby & Jacklin, 1974). Perhaps these gender differences reflect inherited differences that separate males from females. We examined the available evidence in our 1975 book and found no evidence for such inherited sex differences. No recent data have altered this conclusion. There is evidence that starting in infancy, boys and girls tend to be socialized differently, and this is the starting point for our explanation of gender differences in fear and anger.

We see no basis for assuming a gender difference in distress in infancy

(Buss & Plomin, 1975). We assume inherited individual differences in emotionality but not inherited gender differences in emotionality. If our position is correct, there should be no difference between male and female infants in distress. Distress occurs early in life, before the infant becomes aware of its gender. Mothers may treat male infants differently than female infants, but gender role training does not begin in earnest until the second year of life. It is during the second year of life that the child walks, starts to speak, and develops a variety of gross instrumental behaviors. Such instrumentality is necessary for the differentiation of anger from the more primitive distress.

We assume that gender role training in emotionality focuses on anger and fear. In traditional gender socialization, boys are allowed to become angry but not fearful; girls are allowed to be afraid but not angry. These differences are relative; boys are allowed fear if the threat is sufficient, and girls are allowed anger if the provocation is sufficient. But culturally, fear appears to be a more feminine emotion, anger a more masculine emotion.

The difference may be merely one aspect of the larger pattern of gender roles. Girls are allowed to be passive and dependent; that is, they are permitted to retain the subordinate role of the child. A young child is relatively helpless in the face of threat or challenges to its poorly developed instrumentality. It must depend on adults for security, defense, and most of the instrumental acts necessary for survival. The *traditional* feminine role in our culture sustains this pattern, and women are encouraged to depend on men as they once depended on parents. This is not to say that traditional women are without power, but their means of manipulation—indirect appeals and negativism, rather than direct challenges—are those of a subordinate in relationship to a controlling figure.

The angry woman presents a challenge to a man, and the traditional man resents challenge from a woman. Anger in older girls and women may be punished physically but more often by the denial of resources and by a loss of affection. The latter is crucial, for a basic motivation for traditional women is to be loved and admired. Fearful women may be protected and loved by traditional men; angry women, never.

The traditional male role is symmetrically opposite; fear is suppressed and anger allowed. Boys are supposed to be adventurous, self-reliant, and courageous. Courage and sense of adventure cannot become manifest in a safe environment. Only by taking risks and facing threats can a boy demonstrate the virtues appropriate to his gender role. Bravery is a source of esteem for males; cowards are sneered at or pitied. To be afraid is to be a sissy. Thus, boys are taught to inhibit fear.

They are also taught to compete head on. Challenges are met directly, usually with aggression. Given the directness, challenge, and instrumentality that define the male role, it is no surprise that boys are quick to anger. Ask any parent about a typical negative interaction between daughter and son: the daughter taunts and teases her brother, using verbal acts of at least some subtlety; the brother typically responds with anger and physical aggression.

The self-reliance of the male role cannot help but push boys toward anger. Boys are trained to be independent and therefore chafe easily when restricted or forced to comply. Boys will be more negativistic, rebellious, and quarrelsome. In short, gender role training clearly differentiates the emotions of fear and anger: Girls are more fearful and less prone to anger than boys.

Fear versus Anger. When the personality trait of fear is correlated with the trait of anger, on the assumption that each of these traits has a strong inherited component, we expect them to be essentially uncorrelated. This low relationship may conceal entirely different correlations, one for unemotional people and one for emotional people. Unemotional people are likely to be low in both fear and anger, so the bottom part of the emotionality dimension should yield a positive correlation. Emotional people are likely to be either angry or fearful but not usually both. It is true that anyone who is emotional is likely to manifest at least a little fear and a little anger. But we assume that in most emotional people, anger predominates or fear predominates. Emotional individuals who tend to be equally angry and fearful are expected to be rare. Thus the top part of the emotionality dimension (those high in emotionality) is expected to yield a negative correlation between the traits of fear and anger.

This suggestion of a negative correlation, that emotional people are either fearful or angry but not both, may appear paradoxical. After all, what is presumably inherited is an overreactive sympathetic division of the autonomic nervous system. If the sympathetic division fires so quickly and so intensively, should not the person who has a strong fear reaction also have a strong anger reaction? Our answer is that such a positive relationship is rare because at issue here is not the autonomic reaction (the same in fear and rage) but the conditions that produce the reaction. Through classical conditioning, instrumental conditioning, and observational learning, children learn which stimuli incite fear and which incite anger. And they learn to inhibit fear (socialization of males) or to inhibit anger (socialization of females). After various kinds of learning experiences and socialization pressures, those high in emotionality have made a clear differentiation in both the stimuli that incite an emotional reaction and the kind of reaction that occurs. They tend to be fearful or angry, not both.

An analogy to sexual outlet may help to make this point. Humans are born with a sexual arousal apparatus, but there is no built-in tendency to direct this sexual arousal to any particular target or object. In the ordinary course of socialization, most people become sexually aroused by the opposite gender. Once the outlet for the sexual arousal mechanism has been thus differentiated, heterosexuals are not at all stimulated by members of the same sex. Our arousal tendencies may remain strong, but they are limited to particular conditions (heterosexuality). Similarly, a minority develops into homosexuals, who can become strongly aroused by members of the same sex but have no sexual response to opposite-sex partners. There are bisexuals who seem to be aroused by both men and women, but such people are rare. Virtually everyone is either heterosexual or homosexual, not both. This situation is analogous to the one described above: Most people high in emotionality are angry or fearful but not both. As sexual arousal becomes linked to only one set of conditions, so sympathetic arousal becomes linked to one of two psychological reactions, fear or anger.

Matching

The term *matching* refers to whether the individual's level of temperament (in this instance, emotionality) is roughly the same or different from that of immediate companions, or whether the level of temperament is congruent with the nonsocial environment.

If the child and its mother (or other major caretaker) are both low in emotionality, there should be few problems in the interaction, for neither one becomes upset easily. If the child is emotional and the mother is not, there will be emotional turmoil because of the child's temperament, but these problems will be minimized by the mother's lack of emotionality. She will regard the child as difficult but will tend to react calmly to the child's fears or tantrums and therefore partially counteract the child's emotionality. If the child is unemotional, it will offer fewer problems, but an emotional mother will tend to magnify these problems. By presenting a more stressful social environment, she will elevate the child's low level of distress. She may also offer the child an emotional model to be copied. Still, the mother's contribution would appear to be less than the contribution of inheritance, and the child is likely to remain on the low end of emotionality. If both child and mother are high in emotionality, the child suffers from double jeopardy. Its natural tendency to become upset is likely to be intensified by the mother's emotional reactions and by observational learning of her behavior. If the child's high emotionality differentiates mainly into fear, the mother's amplification of the fear might be enough to tilt the child toward neurotic behavior.

Analogous problems may arise in marriage, though by adulthood there is considerably more resistance to change than in childhood. If both spouses are unemotional, the marriage should be calm and relatively free of the anxieties and fights that may occur when two people live together. If one is emotional and the other unemotional, there are likely to be marital problems but solvable ones. If one partner tends to be anxious, the other is available for soothing; and if the unemotional one is sufficiently mature, he or she can allow for the partner's insecurity. If one partner tends to become angry, this form of emotionality is harder to cope with, but a mature, unemotional partner may be able to sooth ruffled feathers and also know when to tread softly or even try avoidance. None of these possibilities is available when both spouses are emotional. If both partners are fearful, they would tend to reinforce each other's anxieties and thereby intensify any neurotic tendencies. Some couples, however, can adjust to such a situation. If one partner is fearful and the other becomes angry easily, an accommodation is possible, the extreme of which is a neurotic, sado-masochistic relationship. Some traditional marriages seem to work on this basis, however, so long as it is the husband who has the temper and the wife, the fears. If both partners tend toward anger, there would seem to be little hope for the marriage. There would be so much fighting and so little soothing that both spouses would become more irritable and anger-prone, and the relationship would necessarily disintegrate.

Concerning the environment, the most interesting possibilities are mismatches. If a young girl is emotional and has most of the emotionality differentiate into anger, she is likely to experience conflict with socializing agents and with peers, especially if her family and friends are traditional. She is likely to be regarded as willful, and in the face of continual pressure to conform to a girl's role (minimal anger) she may become rebellious. The other side of the coin is the emotional boy who is especially fearful. In a traditional setting, he will often be labeled as a sissy and may have to suffer the shame of being regarded as unmasculine as he grows up.

Concerning vocations, only those high in emotionality are likely to have problems. If the job has elements of danger (chance of bodily harm or of losing considerable money), a fearful person might become neurotic. If the job requires cooperation and perhaps even mediation, or if the job requires patience in putting up with delays or perhaps even incompetence, the emotional person who tends to become enraged easily will not be able to adjust. In both instances, there is the possibility of somatic problems developing from such mismatches between temperament and vocation. There are also vocations that involve considerable stress, such as being a surgeon (which may require many hours at the operating table), working in the middle of the New York Stock Exchange, or being an air traffic controller. These occupations would pose a threat to the psychological or physical health of anyone, but emotional people are especially at risk.

SUMMARY COMMENTS

Traditionally, emotion has been divided into the components of feelings, expression, and arousal. Feelings include the cognitions so central to current explanations of behavior. In our theory of temperament, arousal is the crucial component, because it is the only component in emotion likely to yield inherited individual differences.

In deciding which emotions constitute the temperament of emotionality, we start by distinguishing between high-arousal and low-arousal emotions, a distinction that leads to an evolutionary-adaptive account of emotions. In terms of autonomic arousal, we suggest that there are only three high-arousal emotions: fear, rage, and sexual arousal. Though there are surely differences in sexual arousal, such differences have rarely been studied, their origin is unknown, and they are largely irrelevant to early childhood. Therefore we limited the temperament of emotionality to fear, anger, and one other emotion. This other emotion, distress, is assumed to represent primordial emotionality: that which is inherited. It differentiates during infancy into fear and anger, though distress itself persists throughout life.

Having identified emotionality and described its developmental course, we attempt to show how it can account for some of the behavior of children labeled easy and difficult. The well-known gender differences (boys tilt toward anger, girls toward fear) can be explained by inherited gender differences, by gender role socialization, or by both. Our choice is gender role socialization, though continuing research on gender differences in the organization of the brain might eventually cause a reevaluation of this position. Finally, we discuss matches and mismatches in emotionality: between mother and infant, between peers, and between person and environment.

Some of our theoretical assumptions are speculative, others are extrapolations from data, and still others are data-based. Like many other psychologists, we are groping in a dim light, and our hypotheses represent one way of explaining the sparse available evidence. For the most part, those hypotheses are testable, and many of them are currently being tested.

6 Sociability

Sociability is the tendency to prefer the presence of others to being alone. Sociable children prefer group play, like to go to sleep with others in the same room, and in general value interaction with others over the benefits of privacy. Why do we want to be with others? An immediate and reasonable answer is the rewards that others might offer. Such rewards include money, goods, services, and information (Foa & Foa, 1974). These four are properly regarded as the basic elements of economic exchange, the things that are bought and sold every day in the marketplace. They can be bartered for one another—goods for services or information, and services for information—or money can purchase any of the others. These *economic* rewards are different from truly *social* rewards, which are ordinarily not bartered, bought, or sold. Consider the social reward of sympathy; with rare exception, it cannot be obtained for money or any of the other economic rewards, and it is not ordinarily exchanged for other social rewards. Economic rewards are important and worthy of study by economists and other social-behavioral scientists. From the perspective of temperament, however, we are interested only in those rewards that are intrinsically social.

INTERACTION SOCIAL REWARDS

This category includes five rewards that may be given by others: their presence, attention, sharing of activities, responsivity, and stimulation. The term *interaction* denotes that they flow naturally in social situations and are an intrinsic part of social contact (Buss, 1983).

Presence of Others

Like most other primates, ours is a highly social species. Though at times we cherish privacy, only hermits and disturbed persons prefer complete isolation, and there is a strong suspicion that most hermits are disturbed. It may appear redundant to regard the presence of others as a social reward when such presence is a necessary condition for social behavior.

This social reward does resemble other rewards, however, in that animals and humans seek it, are reinforced by it, and find its absence aversive. Most of us prefer that someone is already home to returning to an empty house; just the mere presence of another person can make a house less lonely. Furthermore, we can inquire about when the presence of others is a reward and when it is not. Thus subjects made fearful prefer to wait with others, whereas unafraid subjects prefer to wait alone (Schachter, 1959). It is a reasonable guess that most people prefer to wait alone in a physician's or dentist's office. In brief, though the presence of others is usually rewarding, it is not always so. As Altman (1975) observes:

> The desire for social interaction or noninteraction changes over time and with different circumstances. The idea of privacy as a dialectic process, therefore, means that there is a balance of opposing forces—to be open and accessible to others and to be shut off or closed to others—and that the net strength of these competing forces changes over time. (p. 23)

Time can be an important determiner of whether others' presence is rewarding. After a period of isolation, the presence of others is especially rewarding; after a prolonged period of others' presence, it may become aversive and privacy is now cherished. Solitude is also needed to lick wounds, plot revenge, contemplate a beloved person, or merely reflect about life.

Aside from time and occasion, the presence of others may be regarded as a dimension, the extremes of which tend to be aversive. The dimension is anchored at the low end by the complete absence of others, which is so painful that the isolation cell is used to punish recalcitrant prisoners. In milder form, isolation may be used to punish children, who are required to sit in a corner or to go to their room. One of the worst aspects of the job of night watchman is being cut off from others for the duration of the watch.

At the other extreme is the presence of too many others, which results in a feeling of being crowded. When an elevator car or bus is jammed with people, there is insufficient personal space and strangers cannot avoid touching others or breathing directly on them. When too many people reside in an apartment, no one has the privacy needed for bodily functions, intimacy, or sex. What most of us have experienced at one time or another has been documented by research over the past two decades: The presence of too many others is usually aversive (Altman, 1975; Freedman, 1975).

Thus the presence of others is a dimension anchored at either end by aversiveness (absence or excess). The rewarding part lies in the middle of dimension. The qualitative limits of this rewarding middle depend not only on the social context but also on the personality of the participants; more of this later.

Sharing an Activity

The presence of others is the bare minimum necessary for the term *social* to be invoked. It is a step up in being social to share an activity with others. Most people prefer to eat with others, watch movies or television together, or just watch the sun set with someone else. Many students choose to study in the library with others rather than at home alone; even at home, many prefer to study with at least one other person. Children enjoy playing in a nursery school filled with other children. Notice that all these examples involve people doing something in parallel, without any necessary social interaction. If one pays attention to another or if there is conversation, the social behavior moves beyond the upper limit of the mere sharing of activity. The lower limit approaches the presence of others; there is a fine line between these two social rewards, which may be seen in several examples. In a cafeteria line, others are obviously present, but no activity is shared. After you buy your meal and sit down to eat, if you eat at the same table with a stranger, you are sharing an activity. Similarly, a child waiting in line to enter a school bus is in the presence of others; on the bus and singing group songs, the child is sharing activity. The difference here is between an unorganized cluster of people (presence of others) and a crowd that has organization and a focus (sharing an activity).

Though some shared activities involve only one or two others—playing, eating, or watching television together—many activities involve large numbers of people. Thus movies, concerts, lectures, spectator sports, and virtually all performances require an audience that ranges from hundreds to many thousands. For such passive watching and listening, most people are not bothered by large crowds and, in fact, find crowds invigorating. The more people present, the more intensive is the reaction to the spectacle: people become aroused, cheer louder, boo more lustily, are less annoyed by the lack of personal space, and more excited by being part of a large mass of people. Thus for most shared activities, which usually involve being spectators, even a large number of people sharing the activity is rewarding. In contrast, when people are merely present and not sharing an activity, crowds tend to be aversive.

There are also times when too many people sharing an activity can be aversive. There may be too many children playing the same game at the playground. Similarly, eating at a crowded cafeteria table may be annoying. It is not just the lack of privacy but also the trouble in eating, playing, or doing whatever one is trying to do.

Attention

We usually want more than the company of others, even if they are sharing an activity. We often want them to look at us or listen to us. Why?

A reasonable guess is that we want to have our existence acknowledged and to be offered at least the minimal acceptance implied by receiving attention from another. It is well known that no one likes to be ignored, which causes dejection, anger, or both. When young children are ignored by adults, they tend to clamor for attention, often by crying or regressing.

Being ignored anchors one end of the dimension of attention from others. At the other end is excessive attention in the form of being stared at or examined closely. Children tend to become tense and initially distressed when they suddenly become the center of attention. Imagine a child entering a party or the family dining room, only to discover that all conversation has stopped and that all eyes are on it. Unless the child were uncommonly socially adept or habituated to such scrutiny, it would become flustered and embarrassed. Why do most of us avoid such conspicuousness? Some people report feeling exposed and vulnerable. Also, many children associate being scrutinized with being criticized by adults (for a mistake in appearance or social behavior) or by peers (ridicule or teasing). The residual of this association between being examined closely and negative consequences tends to be an aversion to conspicuousness.

Thus, in common with previously mentioned process social rewards, attention from others is rewarding only in the middle of the dimension. The reason for this appears to be a conflict between two opposing motives. We want acknowledgment that we exist and are at least minimally accepted by others, but we also want privacy from prying eyes and ears to avoid feeling naked and vulnerable.

Responsivity

Merely being present involves no particular behavior, but sharing an activity does; and paying attention to someone implies even more social behavior. When the other person is responsive, there is a true social *interaction*. Thus, in a conversation, the listener not only pays attention but also reacts to the speaker with agreement, disagreement, surprise, interest, and an entire repertoire of responses, which serve as stimuli for continued behavior by the speaker. Such mutual responsivity, the essence of social behavior, may be the principal reason that unacquainted people seek each other's acquaintance.

Why is responsivity so rewarding? What is special about responsivity is that the other person's response is not completely determined by one's own behavior; the other's behavior is to some degree indeterminate and unpredictable. The potential novelty of the other person's response makes it interesting, for we are all rewarded by at least some degree of novelty. And one's own subsequent response is stimulated by the other's previous answer, which means that one's own behavior is partly indeterminate. Such novelty of behavior, one's own and the other person's, offers an increment of *arousal,* which, when it is not excessive, appears to be intrinsically rewarding. Why do we seek such arousal? Why does its absence cause boredom? Here we must fall back on an assumption shared by many psychologists: We are built that way, as are other primates. Responsiveness has been found to be important when infant monkeys are raised with "robot mothers." The infants strongly prefer robot mothers capable of rebound (when touched, they swing and may bump the infant) to absolutely still robot mothers (Mason, 1970). Human infants delight in playing the game of giving an adult a toy or flower, only to have the adult give it back. This interaction resembles the turn taking of conversation.

Compared to the extremes of presence, sharing, and attention, the extremes of responsivity are not particularly aversive. People who are unresponsive and lifeless or who are repetitive and entirely predictable are regarded as dull, and we avoid them. But there are much worse things than boredom; being alone, acting alone, and being ignored have already been mentioned.

The opposite extreme, excessive responsivity, is also a minor annoyance. We recoil from people who, like children, are loud and brash in their responses, those whose emotional reactions are out of proportion to our own behavior, and those whose intensity quickly becomes wearing. Such over-responsivity, however, like the under-responsivity that causes boredom, it is rarely so negative that it cannot be tolerated. Overarousal and underarousal seem to be serious issues, however, for those whose homeostatic mechanisms are not fully in place: infants and young children. Excessive responsivity may frighten an infant or overarouse it to the point of discomfort and tears.

Initiation

This last interaction reward involves not just responding in a social interaction but getting it started. There are people who welcome conversation but remain passive, responding only when another person has taken the lead, especially with strangers or casual acquaintances. Taking the initiative involves the risk of rebuff, which cannot occur if one is merely responsive. Such initiative also requires a higher level of activity, as well as leadership. Those who get things started socially, usually extraverts, are valued for it. They are preferred as acquaintances not only by other extraverts but also introverts, whose reticence requires that someone else take the lead (Hendrick & Brown, 1971).

Like the other social rewards, initiation may be regarded as a dimension. The lower bound, absence of initiation, results in no social exchange even getting started. When two shy children are introduced and left by

TABLE 6.1
Interaction Social Rewards

Reward	Absence	Excess
Presence of Others	Isolation	Crowding
Sharing Activities	Solitary Activities	Interference
Attention from Others	Shunning	Conspicuousness
Responsivity	Boredom	Over-Arousal
Initiation	No Interaction	Intrusiveness

themselves, their interaction is likely to be halting, minimal, or even absent. The upper bound of initiation may involve intrusion into the privacy of others. One danger of excessive extraversion is the likelihood of interfering with couples or trios whose conversation needs no further stimulation. Another source of aversiveness is being more friendly than the relationship or the situation warrants. Most adults recoil from such excess, and in infants it may elicit fear. Thus, as with the other process rewards, initiation is rewarding mainly in the large middle but not in the upper or lower bounds of the dimension.

Activity and Arousal

The interaction rewards are summarized in Table 6.1. They may be aligned on a dimension of psychological *activity* on the part of the person or persons delivering the reward. Presence of others requires nothing more than filling space. Sharing an activity involves doing something, but there is no focus on the recipient or interaction. In watching or listening to another person, there is a focus on the other person, which is psychologically more intense. Responsivity consists of a leap upward in activity, for now the other person is making a social *response* that focuses on the recipient. Initiation, which marks the peak of psychological activity, is self-starting instead of being merely reactive.

Each increment in activity increases the intensity of social *stimulation*, which elevates the recipient's level of *arousal*. The lowest level, presence of others, involves little stimulation or arousal. Sharing an activity (in a crowd watching a football game) offers some stimulation, not just from the game but also from being part of the crowd, and is therefore arousing. Working side by side with others has also been found to be arousing (Zajonc, 1965). Attention from others is highly stimulating and can cause either a pleasant "rush" of feeling or an unpleasant feeling of being too conspicuous. And the still higher level of stimulation that results from responsivity or initiation causes an even higher level of arousal.

We can appreciate these differences in stimulation and arousal when we inquire about technological or animal substitutions for people. The radio or phonograph are sometimes almost as good as the presence of others, perhaps because the auditory stimuli (talk or music) deny complete solitude. These media of communication, however, cannot substitute for any of the more socially stimulating process rewards. Television cannot be considered because it offers strong visual stimulation and so acts as a *distraction,* not a substitute for people, but conversation over the telephone is little different from conversation in person.

A recently developed technological device can substitute for social responsivity: the computer. Advanced computers are responsive in that part of the feedback they offer is indeterminate and therefore novel. Some can be hooked up to a mechanical "voice" that offers a simulated conversation with the user. Responsivity is enhanced by competition in recent generations of computer games. Here the user competes with the computer, which replaces a live opponent. Such computers can substitute for a real person because they offer the responsivity that is the hallmark of social interaction: I talk and you answer, or I try one tactic, and you respond with your own.

Animal pets are, for most of us and especially for children, better substitutes for people than are technological devices. A cat or dog is not only present, but may share an activity. They attend to their owners and even respond to them. Some initiate social interaction.

Neither animals nor computers completely replace people as the source of process rewards, for we do need our own kind. Even children's dolls are not adequate replacements, though they are excellent temporary substitutes. These substitutes, however, help us to focus on the various ways in which other people can be rewarding and how the various rewards differ along the dimensions of activity and social stimulation.

These interaction rewards, which occur naturally when people are together, are part of the process of social interaction, hence their name. There is another class of rewards that are not an intrinsic part of social interaction. They consist of social responses that recipients find rewarding; each response differs in content from the next, hence they are called *content* rewards. They are respect, praise, sympathy, and affection. This sequence assumes an increasing potency of reward and an implied closeness of social relationship, for the content rewards tend to occur mainly in the context of a relationship.

Interaction and content rewards must be regarded as universal incentives. If so, what is the relevance of personality traits? The social rewards are linked to personality traits in two ways. First, some people are likely to prefer certain of the rewards to others, a preference that may be linked to personality traits. Second, some people not only are reinforced by a particular reward but seem desperately to need it, and sociability is especially relevant.

We assume that all the interaction rewards are linked to the trait of sociability. Sociable people are more reinforced by the social rewards, are more motivated to seek them, and are more upset when deprived of them. Sociable people, by definition, prefer the company of others. This means that the presence of others is needed more by them than by unsociable people. Similarly, sociable people strongly prefer to share activities rather than to act alone. They tend to be more distressed when ignored and are most comfortable when receiving a modicum of attention from others. If there is a single social reward that is crucial for sociable people, it is *responsivity,* and this is especially true for those high in sociability. Extremely sociable people are ordinarily not satisfied with the mere presence of others or with sharing an activity; even attention from others does not suffice for long. True, they will accept these social rewards if nothing better is available, but what they really seek is the greater activity and stimulation that occur when another person is responsive. The back-and-forth, give-and-take of two people communicating represents the high point of social behavior.

The extremely sociable person's hierarchy of interaction rewards matches the sequence described earlier. Presence of others is the least in value, and value increases through sharing and attention to the peak of responsivity (and by implication, initiation). For such a person, the mere presence of others may be so little better than their absence as to be regarded as socially unrewarding. Similarly, an extremely sociable person might be unmotivated to seek sharing an activity if the activity were too dull—a faculty meeting for example. These rewards, however, apply mainly to those who are extremely sociable. Moderately sociable people presumably would settle for less stimulating social rewards. Like responsivity, initiation offers the most social stimulation, and both are needed by an extremely sociable person. Sociable people are likely to initiate social interactions because they want the social stimulation; being capable of initiating social interaction, they do not need this reward as much as they need responsivity. The people who desperately need others to initiate social behavior are those who seek social stimulation but are too tense and inhibited to make the attempt on their own: those who are both sociable and shy.

We assume that none of the content rewards is linked to sociability. Everyone likes respect, praise, sympathy, and affection, and sociable people are no different from others in their preference for these rewards. However, there are personality traits linked to the content rewards. Insofar as a concern for status is an important part of respect, formal people are expected to value respect more than others. Praise and affection are the major boosters of self-esteem, so those low in self-esteem especially value these two rewards. Sympathy and soothing are needed whenever people become upset. Who is likely to become distressed easily and intensely? Almost by definition, such people are likely to be high in the temperament of emotionality.

THE NATURE OF SOCIABILITY

These various assumptions about social rewards enable us to specify the nature of sociability. It consists of seeking and being especially gratified by the rewards that flow naturally in social interaction: presence of others, sharing of activities, attention from others, responsivity, and initiation. This sequence of rewards represents increments in reinforcing power. Responsivity may be regarded as the essence of what is sought in social interaction and what is more prized by sociable people. None of this denies the potency of the content rewards, which are universally sought. Respect, praise, sympathy, and affection, however, are not any more reinforcing for sociable people than for others.

Social interaction is obviously not always rewarding, for their excesses may be aversive: crowding, too much attention from others, and the intrusiveness that results from expressive responsivity or initiation. In a sense, social interaction may be a gamble in which one seeks rewards and risks punishments. We assume that sociable people are more strongly motivated to seek the rewards and therefore are more willing to tolerate the punishments: crowding, excessive attention, and intrusiveness.

Sociable people are not any more reinforced by the rewards of relationships (the content rewards) than is anyone else. The process rewards sought keenly by sociable people can be obtained in *any* social interaction and do not require a relationship. The content rewards, in contrast, are ordinarily available only when there is some sort of bond between people. To be sociable, then, is not to be especially susceptible to the joys of relationships but rather to seek out the social rewards, especially responsivity, that can be obtained whenever people get together.

We assume that there is an inherited component in the personality trait of sociability. Like most inherited behavioral tendencies, it is not immutable and can be shifted upward or downward by life events or by other temperaments. Do the negatives of social interaction diminish the inherited tendency to be sociable? Responsivity may be accompanied by excessive crowding, and privacy may be denied; relationships may be dominated by hostility and rejection, so that social interaction tends to become aversive and is less sought after. Other things being equal, however, sociable people experience no more negatives than anyone else. Indeed, because of their strong social motivation, they are likely to develop appropriate social skills and to continue seeking social interaction until they find contexts in which the rewards outweigh the punishments.

As a need to be with people, the trait of sociability must be considered a motive. We suggest that correlated with this motive is a tendency to *respond warmly* to others. Sociable children are more strongly reinforced by process social rewards, which tend to occur naturally in social interaction. When they receive these rewards, they are more delighted than are unsociable children, who place less value on responsivity, attention, and sharing of activities. Sociable children are glad to see others because they anticipate the social rewards they value. Other things equal, then, sociable children tend to smile more, to be more responsive to others, to attend to others more, and to share activities more—that is, they furnish the very social rewards that they find so reinforcing.

Other things may not be equal, however. Individual differences in formality may be important. Formal people are especially concerned with the unwritten rules that govern social behavior: manners, etiquette, forms of address, recognitions of status, and modesty. Their central concern in social behavior is *propriety:* doing what is correct and socially acceptable. They are particularly sensitive to differences between public and private contexts, and they draw a sharper line than most of us between allowable private behavior and allowable public behavior. Intent on doing the right thing and obeying social rules, they tend to be less open, less expressive, and therefore less warm. Informal people are just the opposite and express their feelings openly; as such, they are more likely to be warm in social situations.

Other things equal, sociable people may be expected to possess good social skills. After all, they are especially interested in people and in participating in social events. Their greater participation means that they will have more opportunities to acquire the skills that help in dealing with others. Furthermore, they are likely to value such skills more than most people, for social skills may help them to obtain the social rewards they seek.

It bears repeating that sociable children are less likely to be satisfied with the low-intensity process rewards (presence of others and sharing activities), their motivation being so strong that they need the higher-arousal rewards involved in attention, responsivity, and initiation. For the same reason, they are less likely to be satisfied with technological substitutes for people: various solitary games and computers. Highly sociable children seem to need flesh and blood; they might accept animal pets as substitutes for people, but not machines or games. Finally, given their strong need for people, sociable children are more susceptible to loneliness when deprived of social contacts.

INFANCY

The first relationship in which the temperament of sociability might play a role is that between mother and infant in the first year of life, when the infant is helpless and depends almost entirely on the mother for all its needs. Virtually all mothers start by accommodating to their infants' wants, both physiological and psychological. As a result of maternal adjustments to the infant, any impact of the infant's sociability temperament is likely to be concealed. When the infant is 6 to 8 months old, however, it can move about without maternal assistance, and most infants are sufficiently secure to leave the mother to play with toys or with strangers. Once the infant is no longer completely dependent on the mother, we can discern any impact of the temperament of sociability—both the infant's and the mother's.

Let us consider only the extremes: high or low sociability. If both mother and infant are high in sociability, the mother will be comfortable with the infant's demands for her and others' presence and attention, for sharing activities, and for the mutual give-and-take that occurs beyond the necessary feeding and maintenance routines. Similarly, if mother and infant are both low in sociability, both will be comfortable with the lower frequency of social contact, attention, sharing, and responsivity. Problems may arise, however, when there is a mismatch between the infant's and the mother's sociability temperament. Parenthetically, it may seem paradoxical that a mother's inborn sociability may differ from that of her infant. However, the mother contributes (on the average) only half of her offspring's genes; inherited personality traits are likely to be polygenic; and the lottery that occurs at conception allows for considerable divergence between parents and children.

If the infant is sociable and the mother unsociable, the mother is likely to regard the infant as excessively demanding. It may want more of her presence, attention, sharing of activities, and responsivity than she finds comfortable and regards as adequate. As a result, she is likely to be bothered by her infant and frustrate its need for greater social contact. The infant, deprived of the social rewards it seeks, may become irritable, give up the attempt, and settle for a lower level of social contact, or (and this is most likely) turn to others for the requisite social interaction.

If the infant is unsociable and the mother sociable, she is likely to be disappointed that the child does not seek her out and wish to maintain social contact as much as she expects. She may feel rejected and will have no choice but to accommodate to her infant's weaker need for social interaction. As a result, she may be less affectionate and initiate fewer contacts. If she has other children who are more receptive to such social contacts, she is likely to prefer them to the child whose sociability does not match her own. If this mother-child pair were seen in a laboratory setting after their behavior patterns had become established, an observer might emphasize the mother's apparent indifference to the child. The child's low sociability could be neatly explained by the lack of stimulation and social reinforcement by the mother. This explanation might be correct in some instances, but we suggest that in the majority of cases, the mother is *reacting* to her child's sociability, not causing it.

The infant's sociability temperament may also play a role in the development of stranger anxiety. Other things being equal (emotionality, for instance), a sociable infant is more strongly motivated to interact with strangers and will therefore be more likely to tolerate the higher arousal that accompanies such novelty. Even if a sociable child is initially anxious, the motivation to interact should make the child overcome the fear quicker than a child low in sociability temperament. Also, given that a sociable child seeks more interactions, it meets more strangers and therefore habituates to them. In brief, the temperament of sociability tends to minimize the occurrence of stranger anxiety and if it occurs, to shorten its duration.

Three Attachment Types

On the basis of how infants respond to separation and then reunion with their mothers, Ainsworth (1973, 1979; Ainsworth, Blehar, Waters, & Wall, 1978) has distinguished three types of infants. The *secure* infant allows the mother to leave with minimal protest and greets her warmly when she returns. The *avoidant* infant complains when the mother leaves and tends to ignore her when she returns. The *resistant* infant appears to be angry with the mother when she returns. This typology seems to be able to predict certain aspects of children's social behavior at 2 years (Matas, Arend, & Sroufe, 1978) and at 3½ years (Waters, Wippman, & Sroufe, 1979). Thus, though we should be wary of personality traits that are identifiable on the basis of behavior in a single social context, the typology appears to be useful.

We suggest that two temperaments may affect which kind of reaction the infant manifests in Ainsworth's attachment paradigm. Secure infants are likely to be at least moderately sociable and not especially emotional. Thus, they welcome the opportunity to play with a stranger (sociable), do not react with fear to the mother's absence (unemotional), and welcome her warmly on her return (sociable). Avoidant infants are likely to be unsociable and so play less with the stranger and are less interested in the mother when she returns. Resistant infants are likely to be emotional: They are fearful when the mother leaves and angry with her when she returns. We hasten to add that the temperaments of both infants and mothers comprise only one determinant of what happens between mothers and infants. Other aspects of the infant and the mother's socialization practices are also expected to play a role.

Other temperament researchers have related temperament to attachment types. Chess and Thomas (1982) suggest that "the infant's behavior in the Ainsworth Strange Situation could be appropriately rated under the temperamental categories of approach/withdrawal, adaptability, quality of mood, and intensity" (p. 220). Kagan (1982) states that "there is good reason to believe that the child's temperamental disposition to become distressed in uncertain situations makes an important contribution to behavior in the Strange Situation" (p. 24). Goldsmith and Campos (1982) also mention that attachment types might be related to differences in emotionality that are not specific to the infants' reactions to temporary loss of the mother.

Some evidence supports these hypotheses. Ambivalently attached infants cry nearly twice as much as securely attached infants as early as the first few months of life (Ainsworth, et al., 1978). Securely attached infants are more sociable with peers (Easterbrooks & Lamb, 1979; Liberman, 1977; Pastor, 1981; Waters, et al., 1979), and they are more sociable and less shy with strange adults (Main, 1974; Thompson & Lamb, 1983).

Some attachment researchers explain the relationship between security of attachment and infant sociability as being caused environmentally:

> Securely attached infants are likely to generalize the trust and confidence derived from interaction with their mothers to initial encounters with strangers. Conversely, insecurely attached infants should respond more negatively to strangers because of a history of inconsistent, unhelpful, or unsatisfying interactions with their mothers. (Thompson & Lamb, 1983, p. 185)

Our approach leads to a different interpretation: Children differ initially in sociability and emotionality and these temperaments affect social interaction with both mother and stranger.

Sroufe (1982), a prominent attachment researcher, flatly denies any influence of temperament on attachment: "attachment and temperament are orthogonal" (p. 744). He argues that shy behavior with strangers is irrelevant to Ainsworth's attachment types because wariness of strangers and amount of distress at separation are not used to classify infant attachment. There are also findings that he believes are difficult to explain in terms of temperament. Avoidant children appear to be dependent with their preschool teachers (Sroufe, in press); there is little agreement between infants' attachment classification with their mothers and their fathers (Main & Weston, 1981); and the Infant Temperament Questionnaire which measures the nine NYLS dimensions does not predict attachment classifications (Vaughn, Deinard, & Egeland, 1980). Only the last finding is damaging to a temperament interpretation, but the negative finding might be due to the use of the NYLS instrument. These points notwithstanding, we suggest that there are enough data in support of the hypothesis that temperament relates to attachment classifications to warrant further investigation.

Our remaining speculations concern the mother's temperaments. If she is unsociable and therefore does not offer the infant as much contact and stimulation as it needs, the infant tends to look to others for social contact and so might avoid the mother on her return. If the mother is at least moderately sociable and not especially emotional, her infant is more likely to be a secure baby.

The assumption that the sociability and emotionality of infants and of mothers are related to infants' attachment classifications has received support in an unpublished project by Bretherton, O'Connell, & Tracy (1980). They compared self-reports of mothers and ratings of their infants with infants' behavior in the Ainsworth Strange Situation. Attachment classifications were found to relate to shyness of the infant and sociability of the mother. As will be seen shortly, shyness derives from sociability and emotionality, and thus, by inference, this study supports our predictions.

BEHAVIOR WITH PEERS

When infants are playing with other infants, their behavior may be strongly influenced by the temperament of sociability. In a study involving observations of four infants at play, Bronson and Pankey (1977) discovered two relevant trends:

First, over repeated exposures to series of four-baby play sessions the individual babies became increasingly differentiated, and increasingly consistent, in their inclination to either withdraw from or engage in the situation. Since the cumulative exposure was roughly similar for all babies, the growing firmness of their differing reactions indicates that some sort of within-baby disposition was determining their individual evaluations. Second, the at-

titudes that developed toward the play session experiences were fairly predictive of peer behavor shown in a nursery school setting a year and a half
later. (p. 1182)

The within-baby disposition that was observed here would appear to be
the temperament of sociability, a trait likely to persevere throughout
childhood and surely be seen in a nursery school situation.

Once past infancy, children enter into an increasing range of social
contexts in which they are expected to develop social skills. To be sure,
these skills are at first primitive, consisting mainly of being able to respond verbally and nonverbally to initiations by others and perhaps even
starting an interaction. Children high in sociability temperament, by
definition, are more motivated to acquire such skills and are more rewarded by social incentives. They are more likely to acquire the requisite
skills and therefore enjoy social interactions. Children low in sociability
temperament are less motivated to acquire social skills and are less likely
to endure the negatives of social interaction; as a result, their social skills
may be expected to be poorer and they would therefore receive fewer
rewards in social contexts.

SHYNESS

Sociability and shyness tend to be regarded as more or less the same
personality trait, the idea being that shyness is nothing more than low
sociability. If this equivalence is accepted, shyness cannot be separated
from sociability, by definition. If we are explicit and precise in our usage,
however, shyness and sociability can be defined independently. Sociability is the tendency to affiliate with others and to prefer being with others
rather than being alone. Shyness refers to one's behavior when with
people who are casual acquaintances or strangers: inhibited and awkward, with feelings of tension and distress and a tendency to escape from
social interaction. Given these independent definitions, we can inquire
about the relationship between shyness and sociability (Cheek & Buss,
1981). Items involving shyness were written, a typical one being "I feel
inhibited in social situations," and sociability items were written, a typical
one being "I like to be with people." For college students, the correlation
between the shyness and sociability scales was -.30, suggesting that the
two are related; unsociable people tend to be shy, and sociable people
tend to be unshy. The size of the correlation is modest, however, suggesting that shyness and sociability should be regarded as distinct traits: Some
sociable people are also shy, and some unsociable people are also unshy.

There is also evidence that when people first meet, their behavior is determined not only by the trait of shyness but also by sociability (Cheek & Buss, 1981). Furthermore, the trait of fearfulness correlates .50 with shyness, but only -.09 with sociability; shy people tend to be fearful, but unsociable people are not necessarily fearful.

Confirmatory evidence in infancy comes from a study of 60 infants in which 8- and 9-month-olds rated as emotional by their parents displayed more fear of strangers in the laboratory (Berberian & Snyder, 1982). Because parents rate their children as emotional for many reasons other than their social interactions, these results suggest that even in infancy, emotionality is an important precursor of shyness.

Shyness refers mainly to behavior with strangers or casual acquaintances. Thus most shy children are not tense and inhibited with good friends and members of the family. Sociability, however, refers to the tendency to be with people generally: not only the desire to meet new people (and therefore interact with strangers) but also the tendency to remain in others' company for longer periods of time, and the desire to play with others rather than alone. In infancy, shyness appears mainly in the form of stranger anxiety (wariness), whereas sociability appears in the form of preferring to play with other children and not wanting to be left alone by adults. Thus there are conceptual and empirical grounds for keeping shyness and sociability distinct.

Both shyness and sociability have been found to be heritable. When the California Psychological Inventory was examined for heritable items, one factor consisted largely of shyness items (Horn, Plomin, & Rosenman, 1976). Our EASI I scale contains at least one shy item (and perhaps more, depending on one's interpretation of the items), and it is also heritable (Buss & Plomin, 1975, p. 240). Sociability has been found to be heritable in both the EASI I and the EASI III, as well as in other studies reviewed in the 1975 book and to be discussed later.

Given that both traits are heritable and that they are related, perhaps only one should be considered as a temperament and the other as a derivative. This is our position, of course, and as the title of this chapter indicates, we believe that sociability is the temperament and shyness the derivative. We have several reasons for this position. As mentioned above, shyness refers only to social behavior with people not known very well, whereas sociability refers to the tendency to want to be with (or not be with) people in all kinds of contexts and with whom there are all kinds of relationships. Thus sociability refers to a more generic tendency.

Also, as mentioned above, shyness correlates significantly with fearfulness and also with sociability, but sociability and fearfulness are uncorrelated. This pattern of relationships suggests that a large part of shyness may be attributed to a combination of fearfulness and low sociability. We suggest that the reason shyness has been found to be heritable is its overlap with the temperaments of sociability and emotionality.

It makes sense to regard shyness as fear in social situations, especially in early childhood, before the issue of self-consciousness becomes important. We must be careful to distinguish between shyness and fearfulness in infancy, however. If the child fears only unknown people or is wary in its approach to them, this behavior is shyness. If the child is fearful not only of strangers but also of strange objects, events, and environments, this behavior is fearfulness. Fear behavior, which includes both social and nonsocial contexts, is the more generalized reaction than shyness, which occurs only in social contexts.

Why is there a relationship between shyness and sociability? One possibility lies in the issue of social skills and motivation, discussed earlier. Unsociable children are less rewarded by social incentives (by definition) and therefore find social contacts less enjoyable. Having fewer social contacts, they do not fully develop their social skills and therefore feel insecure and inadequate. Thus the weaker motivation of unsociable children might lead to shyness through undeveloped social skills and lack of opportunity to habituate to strange social contexts (because they are less rewarding).

Consider also the dual nature of shyness (Buss, in press). Fear of strangers, the early developing form, starts in infancy and continues through adulthood; it appears to consist largely of a combination of high fearfulness and low sociability. Self-conscious shyness, the later developing form, starts at roughly the fourth or fifth year of life; it appears to consist largely of acute awareness of oneself as a social object (Buss, 1980). When self-consciously shy, we blush and feel awkward and foolish. The causes of such shyness are being conspicuous, being involved in a breach of privacy or having made a minor social mistake. The autonomic reaction, if any, tends to be the parasympathetic reaction of blushing. In fearful shyness, on the other hand, the cause is social novelty, and the autonomic reaction tends to be the sympathetic arousal of fear. Though there is evidence that the trait of fearful shyness has a genetic component, the trait of self-conscious shyness would seem to be acquired as part of the process of socialization: learning how to act with others and how they might regard us.

If this theoretical account is correct, the only kind of shyness seen in infants is fearful shyness, which has an inherited component. In older children and adults, however, there are two kinds of shyness. The fearful kind, which continues throughout development, has a genetic component, but the self-conscious kind of shyness has no genetic component. Given the complexity of shyness in older children and adults and given its mixed origin, it would appear best to avoid classifying shyness as a temperament. This conclusion would appear to be strengthened by the possibility of deriving the fearful kind of shyness from the temperaments of emotionality and sociability.

EXTRAVERSION AND NEUROTICISM

The modern concepts of extraversion and neuroticism are creative products of Eysenck (1947, 1983). There is a consensus that the first two second-order factors derived from Cattell's major psychometric system of personality (Cattell, Eber, & Tatsuoka, 1970) are nearly identical to Eysenck's extraversion and neuroticism (e.g., Royce, 1973). In our previous formulation (1975), we viewed extraversion as a combination of sociability and impulsivity, as does Eysenck (1983). Though we maintain that impulsivity is still part of the concept of extraversion and the way it is measured, we now suggest that impulsivity plays a minor role in extraversion. The "impulsivity" factor that is typically found among extraversion items is more properly called "liveliness" and correlates much more highly with sociability scales than it does with impulsivity scales (Plomin, 1976b). Eysenck's (1983) own data suggest that components of impulsivity are only minimally related to extraversion, with median correlations of about .20. Our new position is that the people who are typically labeled as extraverts are high in sociability and low in shyness, a possibility not previously considered by extraversion researchers.

In our original measure of sociability (1975) the questionnaire consisted of both sociability and shyness items. To avoid such confounding of two separate personality traits, we have included only sociability items in our new sociability scale:

I like to be with people.
I prefer working with others than alone.
I find people more stimulating than anything else.
I am something of a loner.
When alone, I feel isolated.

Notice that all these items involve affiliativeness or a preference for the company of others, and none involves one's anxious or self-conscious behavior or feelings when actually with others (shyness).

Sociability, we insist, is one of the two crucial components of extraversion. Add unshyness to high sociability, and the result would be an extravert; add unsociability to shyness, and the result would be an introvert. There are data bearing on this issue (Plomin, 1976a). The extraversion scale of the Maudsley Personality Inventory (Eysenck, 1959) was correlated with a "sociability" questionnaire that contained a mixture of sociability, shyness, and sociability-shyness items:

I prefer to do things alone. (reversed)
I almost always prefer to work and study with others rather than alone.
I have more friends than most people.
I am very sociable.
I like to feel independent of people. (reversed)
I tend to be a loner. (reversed)
I prefer parties with lots of people.
I make friends very easily and quickly.
I tend to be shy. (reversed)

The first six items all ask about sociability, but items 7 and 8 combine sociability with shyness, and item 9 is obviously a shyness item. Clearly, this scale is a mixture of sociability and shyness. The fact that this 9-item scale correlates .81 with the Maudsley extraversion scale suggests that extraversion, as defined by Eysenck in his questionnaire measures, is essentially a combination of sociability and shyness.

Extraverts are sociable and unshy; introverts are unsociable and shy. This suggestion makes sense when we visualize the behavior of people at parties. Extraverts are strongly motivated to mix with others and obtain the social responsiveness that is the goal of sociable people. Moreover, there is no shyness (fear or self-consciousness) that would inhibit sociable people from initiating such contacts. Introverts are only weakly motivated to mix with others, for they place a lower value on sociable responsiveness. Introverts are inhibited by either fear or self-consciousness from initiating social behavior or responding adequately to the overtures of others.

Concerning Eysenck's concept of neuroticism (1947), it is obviously related to our temperament of emotionality—specifically, the distress and fear elements of emotionality (but not anger). Neurotics are widely regarded as anxiety-ridden. They tend to become tense, upset, and frightened, and they have considerable difficulty in adapting to the stresses and strains of everyday life. One reason they are so frightened would seem to be the classical conditioning of fear: Previously neutral objects and events become fear inducing because of their link to such unconditioned fear stimuli as being harmed, being threatened with harm, and being in pain. Another cause of heightened fearfulness is the acquisition of fears through cognitive learning: seeing such scary movies as Psycho and Jaws. Some young children, however, are especially prepared to acquire fears by being high in the temperament of emotionality, especially after it has differentiated into fearfulness. Emotional children tend to react with distress more frequently and more intensely, by definition. It follows that there would be more opportunities for classical conditioning by which a broad spectrum of environmental events would come to elicit fear. Furthermore, their reactions to such movies as Psycho and Jaws would tend to be more severe and longer lasting, which would add to the burden of fears already acquired through classical conditioning. Given what is known about the power of phobias, such emotional children would tend to avoid fearful objects and stimuli and therefore not allow any opportunity for their fear to extinquish.

Let us add a note of caution about our account of neuroticism and extraversion. We freely acknowledge the importance of life experiences and learning in the origin of these two personality traits: classical conditioning and cognitive learning in neuroticism, and social rewards and punishments in extraversion. We insist, however, that these causes are effective in leading to neuroticism or extraversion only (or at the least, mainly) in those children who are already prepared to acquire these traits. The necessary preparation, we suggest, consists of emotionality for neuroticism, and a combination of sociability and shyness for extraversion.

CONCLUDING REMARKS

We started this chapter with the question, why do people prefer the presence of others? The answer that others may offer rewards led immediately to the issue of which kinds of rewards. We eliminated nonsocial rewards as not being intrinsic to social interaction and concentrated on social rewards. The interaction rewards of presence of others, sharing of activities, attention, responsivity, and stimulation are assumed to be crucial to sociability. These are the rewards that are especially sought by those high in sociability, and therefore these incentives help to define what we mean by this temperament: the seeking of interaction rewards. We also assume that sociable people tend to offer these process rewards to others, such reciprocation leading to their being seen as warm people.

Together with emotionality, sociability is assumed to influence the mother-infant bond that has been labeled *attachment*. The emotionality and sociability of both mother and infant may be important determiners of the development of the three kinds of attachment types described by Ainsworth (1979).

Shyness traditionally has been closely linked to sociability, and low sociability and shyness have often been regarded as equivalent. Our position is that their relationship is sufficiently weak for shyness to be regarded as distinct from sociability, an assumption confirmed by their correlation, $-.30$. Shyness correlates .50 with the fearfulness component of emotionality. Our interpretation of these correlations is that shyness should not be regarded as a temperament but as a derivative of the two temperaments of sociability and emotionality.

Finally, we attempted to derive two of Eysenck's traits from our temperaments. His extraversion is assumed to be a combination of sociability and emotionality (specifically, shyness). His neuroticism is assumed to derive from emotionality together with classical conditioning of fear and avoidance.

Our approach to sociability has been necessarily wide-ranging, for individual differences in people-seeking have implications for a variety of social behaviors and traits. Again, some of our assumptions are speculative, some have already been confirmed, and others await testing.

7

Theory and Measurement of EAS

In our previous book (1975) we listed four temperaments that lent themselves to the acronym EASI: emotionality, activity, sociability, and impulsivity. We have already discussed emotionality and sociability but have nothing new to write about activity. Construing activity as tempo and vigor still seems appropriate, and the only modification is minor: Tempo and vigor have been found to correlate so well that there is no longer any need to consider them as separate. For reasons to be discussed shortly, we have dropped impulsivity from the list, making the new acronym EAS.

DEFINITION AND CRITERIA

In our previous book, we listed several criteria that defined temperaments, distinguishing them from other personality traits. One that was crucial before remains the crucial criterion now: It is inheritance. This criterion presents a clear challenge: The dispositions we list as temperaments must be sustained by evidence from twin studies and the other behavioral genetic methods reviewed in the next chapter.

One other criterion that we add is presence in early childhood, preferably infancy (the first 2 years of life). This focus on infancy and early childhood is consonant with the interest of most temperament researchers, as discussed in Chapters 3 and 4. Moreover, such early traits are likely to be the foundation on which later personality traits are built.

These two criteria serve to define temperaments as *inherited personality traits present in early childhood*. In terms of the breadth of the personality traits, we prefer to study broad traits, consisting of behaviors that occur in most situations and must therefore be averaged across them (activity) or behaviors that occur in oft-repeated situations (emotionality and sociability). We are of course more interested in traits that are important in the lives of individuals. Early appearance and heritability might be shown for narrow responses (or a single response, such as smiling), traits that occur in only a few contexts, or behaviors that involve trivial aspects of human existence, but we are less interested in these. Beyond this preference for broad and significant traits, there is the issue of the usefulness of different levels of analysis, which we discuss in Chapter 11.

We should also mention that the traditional use of the term *personality trait* excludes intelligence from consideration, for otherwise intelligence would meet both criteria of temperament. The special problems of assessing intelligence and its linkage to cognitive processes rather than motives and noncognitive ways of behaving, however, have set the study of intelligence apart as a discipline separate from the study of personality, and we shall abide by this distinction.

Do inherited personality traits present in early childhood *necessarily* show continuity throughout childhood and adulthood? The answer is No because genes turn on and off during development (see Chapter 8). Nonetheless, we are more interested in traits that are predictive of later development, that is, traits that show some continuity or at least have *residuals* for later personality. What if childhood temperaments simply appeared and then later disappeared, having had no impact on later personality development? An example of such a temperament would seem to be the NYLS dimension of Rhythmicity, which includes cycles of sleep-waking, hunger, and elimination. It is hard to see how an infant's rhythmicity would affect the same individual's behavior in late childhood or in adulthood. Indeed, parental rating instruments based on the NYLS conceptualization exclude Rhythmicity in measuring temperament after early childhood. Such temperaments may be of considerable interest to pediatricians and others who focus on children but not to those interested in personality or development. Any temperament that simply disappears and has no later impact must be considered less important than a temperament that has lasting effects.

We have selected our three temperaments with an eye to personality development and the later appearance of these traits. Emotionality and sociability appear in one form or another in virtually all lists of personality traits and are well represented on personality questionnaires. Activity has been somewhat neglected recently, though it appeared frequently on earlier questionnaires (see Guilford, 1959) and must be considered an important aspect of adult personality. The thrust of these remarks is that having an impact on personality development, either by showing up continuously throughout development or by leaving behind residuals that determine the development of related personality traits, should be considered in selecting temperaments. This characteristic does not attain the importance of the two major criteria, inheritance and early appearance, but surely it is a valuable property of any trait designated as a temperament.

Our definition of temperament as inherited personality traits implies cross-cultural and even cross-species similarities. However, genetic influence is a population concept: The relative influence of genetic and environmental variance can differ among populations in the human species and certainly among different species. The emergence of a cluster of genetically induced individual differences in one culture or species does not mean that genetic variance will necessarily be similarly shaped in other cultures or species. Nonetheless, human populations are similar genetically (at least in comparison to other species) and for this reason we might expect to find similar configurations of genetically influenced individual differences. We might also expect that similar constellations of behavior will emerge in primates, especially the great apes, and perhaps even in other mammals. In fact, as discussed in Chapter 2, EAS temperamental clusters of individual differences have been demonstrated in chimpanzees, dogs, and mice, and evidence for their heritability exists. Though our definition of temperament is compatible with the view that EAS temperaments will be found among genetically similar populations and species, the theory does not stand or fall on cross-cultural or cross-species comparisons. We should also mention that since populations and species differ genetically as well as environmentally, our definition of temperament implies no prediction concerning either the appearance of or etiology of average differences between cultures—such as the Freedmans' (1969) finding that Oriental infants may be less emotional than Caucasian infants—or average differences between species—such as the average difference in sociability between cats and dogs.

IMPULSIVITY

After reviewing the evidence on the inheritance of impulsivity in 1975, we concluded that it was mixed, some research supporting the hypothesis of heritability and other research, not. One difficulty in making a firm decision about impulsivity as a temperament is that it appeared to include several diverse but related behavioral tendencies, which led to this conclusion: "History records many examples of a muddled area being clarified by subsequent research. There is of course the danger of extending the life of a hypothesis far beyond its possible worth, but we suggest that it is much too early to worry about that possibility. Let us at least keep open the question of whether impulsivity is a temperament and so repeat our evaluation of the evidence to date: the case is not yet proved" (Buss & Plomin, 1975, p. 147).

It has been almost a decade since these words were written, but little has occurred that would alter our conclusion. Impulsivity is rarely studied as a personality trait, and when it has appeared in research on temperaments, it is usually in the guise of distractibility (see Chapter 4). There is no better (or worse) case for impulsivity as a temperament now than there was previously.

The multiple components of impulsivity pose a serious problem in stating precisely what this trait is. In our previous book, we listed four components: inhibitory control, as manifested in resistance to temptation and delay of gratification; decision time, as reflected in making up one's mind quickly or being obsessive; persistence in ongoing tasks; and sensation seeking, which involves being bored easily and seeking exciting stimulation. In revising our original EASI questionnaires, we tried a drastic solution for impulsivity. After eliminating decision time and persistence, we divided the remainder into the two (presumably) separate traits of inhibitory control and excitement seeking. These two traits were included in a preliminary form of the revised questionnaire, which was administered to 330 college students. Excitement seeking emerged as a clear factor, but inhibitory control did not. Instead, items from inhibitory control appeared in factors involving the other temperaments, especially activity and emotionality. In retrospect, inhibitory control items loaded on other factors because of the nature of these various traits. Activity, emotionality, sociability, and excitement seeking may be regarded metaphorically as *engines* of behavior in that they involve motives or impulses to behave in particular ways. Inhibitory control may be regarded as *brakes*, modulating and controlling these tendencies to act. As such, particular inhibitory control items would appear on appropriate engine-like factors, with negative loadings. For example, in the above mentioned study of 330 college students, we included an inhibitory control item, "I have trouble holding back my impulses." This item loaded on fear, anger, and activity factors for males; for females, it emerged as a separate factor. Loadings for other inhibitory control items were similarly dissipated across several factors. In brief, the evidence still fails to show that impulsivity possesses sufficient cohesiveness to be considered a trait.

Excitement seeking, on the contrary, does cohere as a trait; is it heritable? Fulker, Eysenck, & Zuckerman (1980) report evidence that one of Zuckerman's (1979) sensation-seeking dimensions is heritable, but sensation seeking comprises only part of our present notion of excitement seeking, which also includes elements of what Fiske and Maddi (1961) call variation seeking. We do not preclude the possibility that excitement seeking is heritable, but in the virtual absence of such evidence, particularly in children, we cannot accept it as a temperament.

Recall we specify two criteria of temperament: heredity and early appearance. Impulsivity and excitement seeking do not meet the second criterion, for there is no evidence of their appearance as personality traits until the fourth or fifth year of life. Thus even if their heritability were clearly established, we could not accept them as temperaments on the basis of our current definition of temperaments. We have surrendered these two traits reluctantly, for there is also no evidence that they originate in any particular environmental determinants. Thus impulsivity and excitement seeking might still be considered as temperaments in a less restrictive conception of temperament than the one we have adopted here.

INFLUENCE OF EAS ON ENVIRONMENT

In Chapters 5 and 6, we discussed how our temperaments might be modified. Let us turn this question around: How might each of our three temperaments influence environment? In attempting to answer this question, we must first deal with the issue of dimensionality of temperament. Each of our temperaments can be divided into the extreme ends and the middle—for example, high and low activity versus medium activity. We assume that people who occupy the middle range of any of our temperaments tend not *to influence* the environment. Indeed, we suggest that the opposite is true: Those in the middle range are most likely *to be influenced* by the environment. Thus an average sociable person is most likely to accommodate to the kind of social reward that is available. Such a person might accept the presence of others or the sharing of activities and not demand responsivity; nor would such a person regard social initiative from others as intrusive. The extremes of sociability, however, are expected to accommodate less to the social rewards that are available. Thus a low sociable person would find extreme responsiveness too arousing, and a high sociable person would find the mere presence of others to be insufficiently rewarding. These extremes would be most likely to seek a different environment or set out to change the social environment. Our discussion will therefore focus only on the extremes of the three temperaments.

Selecting Environments

The example just mentioned represents one way that temperament can affect environment: people select environments that are rewarding or at least comfortable. People high in activity seek an environment that is fast paced and may require considerable energy expenditure, whereas those low in activity prefer a slower pace and a lower energy expenditure. Thus high active people seek out cities; low active people migrate to the countryside or at least suburbia. One extreme prefers the tennis court and the other, the golf links.

Sociable people want to work and play with others, and they are more tolerant of a lack of privacy. Thus the jobs they seek are more likely to involve other people: sales work, acting through committees, and politics. Those low in sociability drift toward more solitary jobs: computer programmer, mathematician, or writer. One extreme tends to find housing in apartments or closely built developments, and the other delights in living in out-of-the way places. One extreme looks for the tennis court or the volleyball court, and the other may be found out in the fields, running or skiing alone.

People high in the temperament of emotionality also select compatible environments, especially the fearful ones. People high in anger do not gravitate toward places or occasions in which they can display their temper, nor do they especially avoid them. Fearful people, though, seek safety and avoid environments that are potential threats. Thus they back off from strange places and people, and they are likely to have a variety of phobias involving fear of high places, dogs, snakes, insects or airplanes, as well as fear of being alone or in a hospital. By seeking situations and places that are safe, they select their environment by elimination (of potential dangers).

In laboratory research, subjects rarely are allowed to choose the environment, a natural consequence of experimental control. In a recent exception, Gormley (1983) allowed his subjects to select activities. Peer ratings of activity correlated with subjects' decision to participate in a more energetic or less energetic experiment. Peer ratings of sociability correlated .53 with subjects' decision to participate in an experiment with others or alone. This experiment would seem to be representative of many everyday life situations in which people select environments. An important determinant of such choice is likely to be temperament.

Affecting Social Environments

Social contexts contain diverse elements, including the locale, the social conventions, and the type of social occasion, but the most important element consists of the people who are interacting. Each person in a group is capable of affecting his or her own social environment. Let us start with the ambience of the social environment that may be attributed to the participants. Suppose an observer is about to enter a conversation involving two other people. What is observed prior to the subsequent participation *sets the tone* for the interaction to follow. The two participants may be highly sociable and engage in an animated conversation, complete with exclamations and considerable expressive behavior. In contrast to such a high sociable dyad, a low sociable dyad might talk quietly, with few expressive gestures and periods of silence. Thus even before the observer entered the conversation, the tone would have been set by the temperament of the participants.

The other two temperaments are less important in setting the tone of social contexts. People high in activity tend to set a fast social pace and those low in activity a slow pace. Emotional people tend to make the situation more taut, either because of their anxious tension or the raw edge of their tendency to be angry. People low in emotionality play no role in setting the tone.

Once the interaction has begun, any participant may affect the social environment by *initiating behavior*. Those high in activity will probably want to speed up the conversation or play a fast-paced game; they might suggest an energetic game or other vigorous activity. Those low in activity tend not to initiate behavior, almost by definition. Social people tend to start conversations, pursue new topics, or suggest actions that increase social contact. Their nonverbal behavior also enhances social interaction. When first meeting people, unshy, sociable people tend to gaze more at others than do shy, unsociable people; those being gazed at more reciprocate by gazing more at the other person (Slivken, 1983). Of course, not everyone welcomes the push by sociable people toward greater responsivity, for it may become intrusive. Some people prefer the more subdued approach of low sociable people, who initiate little but do not intrude, either.

While social behavior is occurring, each of the participants will of course be *reacting* to the social stimuli presented by the others. Only sociability and emotionality are relevant here. Sociable people react positively to sharing activities and the back and forth interaction they find so rewarding. They react negatively to being left out of a conversation and have a low threshold of social boredom. People low in sociability back away from the intrusiveness of those who strive for greater interaction, feeling that their privacy has been invaded. They prefer others who keep their distance and who do not require much responsiveness. Emotional people tend to become insecure and anxious when confronted with strangers or a novel social context, or they easily become angry in the face of real or imagined slights. They prefer situations that are calm to the point of dullness or at least situations that pose no threat or possible insult. Those low in emotionality tend not to react to explosive or threatening social situations and by their lack of reactivity tend to defuse such situations.

By their diverse reactions to social stimulation, people who vary in the temperaments of emotionality and sociability tend to reward or punish the behavior of others. Thus if I know that you are likely to react with fear, I will probably try to avoid threatening you; if you tend to become angry, I will probably try to avoid topics that annoy you. Similarly, if you react with pleasure to my attempt to increase responsivity, I shall continue. If you react by retreating and suggest by your behavior that I am intruding, I am likely to back off and lower the responsivity. In these various ways, people of different temperaments tend to shape the behavior of those around them, thereby influencing the social environment.

Modifying the Impact of the Environment

In addition to selecting or affecting the environment, we may also *modify its impact*. Suppose the locale, the current job, or the current game demands slow-paced behavior that involves little vigor. High active people often find some way to increase the tempo or otherwise expend energy. Thus it is always possible to exercise even in the restricted few feet of a space capsule. When high active people cannot walk, they may be just as energetic in a wheel chair. On a slow-moving job, it may be possible to start doing two different activities simultaneously or at least fill in one's spare time with activities. On the other hand, low active people seem to find ways to diminish the tempo of the environment or minimize the energy expenditure required. There are New Yorkers who do not rush for the subway or try to beat the traffic light, and those who are required to do strenuous manual work may substitute machines for muscle power (riding lawn mowers, hydraulic lifts, electric saws, and so on).

When sociable people find themselves in a relatively isolated environment, they may substitute the telephone for face-to-face conversation or become amateur radio buffs and converse with other radio buffs around the country. They may resort to writing letters and similar slow means of communication, which are better than none at all. If there are geographical barriers, they tend to find ways to surmount them and show up for the dance or debate even if it is on the other side of the mountain. If all else fails, there may be recourse to an imaginary companion, a cognitive adaptation favored by children. People low in sociability also find ways to modify the impact of the environment. Forced to work in a crowded environment—at one desk among many in a large office, for example— they erect physical and psychological barriers around themselves. When in a lively group, they remain on the fringe and are not surrounded by people. One woman told us that when she was at a party required by her husband's job, she fantasied that she was off in the woods by herself and thereby psychologically removed herself from the crowd.

Finally, those low in emotionality tend to react less to anger-arousing or stressful situations. A child may have to put up with emotional parents or with parents who are struggling in their marriage or who disagree over how to discipline the child. There may be the stress of economic hardship or the turmoil of repeated familial relocations. Low emotional children are less affected by such negative familial climates, their temperament

TABLE 7.1
Influence of EAS on Environment

	Activity		Sociability		Emotionality	
	High	*Low*	*High*	*Low*	*High*	*Low*
Select environment	X	X	X	X	X	
Affect social environment						
set tone	X	X	X	X	X	
initiate	X		X			
react			X	X	X	X
Modify impact of environment	X	X	X	X		X

modifying the impact. Those high in emotionality do not moderate the impact of the environment but enhance its impact, almost by definition.

In brief, the temperaments may influence the environment in various ways, which are summarized in Table 7.1. Consider each column of the table from the top down. High activity can influence the environment in all ways except reacting to (reinforcing) others. Low activity is involved with selecting the environment, setting the tone, and modifying the impact of the environment. Both high and low sociability are involved with all possible influences of the environment, as might be expected from this particular temperament. High emotionality is involved with selecting an environment, setting the tone, and (of course) reacting to others. Low emotionality has the least influence on the environment: only reacting to others and modifying the impact of the environment; in the latter, it is the most influential of all the dispositions.

MEASURING EAS

General Issues

Our focus here is on direct measures of the kind that are typically made by observers in the home, nursery school, or playground, or by experimenters in the laboratory. When behavior can be specified as individual responses, these responses have three properties that lend themselves to quantification. The first is *frequency,* which involves merely counting the number of times the response occurs during the period of observation. One variant of frequency combines it with time to yield the *rate* of responding. The second property is the *duration* of response, which requires a reasonable estimate of when it begins and when it ends. The third basic property is *amplitude* of response, which can be measured directly in physical units or estimated in terms of psychological intensity: Cursing is a more intense response than merely criticizing, even when the two responses are equated for loudness (which can be measured with instruments).

Frequency can be used as a measure of all three temperaments, the necessary condition being a precise definition of the behaviors comprising each temperament. For emotionality, an investigator merely counts the number of episodes of distress, fear, or anger for the period under observation. For activity, simple frequency does not suffice, but frequency per unit time (rate of response) is precisely what we want as a measure of tempo. For sociability, frequency is less appropriate, but a count of the number of times others or shared activities are sought might be valuable.

Duration refers to different aspects of behavior in the three temperaments. For emotionality, it refers to the duration of the average episode of distress, fear, or anger. The more intense the emotional reaction, the longer it tends to last. The more distressed the child, the longer it takes to calm it down, a measure called soothability. Neither activity nor sociability lends itself to specific responses, so duration refers not to the time of any particular response but to the time spent in a set of behaviors. For activity, duration consists of the time spent in energetic pursuits, either play or work. For sociability, duration consists of the time spent with people or in shared activities.

Amplitude applies especially to emotionality and activity. For emotionality, it is the objectively measured increase in physiological reactions such as blood pressure, pulse, and galvanic response; or it is the rated intensity of facial and postural expressions of distress, fear, or anger. For activity, amplitude translates directly into vigor, and sociability involves the degree of social responsiveness.

In addition to these three measures of behavior, which derive from basic properties of responses, there are other measures available, which depend more on intervention by an investigator or judgments by an observer. The subject may be allowed a *choice* of activities, which allows an investigator to infer the relative strength of motives or of rewards. An observer can assess the *direction* of behavior, such as approaching or avoiding a stimulus. The intensity of the eliciting stimulus can be assessed to yield a *threshold* of response. Finally, the researcher can assess the subject's reaction when there is a barrier or limitation to motivated behavior, and the subject's attempt to *overcome the obstruction* allows an assessment of motivational strength.

When the three basic measures of response are added to the other measures, the sum is seven classes of measures available for the study of our three temperaments; not all seven measures can be used for each temperament. The following lists divide the measures first by temperament and within that classification, by type of measure.

Emotionality

1. frequency: of crying, shrinking back, hiding, temper tantrums, and so on

2. duration: soothability, or how long it takes for a return to placidity
3. amplitude/intensity: changes in pulse, breathing, blood pressure, and GSR; or intensity of crying, panicky expression, temper tantrum, or pouting
4. direction of response: toward the anger-arousing stimulus in anger, and away from the threatening stimulus in fear
5. threshold: the strength of the verbal or physical threat required to elicit fear; or the degree of frustration or restriction required to elicit anger; in infants, for fear, visual cliff or a looming stranger and for anger, physical restriction

Activity

1. frequency per unit time (rate): walking speed, talking speed, observed tendency to hurry
2. duration: time spent in high-energy activities, persistence in energetic activity after most people have stopped
3. amplitude: tendency to jump or bounce up and down when others are more still; actometer, which measures total amount of movement; crossing more squares in a nursery or playground
4. choice: preference for high-energy games or work; tennis over golf, wrestling over doll play
5. reaction to enforced idleness: seeking an outlet for energy; restlessness

Sociability

1. frequency: number of attempts to initiate contact
2. duration: the amount of time spent with others or in shared activities with others
3. amplitude: degree of social responsiveness
4. choice: preference for being with others rather than being alone, for social rather than solitary play
5. direction: moving toward people rather than away (seeking privacy)
6. restriction: when isolated, an emotional reaction or strong attempts to contact others

Measurement Issues

Each of the temperaments poses problems of measurement. Emotionality offers discrete responses, the amplitude of which can be assessed, but the responses occur infrequently. When children are observed in a nursery school for instance, how many times does a given child cry, throw a tantrum, or react with any other kind of distress during an hour? Most children would react emotionally no more than once or twice in an hour, and such a low frequency makes it difficult to assess individual differences. The major recourses are to amplitude measures and ratings.

Activity involves no discrete responses, for it is more of a background variable, involving style of behaving as much as content. There is considerable short-term variation in tempo and vigor, which may be attributed to variations in the demands of the various activities that occur during the period of observation: playing tag obviously requires more energy than does drawing. The major solution to this problem is sampling behavior repeatedly over many weeks of observation.

Sociability does involve occasional discrete responses, but unlike the other two temperaments, it is a directional motive: a desire to be with others. As a motive, it offers fewer of the basic response dimensions (frequency, duration, and amplitude) and must therefore be assessed by other methods. Preference for social rather than nonsocial activities is a good measure, for it is relatively easy to determine which activities are social and which are not. If preference is to be used as a measure, however, the subject must have a choice of activities; such choice is not always available—infants and prisoners, for example.

Instruments.   There are also issues specific to the conditions under which the research occurs: when the subjects are free-ranging and merely observed versus when they are in the laboratory and under some control. When subjects are being observed without interference, there may be a fundamental problem about how to quantify the behavior. The two major options are objective scores (obtained by an instrument or by having observers count) or rating scales.

Sociability poses problems for measurement by an instrument. Sophisticated psychophysiological measures are available to study emotionality, but unfortunately they are rarely used. The instrument most commonly used to measure one of our temperaments is the *actometer,* which assesses activity. The instrument operates something like a self-winding watch. It can be attached to the limbs of the body, and it offers an entirely objective record of the subject's movements. Such objectivity would seem to guarantee reliability of measurement, even when behavior is sampled for brief periods. Halverson and Post-Gordon (1983) showed that the reliability of actometer readings for nursery school children is low when only a single day's sample of behavior is considered ($r = .18$), but when 10 days of activity were recorded, the reliability rose to .96. When the ratings of activity by various teachers were correlated, the inter-rater reliability of a single day was .88. Evidently, raters can take into account variations in behavior that occur during briefer periods of observation, yielding reliabilities for a single day that are much better than the low one-day reliability of an objective instrument. The increased reliability of actometer readings when they were aggregated also resulted in higher correlations with the teacher's ratings. Thus the one-day correlation between actometer scores and teachers' ratings was .17, but the correlation based on 20 days of observation and recording was .88. There is an important point to be made about ratings by knowledgeable observers: "The much maligned 'global ratings', parent ratings, and clinician ratings may have had an undue bad press. For many applications, well-constructed and well-used ratings of motor activity do a remarkably good job of distinguishing different levels of activity" (Halverson & Post-Gordon, 1983, p. 45).

The reliability and validity of a composited actometer readings has been verified by Eaton (1983). The reliability of 20-minute actometer readings for a single day was .35; when 13 days of actometer readings were composited, the reliability was .88. When composite actometer readings were compared with the composite ratings of children's activity by several nursery school staff members, the correlation was .69. And the composite actometer scores correlated .75 with parental ratings, which led Eaton to comment:

> The correlation with the parent rating is particularly interesting: first, because items on the Colorado Childhood Temperament Inventory scales do not call for the child-to-child comparisons implicit in the teacher rankings; second, because the correlation suggests that child activity level generalizes from the nursery school setting to the home; and third, because the validity of the CCTI activity scale is supported by these findings. (1983, p. 724)

The Laboratory.   Time sampling is an acute problem in laboratory research, for researchers cannot ask subjects to keep returning there repeatedly over many days or weeks. This problem is offset by the gain in precision of measurement and control of behavior that are afforded by laboratory research. Precision and control are not achieved without cost, however. The laboratory situation tends to be artificial, making it difficult to generalize laboratory findings to everyday situations. Control over the subject's behavior is often achieved by stringent limitations on behavioral options. Such limitations are especially troublesome in personality research, in which the subject's preference for one activity or another may be a crucial measure of a personality trait. The problems associated with the laboratory study of personality do not obviate the necessity for such research, for naturalistic observations have their own problems. We need to be aware of the limitations of laboratory research, though, because it is easy to be beguiled by the scientific objectivity of the laboratory and

forget about generalizability. As Moskowitz and Schwarz (1982) conclude, "An artificially structured situation may raise the base rate of a
behavior, but this short, situationally specific behavior count may not
provide a representative sample of behavior. . . . Thus, no matter the
degree of face validity, the generality of measures based on 15-minute
laboratory observations to situations of greater relevance should be demonstrated and not assumed" (p. 527).

Infants. The study of temperament in infants is simplified by the relative absence of socialization pressures and also by the lack of differentiation of behavior. The infant's behavioral repertoire is limited and can
therefore be more fully sampled. The limited response repertoire can also
pose a problem, especially for the temperaments of activity and sociability. Concerning activity, the infant may have insufficient mobility, which
reduces individual differences in energy expenditure. Concerning sociability, the infant is exposed to few social contexts and such exposure is
usually controlled by the caretaker. Thus it may be difficult to assess the
frequency of the infant's social behavior or its preference for social over
nonsocial activities, both of which are excellent measures of sociability.
Emotionality involves more diffuse behavior that can easily be assessed
without recourse to preference or frequency of the acts, and therefore it is
the easiest of our three temperaments to measure in infancy.

The relative undifferentiation of behavior in infancy also presents problems when temperaments are assessed. Early in life, many of the infant's
vigorous movements occur during distress, which means that the energy
expended during distress can easily be confused with the energy of activity temperament. The infant spends most of its waking time in the presence of others, which means that social fear (shyness) may be confused
with nonsocial fear; not all infants who experience stranger anxiety, for
instance, are necessarily high in nonsocial fear. Also, during the first few
months of life, distress is the only negative emotion; fear and anger have
not yet differentiated. If this fact were ignored, it would lead to a confu-
sion between distress and fear (distressed infants being labeled fearful) or
even between distress and anger. Such mistakes are especially likely
because infants may react with distress at 2 months to the same stimulus
that would elicit fear at 8 months. Behavior that is undifferentiated early
in life is easier to assess but is more likely to be misclassified.

Questionnaires

Adult Self-Report. For an adult self-report EAS, five items were written to measure each of the following traits: distress, fearfulness, anger,
activity, and sociability. Fearfulness and anger are assumed to differ-

entiate from distress (see Chapter 5). The fearfulness and anger items are the same as those in the EASI-III (see Buss & Plomin, 1975). The activity items include three items from the EASI-III tempo subscale and two items from the vigor subscale. The distress and sociability items are new.

We administered a questionnaire containing these items and others to 330 students in an introductory psychology class at the University of Texas at Austin. As in all of our questionnaires, items were rated on a scale of 1 (not characteristic or typical of yourself) to 5 (very characteristic or typical of yourself). The items showed good distributional properties: Most means were approximately 3.0 and standard deviations were 1.0. We submitted the 25 items to factor analysis, using standard exploratory factor analytic procedures, such as selection of factors with eigenvalues greater than 1.0 for Varimax rotation.

Factor loadings greater than .30 for the seven factors extracted for rotation are listed in Table 7.2, organized according to their a priori placement on the five scales. It can be seen that the factor analysis generally verified the a priori assignment of items. For each of the five scales, four of the five items load highest on the appropriate factor. The only surprise was that one of the slightly revised activity items (I often feel sluggish and tired) loads highly on distress. In retrospect this makes sense: We had revised the item by adding "and tired," which pushes the item in the direction of neurotic emotionality.

The factor analytic results were much the same when we examined them separately for males and females. The only exception was fear. For males it merged with distress and for females it permeated several factors. Anger, however, was even more distinct factorially when the sexes were considered separately.

To improve the factorial structure of the EAS items, we eliminated the fifth item on each of the scales listed in Table 7.2. The new EAS Temperament Survey and its scoring instructions are listed in Table 7.3.

Table 7.4 represents means and standard deviations for the 5 EAS scales for 220 college women and 110 men. The scores on each of the EAS scales have been divided by 4 (the number of items) in order to express the scores in terms of the 1–5 scale. Though the standard deviations for items are approximately 1.0, the standard deviation for the mean item score within each scale is less then 1.0, because the variance of the mean is reduced by the correlation among the items. Only fearfulness showed a gender difference: Women report being more fearful than men. This mean difference accounts for less than 8% of the variance, which means that an individual's gender tells little about the individual's expected fearfulness. A significant difference in variance was observed for the sexes for distress; men were less variable, though their mean was not different from that of women.

TABLE 7.2

Items and Varimax Rotated Factor Loadings for the Adult EAS Temperament Survey[a]

	E-d	E-f	E-a	Act	Soc	6	7
Distress (E-d)							
I frequently get distressed.	.70						
I often feel frustrated.	.68						
Everyday events make me troubled and fretful.	.57						
I get emotionally upset easily.	.44	.42					
I am almost always calm.[b]						.48	
Fear (E-f)							
I am easily frightened.		.61					
I have fewer fears than most people my age.[b]		.60					
I often feel insecure.	.44	.46					
When I get scared, I panic.	.34	.40					
I tend to be nervous in new situations.	.42	.30					
Anger (E-a)							
I am known as hotblooded and quick-tempered.			.68			.31	
It takes a lot to make me mad.[b]			.65				
There are many things that annoy me.	.41		.54				
When displeased, I let people know it right away.			.46				
I yell and scream more than most people my age.						.59	
Activity (Act)							
My life is fast paced.				.78			
I usually seem to be in a hurry.				.40			
I like to keep busy all the time.				.35			
I often feel as if I'm bursting with energy.				.31			
I often feel sluggish and tired.[b]	-.69						
Sociability (Soc)							
I like to be with people					.70		
I prefer working with others rather than alone.					.63		
I find people more stimulating than anything else.					.57		
I am something of a loner.[b]					.57		
When alone, I feel isolated.							-.45

[a] N = 330 college students, sexes combined. Item loadings greater than .30 are listed.

[b] Item is reversed when scored.

99

TABLE 7.3
The EAS Temperament Survey for Adults[a]

Rate each of the items on a scale of 1 (not characteristic or typical of yourself) to 5 (very characteristic or typical of yourself).

1. I like to be with people. (Soc)
2. I usually seem to be in a hurry. (Act)
3. I am easily frightened. (F)
4. I frequently get distressed. (E)
5. When displeased, I let people know it right away. (A)
6. I am something of a loner. (reversed, Soc)
7. I like to keep busy all the time. (Act)
8. I am known as hotblooded and quick-tempered. (A)
9. I often feel frustrated. (E)
10. My life is fast paced. (Act)
11. Everyday events make me troubled and fretful. (E)
12. I often feel insecure. (F)
13. There are many things that annoy me. (A)
14. When I get scared, I panic. (F)
15. I prefer working with others rather than alone. (Soc)
16. I get emotionally upset easily. (E)
17. I often feel as if I'm bursting with energy. (Act)
18. It takes a lot to make me mad. (reversed, A)
19. I have fewer fears than most people my age. (reversed, F)
20. I find people more stimulating than anything else. (Soc)

[a] Scoring instructions: Reverse Items 6, 18, 19 by setting 5 = 1, 4 = 2, 3 = 3, 2 = 4, and 1 = 5. Then add the scores for the four items on each of the 5 scales and divide each scale score by 4 (number of items per scale) in order to interpret scores in terms of the 1–5 scale.

TABLE 7.4
Means and Standard Deviations for the Adult EAS Temperament Survey

	Women (N = 220)		Men (N = 110)	
	Mean	S.D.	Mean	S.D.
Emotionality				
Distress	2.52	0.86	2.43	0.65
Fearfulness*	2.65	0.73	2.23	0.71
Anger	2.57	0.82	2.70	0.77
Activity	3.35	0.69	3.20	0.62
Sociability	3.81	0.73	3.65	0.81

*$p < .01$ for mean sex difference

TABLE 7.5
Test-retest Reliability for the Adult EAS Temperament Survey

	Test-retest Correlation N = 34
Emotionality	
Distress	.82
Fearfulness	.75
Anger	.85
Activity	.81
Sociability	.85

TABLE 7.6
Intercorrelations among Adult EAS Temperament Survey Scales[a]

	D	F	A	Act	Soc
Emotionality-distress (D)		.63	.28	.14	−.18
Emotionality-fearfulness (F)	.52		.12	−.15	−.16
Emotionality-anger (A)	.37	.17		.26	.10
Activity (Act)	−.08	−.02	.05		.31
Sociability (Soc)	−.04	−.06	−.06	.21	

[a] Males (N = 110) above diagonal; females (N = 220) below diagonal.

Two-week test-retest reliability data were collected at the University of Colorado at Boulder for 34 undergraduate students. Test-retest reliabilities are listed in Table 7.5. As in our previous studies (Buss & Plomin, 1975), test-retest reliability is, on the average, a satisfactory .82.

Table 7.6 presents intercorrelations among the EAS temperaments. As expected from our original theory (Buss & Plomin, 1975), distress correlates substantially with fearfulness and to a modest extent with anger. However, fearfulness and anger do not correlate significantly, a fact already discussed in Chapter 5. Emotionality scales are generally independent of activity and sociability, though a significant correlation emerges for men between anger and activity. As we have found before, there is a modest relationship between activity and sociability.

Parental Ratings. We have also revised our parental rating version of the Children's EASI-II (see Buss & Plomin, 1975) in a study that included the EASI-II items and items based on the nine temperament dimensions of the New York Longitudinal Study (Rowe & Plomin, 1977). As discussed in Chapter 3, six factors emerged from the joint factor analysis of the two sets of items and have been used to form a new instrument called the Colorado Childhood Temperament Inventory. Three of these scales are emotionality, activity, and sociability. Table 7.7 lists the items for the

EAS scales. The emotionality scale is a measure of distress, befitting our theory of the development of emotionality. The activity scale appears to be homologous with the adult scale. However, the sociability scale is better viewed as a mixture of sociability and shyness. It is difficult to assess sociability in young children and most studies measure shyness; also, most researchers do not distinguish between shyness and sociability, as we did in Chapter 6. Therefore, we have included an experimental scale for sociability based on the adult sociability scale in Table 7.2.

The means and standard deviations are shown in Table 7.8. The internal consistencies of the three scales averaged .83. Test-retest reliabilities are

TABLE 7.7
The EAS Temperament Survey for Children: Parental Ratings[a]

Rate each of the items for your child on a scale of 1 (not characteristic or typical of your child) to 5 (very characteristic or typical of your child).

1. Child tends to be shy. (Shyness)
2. Child cries easily. (Emotionality)
3. Child likes to be with people. (Sociability)
4. Child is always on the go. (Activity)
5. Child prefers playing with others rather than alone. (Sociability)
6. Child tends to be somewhat emotional. (Emotionality)
7. When child moves about, he usually moves slowly. (reversed, Activity)
8. Child makes friends easily. (reversed, Shyness)
9. Child is off and running as soon as he wakes up in the morning. (Activity)
10. Child finds people more stimulating than anything else. (Sociability)
11. Child often fusses and cries. (Emotionality)
12. Child is very sociable. (reversed, Shyness)
13. Child is very energetic. (Activity)
14. Child takes a long time to warm up to strangers. (Shyness)
15. Child gets upset easily. (Emotionality)
16. Child is something of a loner. (reversed, Sociability)
17. Child prefers quiet, inactive games to more active ones. (reversed, Activity)
18. When alone, child feels isolated. (Sociability)
19. Child reacts intensely when upset. (Emotionality)
20. Child is very friendly with strangers. (reversed, Shyness)

[a] All but the Sociability items have been taken from the Colorado Childhood Temperament Inventory, the construction, factor analysis, means, standard deviations, reliabilities, and scale intercorrelations of which are described by Rowe and Plomin (1977). The CCTI "Sociability" scale is a measure of shyness, so we have also included a Sociability scale (items 3, 5, 10, 16, and 18) that is based on the adult Sociability measure in Table 7.3. Though it may seem odd to include item 12, Child is very sociable, as a Shyness item, factor analysis indicates that when parents are asked to rate this item, they interpret it as shyness more than sociability. Scoring instructions: Reverse scores for items 7, 8, 12, 16, 17, and 20 by setting 5 = 1, 4 = 2, 3 = 3, 2 = 4, and 1 = 5. Add the scores for the five items on each scale and divide each scale score by 5 (number of items per scale) in order to interpret scores in terms of the 1–5 scale.

TABLE 7.8
Means and Standard Deviations for the EAS Temperament
Survey for Children: Parental Ratings[a]

| | 12 Month | | | | 24 Month | | | |
| | Girls (N = 142) | | Boys (N = 178) | | Girls (N = 142) | | Boys (N = 178) | |
	Mean	S.D.	Mean	S.D.	Mean	S.D.	Mean	S.D.
Emotionality	2.07	0.73	2.12	0.77	2.08	0.76	2.10	0.69
Activity	2.48	0.66	2.50	0.64	2.71	0.60	2.66	0.60
Sociability/Shyness[b]	4.17	0.52	4.25	0.51	4.17	0.47	4.26	0.49

[a] Previously unpublished data from the Colorado Adoption Project (Plomin & DeFries, 1983). Rowe and Plomin (1977) reported means and standard deviations for 182 children of diverse age (1–9 years) and also indicated that the factor structure was similar for boys and girls and for younger and older children. Boys were significantly more active than girls, but no other mean differences emerged for boys and girls or for younger and older children. Similar results are found in these data for 12- and 24-month-olds, though boys are *not* more active than girls.

[b] As explained in the text, the Sociability scale from the study by Rowe and Plomin (1977) mixes shyness and sociability. An experimental sociability scale devoid of shyness items is included in Table 7.7, though no standardization data are as yet available for it.

available for 31 children with an average age of 3.6 years, the interval between ratings being one week. The test-retest correlations were .72 for emotionality, .80 for activity, and .58 for sociability/shyness. The first two correlations are adequate, but the last raises a question about the stability of the sociability/shyness scale.

For 182 children, ranging in age from 1 to 9 years, the three scales were intercorrelated. Of the three correlations, only the .16 correlation between activity and sociability/shyness was statistically significant, though these two temperaments obviously are not closely related.

Teacher Ratings. The field of temperament has moved beyond parental ratings to include other sources of information, and teachers may be especially knowledgeable. The parental rating form of the EAS Temperament Survey for children is not completely appropriate for teacher ratings because the school situation differs from the home. Therefore, we constructed an experimental teacher-rating version of the EAS Temperament Survey for children, which is currently being used in the Colorado Adoption Project (Plomin & DeFries, 1983) for first and second graders. Table 7.9 lists the items for the teacher rating instrument.

TABLE 7.9
The EAS Temperament Survey for Children: Teacher Ratings[a]

Rate each of the items for your student on a scale of 1 (not characteristic or typical of the child) to 5 (very characteristic or typical of your child). If you have not had the experience of observing the child in any of the following situations, please mark "not observed."

1. Child tends to by shy. (Shyness)
2. When with other children, this child seems to be having a good time. (Sociability)
3. Child cries easily. (Emotionality)
4. At recess, child is always on the go. (Activity)
5. Child tends to be somewhat emotional. (Emotionality)
6. When child moves about, s/he usually moves slowly. (reversed, Activity)
7. Child makes friends easily. (reversed, Shyness)
8. Child is full of vigor when s/he arrives in the classroom in the morning. (Activity)
9. Child likes to be with people. (Sociability)
10. Child often fusses or cries. (Emotionality)
11. Child likes to chat with neighbors. (Sociability)
12. Child is very sociable. (reversed, Shyness)
13. Child is very energetic. (Activity)
14. Child takes a long time to warm up to strangers. (Shyness)
15. Child prefers to do things alone. (reversed, Sociability)
16. Child gets upset easily. (Emotionality)
17. Child prefers quiet, inactive games to more active ones. (reversed, Activity)
18. Child tends to be a loner. (reversed, Sociability)
19. Child reacts intensely when upset. (Emotionality)
20. Child is very friendly with strangers. (reversed, Shyness)

[a]The items in this table have been revised from those in Table 7.7 in order to make the questionnaire more appropriate for use with teachers. The "Sociability" scale in Table 7.7 (derived from the CCTI) is a measure of shyness, so we have included here a true Sociability scale that is based on the adult Sociability scale in Table 7.1. Scoring instructions: Reverse scores for items 6, 7, 12, 15, 17, 18, and 20 by setting $5 = 1, 4 = 2, 3 = 3, 2 = 4$, and $1 = 5$. Add the scores for the five items on each scale and divide each scale score by 5 (the number of items per scale) in order to interpret scores in terms of the 1–5 scale.

8 Behavioral Genetics

Behavioral genetics studies the extent to which genetic differences among individuals can account for the observed behavioral and personality differences in a population. Its focus is not on universals but on individual differences. Behavioral genetics is descriptive: It considers what is in a population rather than what could be or what should be. When behavioral genetic research points to a genetic influence for a particular behavior, it means only that genetic differences among individuals account for some of their observed differences in behavior. It does not mean that this is the natural order of things or that environmental influences make no difference.

The relationship between genes and behavior is complex. One gene can be involved in several different kinds of behavior, and several different genes can be involved in a single behavior. In fact, no single major gene has been implicated in the origin of any personality trait or any other psychological behavior. Genetically influenced personality traits are more likely to originate in the action of multiple genes (polygenic inheritance), which are likely to yield a normal distribution of the trait being studied.

Genetic influences are indeed just influences: tendencies that nudge development in one direction rather than another. Genetic influence does not refer to an individual but to an average effect of genetic variation in a population. One person might differ from the population average primarily for genetic reasons, another primarily for environmental reasons. Changing environmental contingencies in the population could alter the mix of genetic and environmental variance; changing environmental contingencies for an individual can certainly change behavior. Heritability, a much-maligned descriptive statistic, describes the extent to which genetic variance can explain phenotypic variance in a population. If heritability is 1.0 for a particular behavior—and no behavioral example even comes close to this condition—genetic variance can account for all of the observed variance. Even with a heritability of 1.0, however, a novel environmental influence could substantially alter the behavior, just as a new gene mutation could alter behavior for a trait whose heritability is zero.

Some scientists assume that genetic influences are locked at full throttle at the moment of conception. To the contrary, developmental genetics focuses on the role of genes in the regulation of developmental change. Genes are just as likely to be sources of change as they are of continuity, and exploration of these effects is at the heart of the new interdisciplinary field of developmental behavioral genetics (Plomin, 1983b).

MAJOR METHODS

Our goal here is to present sufficient background material to understand research on heritable personality traits. Readers already possessing this knowledge should skip this section, and others may wish to consult textbooks of behavioral genetics for a detailed exposition: Dixon & Johnson (1980), Fuller & Thompson (1978), Plomin, DeFries, & McClearn (1980), and Vale (1980).

Research with Animals

Animal behavior is studied not only because humans share certain personality traits with other animals, but also because breeding can be controlled, environment can be controlled, and many generations of quick-breeding animals can be studied. The major methods used for nonhuman animals—mostly mice because of their small size, rapid reproduction, and mammalian status—are family studies, studies of inbred strains, and selection studies. Family studies compare genetically related individuals in order to examine the extent of genetic influence. Of course, familial resemblance does not prove genetic influence because resemblance could be mediated environmentally rather than genetically. With nonhuman animals, controlled breeding makes it possible to obtain hundreds of half-sibling offspring of the same sire. Comparing the similarity of relatives that share different degrees of heredity—such as full siblings and half siblings—permits estimates of genetic influence, though caution is required in the interpretation of all family studies because environmental similarity might covary with genetic relatedness.

An inbred strain is derived from brother-sister matings for 20 generations. This severe inbreeding produces animals that are virtually clones. Differences *within* an inbred strain thus provide an estimate of nongenetic variation, whereas differences *between* inbred strains reared in the same laboratory environment can be used to estimate genetic influence. Prenatal cross-fostering (ovary and embryo transplants) and postnatal cross-fostering can be used to eliminate prenatal and postnatal environmental explanations of the difference between inbred strains. A powerful method for analyzing genetic and environmental sources of variance using inbred strains, called *diallel analysis,* involves the complete intercrossing of several strains.

Selection studies provide the clearest evidence of genetic influence. If heredity is important for a character, we ought to be able to select successfully for it, as animal breeders knew for centuries before the mechanisms of heredity were understood. The extent of genetic influence is assessed in selection studies by considering how fast selection occurs. The success of selective breeding for various traits in dogs, for behavior as often as for morphology, is the most dramatic illustration of genetic diversity. Consider, for example, the 49-fold difference in weight between a Chihuahua and a Saint Bernard. An interesting book on the behavioral aspects of selection in dogs is one by John Paul Scott and John Fuller (1965), who conducted an extensive two-decade research program on five representative breeds, described in Chapter 2.

Human Twins

The basic methods of human behavioral genetics are family, twin, and adoption studies. We are in the odd position of having more personality data on twins and adoptees than on more usual types of family members. Though family studies yield ambiguous data in the sense that hereditary and environmental influences are not separated, family studies do reveal familial resemblance, a prerequisite for genetic influence.

The twin method can be viewed as a natural experiment in which pairs of individuals in one group (identical twins) are the same genetically, and pairs in the other group (fraternal twins) are only half as similar genetically. If heredity influences a character, identical twins should be more similar for the character than are fraternal twins. If identical twins are no more alike than are fraternal twins, the trait under study is not inherited. Quantitative estimates of the proportion of observed variance that can be explained by genetic variability can be derived from the difference in correlations between members of identical and fraternal twin pairs. This proportion is called heritability. The method most frequently used to estimate heritability from twin data is based on the twofold greater genetic similarity of identical twins as compared to fraternal twins: The difference between the identical and fraternal twin correlations is simply doubled (Falconer, 1960). For example, the typical identical twin correlation for height is .95; for fraternal twins, the correlation is about .50. The pattern of twin correlations suggests that individual differences in height are largely genetic. Doubling the difference between identical and fraternal twin correlations suggests that 90% of the variance in height is due to genetic variance.

One factor that can affect this estimate of genetic influence is assortative mating: the tendency of like to mate with like. Thus tall women are more likely to mate with tall men, and intelligent women are more likely to mate with intelligent men. As parents, they are genetically more similar than are parents who are randomly selected. This greater similarity of parents who mate assortatively tends to make fraternal twins more alike, but it cannot increase the correlation between identical twins, who are genetically identical, by definition. Thus, the overall effect of assortative mating is to make the correlation between fraternal twins higher and therefore closer to the correlation between identical twins, thereby lowering the estimate of heritability.

Another factor that affects the estimate of genetic influence is nonadditive genetic variance, a concept too complex to discuss here (see Plomin et al., 1980, pp. 212–213, for a discussion). It needs to be mentioned, however, for its effect is opposite to that of assortative mating on the estimate of genetic influence. Because assortative mating and nonadditive genetic influence have counterbalancing effects, it is assumed that the usual formula for estimating heritability—doubling the difference between correlations for identical and fraternal twins—provides a reasonable estimate.

The twin method assumes that the environmental similarity shared by pairs of identical twins and pairs of fraternal twins is roughly the same. Both types of twins share the same womb, are reared in the same family, and are the same age and same sex (only same-sex fraternal twins are usually used for comparisons with identical twins, who are always the same sex). It has been suggested, however, that identical twins may be treated more alike than are fraternal twins, and therefore the closer resemblance of identical twins might be due to fewer environmental differences as well as to greater genetic similarity.

One could argue the other way, though: that identical twins are treated *less* alike than fraternal twins. We know that this is closer to the truth prenatally, for identical twins have larger birth weight differences than do fraternal twins. With regard to postnatal environment, one could argue that identical twins contrast themselves and are contrasted by others, accentuating any differences that exist in an attempt to define separate identities.

Identical twins tend to be dressed more alike by their parents, and they spend more time together than do fraternal twins. For these and other variables, however, the difference between identical and fraternal twins is so slight that it cannot account for the much higher trait correlations in identical twins (Plomin et al., 1980, pp. 295–299).

Whatever the differences in how the two kinds of twins are treated—small or large—the question remains what the effects of these differences are on personality. Fraternal twins who mistakenly thought they were identical, or whose parents thought they were identical, are no more alike in personality than are correctly identified fraternal twins (Scarr, 1968; Scarr & Carter-Saltzman, 1979). Loehlin and Nichols (1976) investigated whether adolescent identical twins who had been treated alike resemble each other more in personality; they do not. The absence of a significant impact of differential treatment of twins on their personality has been confirmed in several other studies (see Plomin et al., 1980).

Adoption Studies

Studies of adopted children separate the effects of heredity from the effects of familial environment. Resemblances between the biological parents and their children reveal the impact of heredity; such parents do not rear their children and so have no (familial) environmental impact on them. Similarities between the adoptive parents and their adopted children reveal the impact of family environment; such parents are unrelated to the adopted children and so heredity is not involved.

Selective placement, in which adoption agencies match adoptive parents to the biological parents of the adoptees, introduces a possible confound. The bases of selective placement have tended to be intelligence and social status, not personality. Thus selective placement seems not to pose a problem when personality is the focus of study.

Adoption studies can reveal *genotype-environment interaction:* the differential impact of environmental factors on children of different genotypes. The typical environmental analysis asks whether an environmental influence has an *average* effect across all children. Such influences are rare. More likely, an environmental factor greatly affects some children but not others. The environment could also have different effects for children who differ genetically. For example, even if explosive parental discipline does not relate to children's emotionality on the average, it might affect children who are predisposed to be emotional, triggering emotional behavior. Assessment of genetic and environmental main effects and their interaction is described by Plomin, DeFries, & Loehlin (1977).

GENOTYPE-ENVIRONMENT CORRELATION

This concept refers to the differential exposure of individuals to environment. Children with a genetic tilt toward activity tend to seek out situations that require vigor or a rapid tempo rather than situations involving slow-moving, low-energy behavior. Thus their genetic propensity (activity) is correlated with environmental influence (energetic rather than sluggish).

Three types of genotype-environment correlation have been proposed, and methods for assessing them have discussed (Plomin et al., 1977). The *passive* type, which is most often considered in quantitative genetic analyses, emerges from the usual situation in which family members share both heredity and family environment. For example, sociable children are likely to have sociable parents and siblings who provide sociable environments for them. The *reactive* type involves a differential response to children that is correlated with their genetic propensities. For example, school children might recognize emotional tendencies in one child and deliberately elicit such outbursts. The *active* type of genotype-environment correlation occurs when individuals induce changes in environments to make them fit better with their genetic propensities. Active children, for example, are difficult to restrain because they can turn quiescent situations—such as the back seat of a car—into sprightly, vigorous situations. Though we usually think of positive correlations between genetic dispositions and environmental factors, negative genotype-environment correlation is also possible, for example, when teachers attempt to damp the bounding of a highly active child. A general theory of development fashioned around these types of genotype-environment correlation essentially posits a shift from the passive to the reactive and active varieties during childhood (Scarr & McCartney, 1983).

Recent work by David Rowe (1983) suggests a mechanism by which genotype-environment interaction might occur. In two studies, he found that children's perceptions of the love in their homes are significantly affected by genetic differences. This suggests one process by which genotypes interact with environments: The perception of parental love differs according to genetic dispositions. Perceptions of control by children, on the other hand, are largely a family affair, uninfluenced by genetic differences among the children.

STRUCTURAL MODELS

Family, twin, and adoption designs each make assumptions concerning assortative mating, additive and nonadditive genetic variance, the comparability of identical and fraternal twin environments, and selective placement. Rather than considering each experiment separately, behavioral geneticists have moved in the direction of analyzing the combined data from several experiments. Structural models are superior to the piece-by-piece approach in several ways. They permit analysis of all data simultaneously, make assumptions explicit, permit tests of the relative fit of the model, and allow tests of different models. Modeling basically involves fitting a series of overdetermined simultaneous equations (usually formed by path analysis) to estimate genetic and environmental parameters that best fit observed familial correlations.

DEVELOPMENTAL BEHAVIORAL GENETICS

Different sets of genes have their maximum influence at different times during the life of an individual. Thus one set of genes determines the secondary sex characteristics of males during adolescence, and another set determines the loss of hair on the head during middle age. Similarly, particular environments can influence individuals at different times during their lives. Using cross-sectional data, we can ask whether the mixture of genetic and environmental influences changes in development. For example, do twin studies find waning genetic influence on temperament as children experience more varied environments outside the home? Methods for answering such questions have been proposed (Ho, Foch & Plomin, 1980).

Even more informative is the *longitudinal* analysis of genetic and environmental contributions to change and continuity in development. One approach has been used in the analysis of longitudinal data from the Louisville Twin Study (Matheny, 1983). Developmental changes (spurts and lags) have been analyzed, using repeated-measures analysis of variance for identical and fraternal twins.

Phenotypic stability can be mediated genetically or environmentally. If there is no stability, the genetic and environmental factors that affect the character do not correlate across age. Genetic correlation describes the overlap among the genetic systems that affect a character at two ages. Similarly, an environmental correlation reveals the extent to which environmental factors that affect a character at one age also affect the character at another age (Plomin & DeFries, 1981).

ENVIRONMENT: FAMILIAL AND INDIVIDUAL

Behavioral genetics methods can distinguish two kinds of environmental components (Rowe & Plomin, 1981). The first, which we shall call *family-similar,* includes environmental influences shared by all members of a family but different from environmental influences in other families. In an adoption study, pairs of unrelated children adopted into the same home share only that familial environment. The correlation between such pairs of children represents variance due to family-similar environment. This variance has been found to be negligible (Rowe & Plomin, 1981).

The other environmental component, which we shall call *individual experience,* consists of the environment particular to each individual; such differential environment renders members of a family different from each other. Identical twins, having the same genes, can differ only for environmental reasons. For twins in the same family, any family-similar environment would not contribute to differences between the twins. Therefore, any environmental influences, by definition, involve individual experiences. For personality, the correlations for identical twins are usually around .50. By subtraction from 1.00, we infer that half the variance is environmental variance of the individual experience kind (minus any variance due to error of measurement).

DIFFERENTIAL HERITABILITY

Are some personality traits more heritable than others? Part of the difficulty in demonstrating differential heritability is lack of statistical power. Given the usual identical and fraternal twin correlations of .50 and .30, respectively, it may be difficult to demonstrate significant heritability. Power analyses (Cohen, 1977) show that a sample of 250 identical and 250 fraternal twin pairs is needed to detect a significant ($p < .05$) correlational difference of this magnitude 80% of the time. For samples of 50 pairs of each type of twin, a significant difference between the typical identical and fraternal twin correlations will be detected only about a third of the time. Lack of power is a more severe problem when the heritabilities of two traits are compared. With 100 pairs of each type of twin, a heritability of .40 based on an identical twin correlation of .50 and a fraternal twin correlation of .30 has a standard error of $\pm$ .24. This means that we could not discriminate the typical personality heritability of .40 from another trait whose heritability is zero, given 100 pairs of each type of twin. With 1,000 pairs of each type of twin, researchers can detect such differences but still cannot discriminate the usual heritability of .40 from a more modest heritability of .20.

With the issue of statistical power as prelude, we can now examine data on differential heritability. Some personality traits—perhaps tolerance or wanting to make a good impression—should show less genetic influence than other traits. Loehlin and Nichols (1976) noticed that in their large adolescent twin sample, participants in the National Merit Scholarship Qualifying Examinations, all the scales of the California Psychological Inventory CPI—including Tolerance and Good Impression—manifested differences between identical and fraternal twin correlations of about .20, suggesting a heritability of about .40. For example, for CPI Tolerance, the identical and fraternal twin correlations were .53 and .33, respectively. For Good Impression, the correlations were .47 and .28. They concluded:

> Thus, in the CPI data, we fail to find evidence of any consistent tendency for some scales to show greater differences in identical-fraternal resemblance than other scales do; the identicals are consistently more alike than the fraternals but about equally so on the various scales. (p. 28)

Loehlin and Nichols also examined clusters of items from the CPI as well as from an objective behavior inventory, adjective checklists, self-concept measures, and interests and attitudes. Similar results were found in their survey of other twin studies:

> In short, for personality . . . the existing literature appears to agree with our own finding that, while identical-twin pairs tend to be more similar than fraternal-twin pairs, it is difficult to demonstrate that they are consistently more similar on some traits than on others. (p. 46)

Zonderman (1982) applied model-fitting analyses to the data of Loehlin and Nichols (1976) and found evidence for differential heritability for the 18 CPI scales: the more heritable CPI scales are those in the second-order CPI factor of Extraversion (Nichols & Schnell, 1963). Carey, Goldsmith, Tellegen, & Gottesman (1978) combined data from three twin studies using the CPI and also concluded that scales in the CPI Extraversion factor showed the highest heritabilities. However, Loehlin (1978) did not accept this conclusion because the study focused on identical and fraternal twin correlations rather than on the *differences* between identical and fraternal twin correlations.

Horn, Plomin, and Rosenman (1976) suggested that the lack of differential heritability for the CPI scales might be due to item overlap: 38% of the 480 CPI items overlap at least two of the 18 scales. New CPI scales were created, eliminating the overlapping items. The twin results for these new scales provided some evidence for differential heritability, with two scales—Responsibility and Femininity—showing heritabilities near zero. Cross-validation criteria were used to isolate 41 reliable CPI items that showed heritable influence. When these heritable items were submitted to factor analysis, the largest factor consisted mainly of shyness items—for example, "It is hard for me to start a conversation with strangers."

With the exception of Extraversion-related traits, there is a consistent .20 difference between identical and fraternal twin correlations for diverse personality traits. This conclusion is based on research with self-report questionnaires. Perhaps identical twins merely *perceive* themselves as more similar than fraternal twins, a thought that led us to conduct several twin studies using parental ratings of children's personality. Parents see their children over long periods of time and in many situations, so they might be an excellent source of information about their twin children. However, several twin studies using parental ratings revealed that all traits appeared to be influenced by heredity. One difference from the self-report data is that parental rating data usually yield fraternal twin correlations that are low, sometimes even negative in direction (Plomin, 1981). There may be a tendency to contrast fraternal twins, rating one co-twin as the active one and the other as the inactive one, though the twins really are not very different in activity level.

At least one exception to the rule of no differential heritability can be found for parental ratings. Rowe & Plomin (1977) included items designed to assess the nine temperament dimensions of the New York Longitudinal Study. A factor analysis yielded a cluster of items that could only be called a Reaction to Foods; this factor showed no heritability in a twin study of 2- to 6-year-old twins (Plomin & Rowe, 1977) and in an unpublished twin study of 5- to 10-year-old twins (study described in Plomin & Foch, 1980).

One might argue that parents have a general impression about the twins' similarity and that parents of identical twins generally regard their children as more similar than do parents of fraternal twins. If there is such a bias, it is shared by mothers and fathers because similar results are obtained when twin correlations are derived from the mother's ratings of one twin and the father's rating of the other twin (Plomin, 1976a).

Perhaps the finding is real: Self-reports and ratings of personality are all moderately heritable. In their book, Loehlin and Nichols offered a hypothesis to explain this possibility. Based on a theory of Allen (1970), they suggested that:

> If the heritability of a trait is low, gene mutations affecting the trait will tend to accumulate, increasing its genetic variance. Once the genetic variance becomes large enough relative to environmental variation so that the heritability of the trait is appreciable, stabilizing natural selection will begin to operate on the trait to slow and eventually to stop further increase in its genetic variability and hence to hold heritability at a stable level. . . . Generally speaking, then, on this hypothesis all traits tend toward moderate levels of heritability because the genetic component of variation of any trait tends to increase until the process of natural selection can "see it" against the background of environmental variation present and hold it stable. (1976, p. 90)

Loehlin has suggested another possible explanation for the lack of evidence for differential heritability of self-report personality questionnaires

(1982). His argument begins by noting that two major higher-order factors, Extraversion and Neuroticism, are found in many personality questionnaires. Both traits appear to be substantially heritable. For example, in a recent Swedish study (Floderus-Myrhed, Pedersen, & Rasmuson, 1980) using nearly 13,000 twin pairs, the twin correlations for Extraversion were .47 (identical) and .20 (fraternal) for males; for females, the correlations were, respectively, .54 and .21. These twin correlations suggest a heritability of .54 for males and .66 for females. For Neuroticism, the heritabilities are similar: .50 for men and .58 for females. Loehlin (1982) also reanalyzed his National Merit data to form seven orthogonal factor scales from the items of the CPI, two of which were Extraversion and Neuroticism. These two scales yielded the expected high heritabilities; other scales such as Stereotyped Masculinity, Intolerance of Ambiguity, and Persistence yielded much lower heritability estimates. Loehlin suggested that Extraversion and Neuroticism are such pervasive super-traits that they mask the differential heritability of other, unrelated traits. This suggestion is relevant to our approach to temperament because sociability is a component of Extraversion, and Neuroticism is related to emotionality.

TEMPERAMENT—ENVIRONMENT INTERACTION

Interactions represent conditional relationships: The relationship between X and Y depends upon another variable, Z. For example, emotionality in early childhood might predict adjustment problems in school only for children who experience certain environmental stresses. Temperament interactions can treat temperament as an independent variable, as a dependent variable, or as both an independent and a dependent variable (Plomin & Daniels, 1984). Most research on temperament interactions has been of the first type: The interaction between temperament and environment has been used to predict outcome measures such as school performance and adjustment. Genotype-environment interaction is an example of the second category, in which temperament is treated as a dependent variable predicted by genetic factors, environmental factors, and their interaction. No research of the third type has been reported but an example would be stability between temperament in infancy and temperament in childhood as a function of environmental stability, which Sameroff and Chandler (1975) refer to as transactions.

We suggest that these interactions should be analyzed as statistical interactions in a standard analysis of variance. For example, in the classical two-by-two analysis of variance, one routinely determines the variance of the dependent variable explained by the main effects of the independent variables; after removing this variance, one examines the variance explained by the interaction of the main effects. The significance of the interaction term indicates whether the joint effects of the two independent variables acting together are related to the dependent variable beyond the separate influence of each of the independent variables, which is precisely what an interaction is.

However, analysis of variance is limited to dichotomous or discontinuous variables, whereas most measures used in temperament research are continuous. Even difficult temperament, once viewed as discontinuous, is now conceptualized as a continuous easy-to-difficult dimension. When such continuous variables are divided at the mean to fit the procrustean mold of analysis of variance, much of the information in the distribution is lost. The most general approach to the analysis of temperament interactions is hierarchical multiple regression (Cohen & Cohen, 1975), which permits analysis of both continuous and discontinuous data, provides tests of the significance of interactions, and permits tests of different models of interaction such as quadratic interactions.

Hierarchical multiple regression can be conducted with any general regression program (Plomin & Daniels, 1984). The simplest model predicts a dependent variable from two independent variables and their interaction:

$$\hat{Y} = b_1X_1 + b_2X_2 + b_3X_1X_2 + C$$

Using the first category of temperament interactions, one can predict behavioral problems $(\hat{Y})$ from temperament (X_1), environment (X_2), and their interaction (X_1X_2). C refers to a regression constant. X_1 and X_2 are analogous to main effects in an analysis of variance. The two-way interaction (X_1X_2) is represented by the product of the main effects from which the main effects have been partialled, as in the analysis of variance procedure for estimating interactions. The main effect of temperament is tested by b_1, the partial regression of children's behavioral problem scores on children's temperament scores. The main effect of environment is tested by b_2, the partial regression of behavioral problems on the environmental measure. The interaction between temperament and environment is tested by b_3 which indicates that the relationship between temperament and behavioral problems changes as a function of the children's environment.

The significance of the main effects and the two-way interaction is tested sequentially (hierarchically). During step 1, b_1 and b_2 are estimated from Y, X_1, and X_2. The product X_1X_2 is added to the regression equation during step 2. The change in the multiple R^2 due to the product entered during this second step is attributed to the interaction and can be tested for statistical significance.

Hierarchical multiple regression can accommodate several independent variables and their higher-order interactions. Even nonlinear interactions, such as threshold effects, can be studied by including the square of the interaction term, which assesses the quadratic interaction expected when the interaction between temperament and environment emerges only after a certain threshold of environment has been exceeded. In brief, this approach is more powerful than other approaches to the analysis of interactions.

9 Heredity and the EAS Temperaments

Behavioral genetic research relevant to the EAS traits in childhood has flourished since our 1975 book, when there were only a handful of parental rating studies of twins. Now there are a dozen parental rating twin studies, as well as observational studies using global ratings and specific behaviors.

Not all this research is relevant to our revised theory, which focuses on the EAS traits in early childhood. Most behavioral genetic research in the area of personality involves self-report data for adolescents and adults. We include none of these data, though not because of lack of support of our theory. In fact, these data clearly support it. The best case for heritability can be made for extraversion and neuroticism, which are related to our temperaments of sociability and emotionality, respectively. We have excluded studies of adolescents and adults because our abiding interest is personality development in childhood.

Small studies posed a problem for our review. Given the usual pattern of twin correlations, for example, studies with fewer than 20 pairs of twins of each type can show significant genetic influence only if they violate the twin model. Therefore, we have excluded small studies from our review.

We also selected only studies that measured traits similar to our EAS temperaments. We have not relied solely on trait labels reported in studies but have examined individual items to understand what was really measured and how it relates to emotionality, activity, or sociability. When our interpretation of a measure differs from the author's label for it, we discuss our decision. We are also aware that measures in infancy are often dictated more by what researchers *can* study than by what they want to study.

The review of behavioral genetic research on temperament is organized around measurement techniques because the results differ somewhat according to the method employed: parental ratings and interviews, observational studies using global ratings, and studies measuring specific behaviors. The vast majority of the studies used twins, but there are a few family studies and adoption studies.

PARENTAL RATINGS

EAS Measures

Twin Studies. How do the EAS traits fare in twin studies using parental ratings? Table 9-1 summarizes the results of our various twin studies using several versions of EAS measures. From the first study by Buss, Plomin, and Willerman in 1973, these twin studies have supported the hypothesis that the EAS temperaments display an inherited component. Though some of the samples are not large, they are of respectable size, and the findings are consistent across different ages and across different measures. The size of the correlations varies from study to study, probably because of procedural differences. For example, the study by Buss et al. (1973) used a 20-item questionnaire in a sample of children ranging from less than a year to 16 years old, with an average age of 55 months. In contrast, the study by Plomin (1974) used a 56-item questionnaire and included children who ranged in age from 2 to 6 and were 42 months old on the average. Despite these fluctuations, the differences between the identical twin correlations and the fraternal twin correlations remained stable.

The average twin correlations across these studies are presented in Table 9.2. The differences between the identical and fraternal twin correlations are highly significant but too large to be accommodated by the classical twin model. Fraternal twins, like other first-degree relatives, share half their heredity and should thus be approximately half as similar as identical twins. However, for all three EAS traits, the fraternal twin correlations are not significantly greater than zero. This problem is particularly obvious for activity; in two of the four samples, the fraternal twin correlation is significantly *negative*. One explanation for lower-than-expected fraternal twin correlations may be nonadditive genetic variance, but nonadditive genetic variance cannot produce negative correlations. A post hoc speculation is *contrast*. Parents might contrast their fraternal twins, labeling one as active and the other as inactive. The twins might contrast themselves and become more differentiated behaviorally. One twin partner, who might be slightly more active than the other, converts this slight edge into a consistent advantage in initiating activities, and the other twin relinquishes the initiative to his partner. Why does this not also happen for identical twins? Presumably, identical twins are so alike behaviorally that contrast is difficult.

In one study (Plomin, 1974), some of these issues were explored by comparing two procedures: (1) each parent rated both twins, yielding an average *(midparent)* rating; and (2) each parent rated only one twin, which yielded *cross-rating* correlations. For the midparent ratings (aver-

TABLE 9.1
Twin Studies Using EAS Questionnaires

Reference	Questionnaire	Sample	EAS scale	twin correlations	
				identical	fraternal
Buss, Plomin, & Willerman (1973)	20-item EASI-I	78 identical 50 fraternal	Emotionality	.63	.10
			Activity	.79	.16
		mean age: 55 months	Sociability	.58	.23
Buss & Plomin (1975)	20-item EASI-I	overlaps Buss et al. (1973) but larger and more homogeneous in age	Emotionality	.64	.03
			Activity	.62	.09
		81 identical 57 fraternal	Sociability	.62	.13
		mean age: 55 months			
Plomin (1974)	54-item EASI-III	60 identical 51 fraternal	(midparent ratings)		
			Emotionality: distress	.47	.10
		mean age: 54 months	Emotionality: fear	.70	.38
			Emotionality: anger	.57	−.12
			Activity: tempo	.41	−.41
			Activity: vigor	.57	−.14
			Sociability	.47	−.12

Study	Measure	Sample	Trait		
			("cross-ratings" — see text)		
			Emotionality: distress	.17	.03
			Emotionality: fear	.30	.09
			Emotionality: anger	.17	−.10
			Activity: tempo	.16	−.39
			Activity: vigor	.27	−.10
			Sociability	.20	−.10
		29 identical 30 fraternal	("parents in agreement" subsample—see text)		
			Emotionality: distress	.66	−.02
			Emotionality: fear	.76	.41
			Emotionality: anger	.47	.04
			Activity: tempo	.64	−.45
			Activity: vigor	.65	−.18
			Sociability	.55	−.13
Plomin & Rowe (1978)	CCTI	36 identical 31 fraternal mean age: 43 months	Emotionality	.70	.06
			Activity	.65	−.38
			Sociability	.48	−.16
Plomin, unpublished (see Plomin & Foch, 1980, for description of study)	CCTI	51 identical 33 fraternal mean age: 7.6 years	Emotionality	.60	.27
			Activity	.73	.05
			Sociability	.56	.05

TABLE 9.2
Average Twin Correlations for EAS Questionnaires in Table 9.1[a]

Reference	Sample	EAS scale	twin correlations	
			identical	fraternal
Buss & Plomin (1975)	228 identical	Emotionality	.63	.12
Plomin (1974)				
Plomin & Rowe (1978)	172 fraternal	Activity	.62	−.13
Plomin (unpublished)				
	mean age: 61 months	Sociability	.53	−.03

[a] The Buss et al. (1973) study was not included because of its wide age range and its overlap with Buss & Plomin (1975). The three Emotionality scales and the two Activity scales in Plomin (1974) were averaged.

age of mother's and father's ratings) the identical twin correlations were slightly lower than the ratings of either the mothers or fathers, but the fraternal twin correlations were similar. Thus, when one person rates both identical twins, the twins' similarity may be artificially enhanced. However, these data do not support the hypothesis that fraternal twins are contrasted—unless both parents share the bias. The cross-rating twin correlations, listed in Table 9.1, refer to the average of the correlations between the mothers' ratings of cotwin A and the fathers' ratings of cotwin B. These correlations are lower, as we would expect from the low average correlation between mothers' and fathers' ratings ($r = .39$). The identical twin correlations for the cross-rating data should not exceed the correlation between the parents' ratings. On this basis, the cross-rating EAS data are similar to the midrater data: larger-than-expected differences between identical and fraternal twin correlations and negative fraternal twin correlations. These data suggest that if there is a bias in parental rating data, it is not limited to one parent rating both twins.

Low agreement between mothers and fathers may have clouded the analyses of midrater and cross-rater data. Therefore, we selected a subset of families in which parents agreed on the ratings of their twins. The absolute differences between the parents' ratings of the two children in each family on each of the EAS scales were averaged. However, the twin results were very similar for both midrater and cross-rater data to the results described above for the entire sample.

One other attempt was made to explore the source of the lower-than-expected fraternal twin correlations using parental ratings by constructing a scale designed to show *no* genetic influence. It consisted of three items reflecting learning within the family: Child picks up after himself; child blows his nose as needed; child brushes his teeth daily. Though the twin correlations for this *nongenetic* scale suggested some genetic influence, the correlations were different from those of the EAS scales. The identical twin correlation was .89 and the fraternal twin correlation was .69, suggesting substantial shared family environmental influence, as expected. As one of us (Plomin, 1974) has written;

> It is tempting to suggest that the .20 difference between the identical and fraternal twin correlations on the "nongenetic" scale represented a bias that inflated the identical-fraternal difference on the EASI scales. If this were true, correcting for the bias would yield much more reasonable estimates of heritability for the EASI scales, but these thoughts are highly speculative. (p. 42)

Family Study. Though the pattern of twin correlations suggests bias, its source could not be pinned down. This is one of the reasons why we decided to collect familial data from relatives other than twins. Since we were using parental rating instruments, a reasonable first step was the collection of parent-offspring data. Of course, the great difference in age of parents and their offspring could lead to genetic and environmental differences between parents and their offspring, but it is important to compare twin data to other familial data. Parents rated themselves and their spouses on an adult version of the EASI-III Temperament Survey, and these scores were correlated with midparent ratings of the temperament of their children. These data provided some novel checks on the validity of parental ratings. For example, the average correlation for the EAS traits between the spouses' self-report and ratings by the other spouse was .54, which supports the validity of the parental ratings. The design also revealed whether parents project their own personality into their ratings of others. Each parent's rating of his or her spouse was correlated with his or her own self-report. This analysis revealed no tendency for parents to project their personality into their ratings of others. Similar analyses yielded no evidence that parents project their own personality into ratings of their children (Lyon & Plomin, 1981).

Table 9.3 lists the parent-offspring correlations for the EAS traits. Though the correlations are low, they are higher than the fraternal twin correlations, especially for maternal emotionality and sociability. The fact that parents share only half of the additive genetic variance with their offspring means that these correlations do not reflect nonadditive genetic variance (which is likely to be important in temperament). The correlations are further limited by any genetic differences that occur between early childhood and adulthood, as well as methodological differences between adult self-report and parental ratings of children's temperament. Nonetheless, if the correlations in Table 9.3 were due solely to genetic similarity between parents and offspring, they would suggest heritabilities

TABLE 9.3
Parent-Offspring Correlations for EAS Measures for 137 Families.

	Correlation between midrater estimates of children's EAS and:			
	Mothers' self-rating of EAS	Fathers' self-rating of EAS	Fathers' ratings of mothers' EAS	Mothers' ratings of fathers' EAS
Emotionality: distress	.34	.00	.25	− .03
Emotionality: fear	.38	.19	.41	.23
Emotionality: anger	.25	.18	.16	.18
Activity: tempo	.06	.12	.08	.04
Activity: vigor	.14	.12	.10	.10
Sociability	.26	.11	.23	.16

of .20 to .40 on the average. However, the correlations could be due solely to shared family environment. One aspect of the data strongly suggests environmental influence: Mother-offspring correlations are twice as large as father-offspring correlations on the average. The results are consistent for parents' self-report and for the ratings by the spouse. Anger and Activity do not show a clear maternal effect, however.

Adoption Study. An adoption study can distinguish genetic influences from environmental influences. The Colorado Adoption Project (CAP) is an ongoing investigation of biological parents, the children they allow to be placed in foster homes, adoptive parents, and the nonadoptive children of normal parents. Nonadoptive and adoptive parents are matched on several demographic variables including social class (details may be found in Plomin & DeFries, 1983). All parents complete a 3-hour battery of psychological measures, including a version of the EAS that is based on factor analyses of the EASI-III. Temperament measures for the children include mothers' and fathers' ratings on the CCTI, tester ratings on the Infant Behavior Record, and ratings made from videotaped interactions between mothers and infants in structured situations. The oldest children are now 7 years of age, and teacher ratings on temperament and behavioral problems are being collected, but the sample is large enough for analysis only at 12 and 24 months.

The CAP design is particularly powerful in that it includes biological parents who share heredity but not family environment with their children, adoptive parents who share family environment but not heredity with their children, and parents who share both heredity and family environment with their children (nonadoptive parents). However, because analyses to date involve infants, the parent-offspring design of the CAP is limited in detecting genetic influence. If parent-offspring correlations were in the range of .10 to .20 as the family data suggest, and if some of this relationship were due to shared family environment rather than shared heredity, the correlations between biological parents and their adopted-away infants would necessarily be low and almost certainly not significant. Indeed, parent-offspring correlations for the adult EAS and infants' CCTI and Infant Behavior Record yield little evidence for genetic influence, though at 24 months the pattern of parent-offspring correlations for Sociability is consistent with genetic influence (Daniels & Plomin, 1984).

Summary. We have reviewed twin and family data that used the EAS parental rating instruments. Our earliest work focused on the twin method, which was a reasonable way to test the hypothesis of heritability of the EAS traits. The twin data suggested substantial genetic influence, thereby supporting EAS theory. In retrospect, however, biases may have inflated the difference between identical and fraternal twin correlations. One position is that this excessive difference in correlations results solely from biases inherent in parental ratings. However, this position cannot explain why the contrast effect is not found for identical twins. Also, if parental ratings involve bias, why does bias occur in *both* midparent ratings *and* cross-ratings (in which each parent rates one twin)?

The family data are also consistent with the hypothesis of genetic influence on the EAS traits, though they involve an upper limit of heritability: If all the familial resemblance were due to heredity rather than shared family environment, the upper limit is about 40% for Emotionality, 20% for Activity, and 30% for Sociability. Though our adoption results are restricted to infancy at this time, we find a small but significant genetic relationship between parents and offspring for Sociability.

Other Parental Ratings

In addition to our EAS studies, parental reports have been used in seven other twin studies of children, five of them since the publication of our 1975 book. As shown in Table 9.4, no two studies use the same measures, but all include at least one measure relevant to EAS.

Scarr (1969) used Gough's Adjective Checklist to obtain maternal ratings of girls in middle childhood. The twin results suggested that two EAS-like scales, Need for Affiliation (Sociability) and Counseling Readiness (Emotionality) were among the most heritable scales. Other Adjective Checklist scales such as dominance, succorance, and nurturance showed no evidence of genetic influence.

At the start of a longitudinal study, Wilson, Brown, and Matheny (1971) found significant genetic influence for several emotionality-related behav-

TABLE 9.4
Twin Studies Using Other Parental Rating Measures

Reference	Sample	Measure	Results	
			Identical	*Fraternal*
Scarr, 1969	24 identical 28 fraternal girls 6–10 years	Maternal ratings of children on Adjective Checklist (Gough, 1960)		
		—counseling readiness (Emotionality)	.56	.03
		—need for affiliation (Sociability)	.83	.56
Wilson, Brown & Matheny (1971) (earlier reports by Brown et al., 1967; Vandenberg et al., 1968)	95 identical 73 fraternal longitudinal from 3 to 72 months	Parental ratings of specific behavioral differences:	Mean twin concordance from 6 to 72 months (%)	
		"Temperament" cluster (Emotionality)		
		—temper intensity	49	32
		—irritability	52	36
		—crying	57	35
		—temper frequency	25	17
		"Sociability" cluster (Sociability)		
		—seeking affection	37	26
		—accepting people	44	30
		—smiling	43	31
Matheny, Wilson, Dolan, & Krantz (1981)	68–72 identical 39–48 fraternal longitudinal from 3 to 72 months	Parental ratings of specific behavioral differences:	Mean twin concordance from 6 to 72 months (%)	
		"Temperamental" cluster (Emotionality)		
		—temper frequency	40	23
		—crying	53	35
		—irritability	45	26
		Activity	42	22
		"Sociability" cluster (Sociability)		
		—smiling	52	37
		—accepting people	50	24
		—cuddling	43	23

Study	Sample	Measure		
Willerman (1973)	54 identical 39 fraternal 3–12 years	Werry-Weiss-Paters Activity Scale (Werry, 1970)		
		Activity	.88	.59
Cohen, Dibble, & Grawe (1977)	181 identical 84 fraternal 1–5 years	Childhood Personality Scale (Dibble & Cohen, 1974)		
		Zestfulness (Activity)	.78	.54
		Sociability	.69	.24
Matheny & Dolan (1980)	68 identical 37 fraternal 7–10	Maternal ratings on 23 bipolar scales organized into 6 factors:		
		Emotionality ("tense, emotional, quick-tempered")	.45	−.11
		Sociability ("socially bold, outgoing, not a loner")	.56	.06
O'Connor, Foch, Sherry, & Plomin (1980)	54 identical 33 fraternal 7.6 years mean age	Conners (1970) Symptom Rating questionnaire		
		Emotional	.71	.31
		Shy	.69	.27
Goldsmith & Campos (1982)	29 identical 31 fraternal 9 months	Infant Behavior Questionnaire (Rothbart, 1981)		
		Activity level	.75	.57
		Distress to limitations	.77	.35
		Fear	.66	.46

iors. A sociability cluster also indicated some genetic influence. Activity was not measured. A follow-up report a decade later (Matheny, Wilson, Dolan, & Krantz, 1981) yielded similar results for emotionality and sociability clusters, and an added activity item also suggested genetic influence. In this study the data were collected by interview, using items that asked whether the twins were the same or different on a variety of behaviors. Though this method does not yield data amenable to parametric analysis, an advantage is that it does not require parents to make an absolute judgment of their children's temperament. The data are strictly relative, comparing one twin to the other. Parenthetically, there were behaviors that revealed no genetic influence—toilet-training problems, for example.

Willerman (1973) measured activity with the Werry scale (1970), which assesses specific behaviors (such as "gets up and down") in specific situations (such as "during meals" and "television"). As typically occurs in rating studies using specific behaviors, the twin correlations are high, but the difference between the identical and fraternal twin correlations is nonetheless substantial.

Another parental rating instrument, the Childhood Personality Scale (CPS; Dibble & Cohen, 1974), was used to study twins from 1 to 5 years of age (Cohen, Dibble, & Grawe, 1977). The CPS consists of 48 items in 24 categories which yield five factors. One factor, Sociability-Shyness, includes items such as "Shies away from getting attention" and "Smiles to a friendly person." Another factor, labeled Zestfulness (ebullience), seems related to Activity and includes such items as: "Lies down, rests his head, or falls asleep instead of playing," "Seems to have little zest for normal activities, acts tired," and "Sits without doing anything unless another person tries hard to get him interested." Both scales show significant genetic influence, and both illustrate the trend toward higher twin correlations for measures of specific behaviors.

Yet another parental rating approach was reported by Matheny and Dolan (1980). Mothers rated their children on 23 bipolar rating scales, comprising six factors, two of which were labeled Emotionality and Sociability. (An "Activity-Distractibility" factor consisted of just two items, "overly active" and "inattentive," which, though showing genetic influence, is not the same as our EAS Activity.) Both the Emotionality and Sociability factors showed significant genetic influence, but one of the six scales, Tough-minded, showed no significant genetic influence. Matheny and Dolan (1980) concluded:

> According to method, behaviors, and the age of the twins, previous efforts by Buss and Plomin (1975) were most comparable to the present study. Buss and Plomin isolated emotionality, activity, sociability, and, to a lesser extent

impulsivity, as the primary factors of a temperament theory of personality development, and presented evidence from highly homogeneous scales that there was a pronounced genetic influence on these four temperaments. The first three of their factors were identified in the present study, and both lines of investigation indicate that emotionality, sociability, and activity are iso-lable, and genetically influenced, aspects of children's behavior. (pp. 232–233)

One parental rating twin study focused on specific behavioral problems in children averaging 7½ years of age (O'Connor, Foch, Sherry, & Plo-min, 1980). The 54 identical twin pairs and 33 same-sex fraternal twin pairs were rated by their mothers on the Parent Symptom Rating (PSR) questionnaire (Connors, 1970). Factor analyses of the 73 PSR items led to the construction of 12 scales, three of which appear to be relevant to the EAS traits. An Emotional factor had as the three highest loading factor items "feelings easily hurt," "feels cheated," and "afraid that people don't like him." Though leaning toward neuroticism, this factor correlated .58 with CCTI Emotionality and thus provides data relevant to Emotionality. A Shyness scale of the revised PSR ("shy," "afraid of new situations," "afraid of people") correlated − .69 with CCTI Sociability, which sup-ports our contention that CCTI Sociability consists of both shyness and sociability. A Restless factor from the PSR might appear to be related to EAS Activity, for it includes items such as "restless," "can't keep still," and "always into things." This emphasis on fidgeting rather than tempo or vigor may be why it correlates only .38 with CCTI Activity. Therefore we omitted this factor from Table 9.4.

Both the Emotional and Shy PSR scales yield estimates of significant and substantial genetic influence. The pattern of results is comparable to other studies using parental ratings of somewhat specific items, and it supports the hypothesis of heritability for Emotionality and Sociability.

An ongoing study by Goldsmith and Campos (1982) focuses on observa-tional and experimental measures of temperament in infancy. Their twin results for the Infant Behavior Questionnaire (Rothbart, 1981) yield the typical pattern of results for questionnaires employing specific behaviors: high correlations for both identical and fraternal twins and significant differences between identical and fraternal twin correlations.

Few studies of familial resemblance in normal, unselected families are relevant to childhood temperament. Beyond the studies mentioned earlier that used the EAS measures, there is only one study of activity level (Willerman, 1973) that related parental ratings of children on the Werry-Weiss-Peters Activity Scale with self-ratings of the parents as they re-membered themselves in childhood. The correlation between mothers and their infants was .48; for fathers and the infants the correlation was

.42; there were 43 families with children from 34 to 70 months of age. Similarly, Caldwell and Herscher (1964) discovered a correlation of .40 between a self-report of mothers' "energy" with the mothers' ratings of the energy of their 1-year-old infants in 30 families.

In summary, behavioral genetic studies using parental ratings other than the EAS measures find similar results for EAS-related measures: Emotionality, Activity, and Sociability show genetic influence in studies of twins in childhood. This conclusion is strengthened by the diversity of measures. They include an adjective checklist, interviews, direct ratings of differences within twin pairs, a situationally specific measure of activity, bipolar scales, and ratings of behavioral problems. These studies also provide some evidence for differential heritability, which the EAS measures cannot provide because they assess only the EAS traits.

These various studies used either global ratings or ratings of specific behaviors. Research using parental ratings of specific behaviors (Cohen et al., 1977; Goldsmith & Campos, 1982; O'Connor et al., 1980; Willerman, 1973) generally yield higher twin correlations than do studies using parental ratings of global judgments (Matheny & Dolan, 1980; the EAS studies discussed in the previous section). Specific ratings produce identical twin correlations of about .75 and fraternal twin correlations of about .40; for global ratings involved in the EAS measures and in the study by Matheny & Dolan (1980), the identical and fraternal twin correlations are usually about .50 and .00, respectively.

What could account for this difference? One possibility is that global ratings involve more error because the rater is asked to integrate over time and across behaviors. Ratings of specific behaviors require the rater to integrate over time but not across behaviors. Error would reduce twin correlations. However, an explanation based simply on error cannot be correct because global ratings show higher test-retest reliabilities than do ratings of specific behaviors. If parents are reliable in rating one child from time to time, why would they not also be reliable in rating two children at the same time? Our guess is that the answer is not error but that global ratings are more subject to contrast effects than are ratings of specific behaviors. Support for this hypothesis comes from the near-zero correlations for fraternal twins and especially from the significant negative correlations for Activity. However, it is too early to discard global rating measures; we certainly do not want to use ratings of specific behaviors just because they yield a pattern of twin correlations more consistent with genetic influence. The "true" pattern of correlations based on observations of the children may be more like the pattern produced by global ratings than by ratings of specific behaviors. We return to this issue shortly.

OBSERVATIONS

Of the few observational twin studies related to the EAS traits, several have so few twins that their data are likely to be unreliable (Freedman, 1974; Reppucci, 1968; Van den Daele, 1971). The remaining studies fall into two categories: global rating scales and observations of specific behaviors.

Global Rating Scales: Infant Behavior Record

The use of parental ratings assumes that parents know their children well and can average their behavior across situations and time. Observational studies trade off observations over many situations and over long periods of time in favor of greater precision and objectivity in observation. However, observational studies can select situations that are *behavior intense:* situations that frequently elicit the target behaviors. One of these is the demanding situation involved in infant mental and motor testing. Nancy Bayley (1969), recognizing that the testing situation provides a window through which children can be observed, developed the Infant Behavior Record (IBR), which testers use to rate infants' behavior following administration of the Bayley mental and motor tests. The IBR consists of 30 items representing broad dimensions of infant behavior such as social responsiveness, activity, and attention, as well as more specific behaviors such as mouthing and banging. Matheny (1980) found three factors at 3, 6, 9, 12, 18, and 24 months of age: Test Affect-Extraversion, Activity, and Task Orientation, factors that have been replicated in our own work and in a study of about 1200 Dutch infants (van der Meulen & Smrkovsky, 1982). Test Affect-Extraversion appears to be related to Sociability. It includes ratings of the infants' social responsiveness to the tester (not to the mother or other persons), though it has the flavor of cooperativeness, endurance, and happiness as well. The Activity factor includes IBR items of activity, body motion, and energy and would thus appear to be an adequate representative of our Activity dimension, though situational specificity is likely because the infant is not permitted to move about freely. Task Orientation includes attention span, goal directedness, and object orientation and thus appears to be in the realm of impulsivity. Matheny (1983) has reported rater reliabilities of .87, .79, and .82, respectively, for the three factors.

Though we expected that parental ratings of infants' general activity would not relate strongly to testers' ratings of infants' activity during Bayley testing, we examined these intercorrelations using data from the Colorado Adoption Project. The correlations, presented in Table 9.5 for 270 infants tested at both 12 and 24 months, confirm our suspicion. CCTI

TABLE 9.5
Contemporaneous Correlations between Midparent Ratings on the CCTI
and Tester Ratings on IBR Factors for 12- and 24-month-old Infants in the
Colorado Adoption Project

	Adopted N = 129–143			Nonadopted N = 100–116		
	CCTI Emo	Act	Soc	CCTI Emo	Act	Soc
12 months						
IBR Activity	.05	.03	.01	− .11	.04	.05
IBR Test Affect-Extraversion	− .19*	.00	.17*	− .07	.02	.25*
24 months						
IBR Activity	.01	.17*	.07	.07	.08	− .17
IBR Test Affect-Extraversion	.00	.08	.31*	− .07	.12	.36*

$*p < .05$

Activity shows a significant relationship to IBR Activity in only one of four comparisons, perhaps because of the situational specificity inherent in the IBR Activity measure. For CCTI Sociability, midparent ratings at 12 and 24 months correlate significantly with IBR Test Affect-Extraversion as rated by the tester; the correlations are somewhat higher at 24 months than at 12 months.

Twin Studies.   Matheny (1980) reported twin correlations for the IBR factors for infants tested at 3, 6, 9, 12, 18 and 24 months of age as part of the longitudinal Louisville Twin Study. Each member of the twin pair was tested and rated by a different examiner. The twin correlations, listed in Table 9.6, suggest genetic influence for both IBR factors. For the Test Affect-Extraversion factor, the average correlations during the first two years are .50 for identical twins and .14 for fraternal twins, with no discernible developmental change in the correlations. For the Activity factor, the average twin correlations were .40 and .17, respectively, with an apparent trend toward increasing heritability in the second year of life.

In an earlier report, Matheny, Dolan, and Wilson (1976) summed the IBR ratings at 3, 6, 9, and 12 months to obtain a *first year* score for each item, and they added the ratings at 18, 24, and 30 months to obtain a *second year* score. We examined the IBR items and found four that seem to assess the same behaviors as our EAS temperaments. We have listed the twin correlations for these items (numbers 2, 5, 14, and 25) in Table 9.7. These data indicate significant heritability for fearfulness in the second year, for activity in the first and second year, for energy in the second year, and for sociability in the first year. These findings offer strong

TABLE 9.6

Twin Correlations for Two Factors of the Infant Behavior Record from the
Longitudinal Louisville Twin Study (Matheny, 1980)[a]

| | Twin Correlations | | | | | | | |
| | 6 months | | 12 months | | 18 months | | 24 months | |
	MZ	DZ	MZ	DZ	MZ	DZ	MZ	DZ
Test Affect- Extraversion	.55	.10	.43	.07	.49	.37	.53	.03
Activity	.24	.11	.33	.28	.43	.14	.58	.14

[a] MZ refers to identical twins; DZ to fraternal. N of MZ = 72–91 pairs; N of DZ = 35–50.

TABLE 9.7

Twin Correlations for EAS-Related Items of the Infant Behavior Record from
the Longitudinal Louisville Twin Study (Matheny, Dolan, & Wilson, 1976)

| | Twin Correlations | | | |
| | 3–12 months | | 18–30 months | |
	identical N = 55	fraternal N = 27	identical N = 47	fraternal N = 27
IBR Fearfulness item	.74	.54	.65	.22
IBR Activity item	.34	− .06	.52	.08
IBR Energy item	.44	.26	.81	.22
IBR Responsiveness to Persons item	.63	.34	.44	.45

support for the heritability of the EAS temperaments, especially in light of the fact that each member of the twin pairs was rated by a different examiner.

The longitudinal nature of these data permitted Matheny (1983) to analyze the concordance of identical and fraternal twin pairs for patterns of change on the IBR during infancy. Stability was statistically significant but modest, as seems to be the rule in infancy. Matheny used a repeated measures analysis of variance to assess the similarity of twin partners' profiles of change. For 66 identical and 40 fraternal twin pairs at 12, 18, and 24 months of age, the twin correlations were significantly higher for identical twins than for fraternal twins. For the Test Affect-Extraversion factor, the correlation for identical twin profiles was .37 and for fraternal twins, .21. For the activity factor profiles, the correlations were .52 and .18, respectively. Thus, according to Matheny (1983), genetic factors are involved in the stability and instability of these EAS-related traits in infancy:

> The correlations show, within the context of behavioral transitions, that the sequences of individual differences of change are partially regulated by genetic influences. In effect, the data from twins show that perturbations or instabilities in temperament do not vitiate the concept of temperament, but permit the concept to include a constitutional basis for the regulation of developmental change. (p. 359)

Matheny's (1983) analysis of developmental profiles suggests genetic influence on change and continuity in development. An earlier study analyzed temperamental change from one setting to another. The same repeated-measures analysis of variance was used for "adaptability" scores in the test situation and in a playroom setting (Matheny & Dolan, 1975). In the test situation, this score involved IBR items and was much like the Test Affect-Extraversion factor, which is related to Sociability. However, in the playroom setting, the measure appears to assess Emotionality, for it includes ratings of the child's initial distress when the mother leaves, the quality of the child's adjustment during the play period, and its involvement with toys and play. The authors report that high-scoring children "cried, required constant soothing and were not involved with play" (p. 1107). The scores in the two situations correlated from .26 to .42 from 9 to 30 months of age. For the purpose of this analysis, it does not matter whether the same dimensions are being measured in the two situations; the goal is to assess the etiology of score *profiles* across the two situations. The analysis strongly suggested that genetic influences are important determinants of profiles of scores across the two situations. The average identical twin correlation was .67 and the average fraternal twin correlation was .33. This novel analysis appears useful in exploring the genetic and environmental determinants of temperament.

Another longitudinal twin study using a tester rating instrument similar to the IBR has been reported by Goldsmith and Gottesman (1981). They analyzed twin data from the national Collaborative Perinatal Project for children who were 8 months, 4 and 7 years of age. The items differed at each age, and several of the factors are difficult to square with EAS. At 4 years, an Irritability factor emerged which appears to be related to Emotionality, including among its highest loading items, "degree of irritability" and "emotional reactivity" (though it also includes cooperation and dependency). At 7 years, one factor was labeled Fearfulness ("fearfulness," "concern when separated from mother," "self-confidence," and "friendly vs. shy with examiner") which seems to be related to EAS Emotionality. Twin correlations for the two relevant factors are presented in Table 9.8. Though the other data in the study suggest a modest genetic influence, the data for the two EAS-relevant factors suggest substantial genetic influence.

TABLE 9.8
Twin Correlations for EAS-Related Factors from the Collaborative Perinatal
Project (Goldsmith & Gottesman, 1981)

	Twin Correlations			
	Identical		*Fraternal*	
	N	r	N	r
4-year Irritability	107	.57	82	.19
7-year Fearfulness	113	.39	82	.12

In addition to lending support to the EAS temperaments, the last two studies yield twin results similar to those of parental ratings. The fraternal twin correlations are greater than zero, but they are still too low in comparison to the identical twin correlations. Different trained observers rated each member of a twin pair, which suggests that the twin results using parental ratings are not due simply to a rating bias on the part of the parents. Rather, these data suggest that the behavior of the twins themselves is responsible for the pattern of twin correlations: a contrast effect in which fraternal twins accentuate any existing differences between themselves. Though the IBR is only partially relevant to the EAS traits, it offers the important advantages of assessing infants' reactions to a standard, mildly stressful situation and of providing comparable data across studies.

Global Rating Scales: Other Measures

There is surprisingly little behavioral genetic research using observer ratings other than the Infant Behavior Record. One exception is a study by Scarr (1966, 1969), mentioned earlier, in which 24 identical and 28 fraternal twin pairs (girls 6–10 years old) were rated on the Fels Behavior Scales (Richards & Simons, 1941) in the home. Each child was rated by a different tester. One rating scale was *social apprehension,* which appears to be roughly the same as shyness. Another was *friendliness,* which is likely to be related to Sociability. The identical twin correlations were .88 and .86, respectively for the two scales; the fraternal twin correlations were .28 for both scales.

In a study mentioned earlier, Matheny and Dolan (1975) used the IBR in rating emotionality-like behaviors in a playroom setting: child's initial distress upon the mother's departure, the quality of the child's adjustment during the play period, and the child's involvement with toys and play. The three scales intercorrelated from .54 to .85 and were combined. The composite measure, which we view as primarily Emotionality, showed substantial genetic influence in a twin analysis involving 25–57 identical twin pairs and 19–34 fraternal twin pairs at 9, 12, 18, 24 and 30 months of age. The average identical twin correlation was .66, and the average fraternal twin correlation was .30. The twins were usually rated by the same person, though the twins were observed separately. Of relevance to our previous discussion of contrast effects, 23 pairs rated by different examiners were rated as *more* similar than the 58 pairs rated by a single examiner. Given the small samples, the differences were not significant but they suggest that even an objective observer rating the twin partners at different times might tend to contrast them. Comparing ratings of twins by a single person with ratings by different persons should pin down when contrast effects occur.

These studies, as well as the ones mentioned in the following section, include observations of specific behaviors in addition to more global ratings. For example, a twin study by Lytton et al., (1977), described in the following section, included ratings similar in generality to the IBR items, but none was relevant to the EAS traits. Two ongoing studies primarily use global ratings but also incorporate specific behavioral observations. The Louisville Twin Study has recently been extended to include structured laboratory vignettes designed to elicit emotionality, activity, sociability and attention (Matheny & Wilson, 1981). These data will be approached primarily by use of IBR-like ratings, though some specific behavioral observations are also planned. No twin comparisons have yet been reported, and we await the results of this study with considerable interest because of its EAS formulation. Another ongoing longitudinal twin study has focused on assessment of arousal (Goldsmith & Campos, 1982). Preliminary results indicate low-to-moderate heritabilities of fear and activity measures using approach to strangers, visual cliff, and free-play situations.

Observations of Specific Behaviors

Though the distinction between observations that employ global ratings and those that focus on specific behaviors is not sharp, it can be drawn by noting whether the focus is on global ratings such as "activity" (characteristic of the IBR) or on specific behaviors such as number of quadrants the child enters. The two ongoing studies just mentioned (Goldsmith & Campos, 1982; Matheny & Wilson, 1981) include both kinds of ratings, and two other observational investigations, conducted in the spirit of ethology, focus on specific social responses of infants. One study of 2½-year-olds assessed social interaction between mothers and their infants (Lytton et al., 1977). Measures of attachment (a combination of seeking attention, help, and proximity) and compliance, both reliably assessed in a standardized situation, revealed no genetic influence and no shared (family-similar) environmental influence. Observational ratings of specific behaviors in unstructured settings also showed no evidence of genetic influence, though shared family environment appeared to be more important for these measures. This latter result may be due to procedural artifacts in that a single rater rated both twins. However, because such measures of mother-infant interaction as dependence and compliance appear to be minimally related to the EAS traits, this novel study is not particularly relevant to our theory.

A similarly designed study assessed the social responses of infants to both mother and a stranger (Plomin & Rowe, 1979). Members of 21 identical twin pairs and 25 same-sex fraternal twin pairs with an average age of 22 months were observed in their homes, using time-sampled observations of specific behaviors in seven situations. Each twin partner was rated by a different observer who took an unobtrusive position in the home, kept a neutral facial expression, and did not return overtures for attention from the children. Social responding to the stranger and to the mother were recorded in alternating 15-second intervals. The first situation, *warm-up,* included measures of the children's social responding to the mother and to the stranger, who were engaged in discussing the project and attempting to avoid interacting with the children. The measures included infants' approaches, proximity, touches, positive vocalizations, smiles and looks. In the second episode, *stranger approach,* the stranger enticed the children to play with him using a standard protocol. The third situation involved play with the stranger using an interactive toy. The other situations included play with the mother, cuddling with the stranger and mother, and separation from the mother.

In the first three situations, social responding toward the stranger suggested genetic influence, whereas the same social responding directed toward the mother showed no genetic influence. As in the study by Lytton et al. (1977), few genetic effects were found. The only genetic effects were for social responding to the stranger, especially during the warm-up situation when the stranger's novelty was greatest.

The twin correlations for the major measures showing adequate variability toward mothers and strangers during the warm-up situation are listed in Table 9.9 separately in terms of responses to mother and stranger. With the exception of smiling, the differences between the identical and fraternal twin correlations are greater—and in most cases, much greater—for social responding toward the stranger than toward the mother. We interpret these results in terms of sociability and shyness. Few behaviors in the later situations yielded patterns of twin correlations suggestive of genetic influence, probably because the stranger becomes familiar as the home visit proceeds.

TABLE 9.9
Twin Correlations for Observations of Specific Social Responses to Mother
and Stranger (from Plomin & Rowe, 1979)[a]

	Social Responding to Mother		Social Responding to Stranger	
	Identical	Fraternal	Identical	Fraternal
Approach	.14	− .03	.50	− .05
Proximity	.23	.11	.40	− .03
Positive vocalizations	.56	.46	.58	.34
Smiling	.19	.19	.08	.25
Looking	− .01	.11	.67	.08

[a] 21 pairs of identical twins and 25 pairs of fraternal twins

TABLE 9.10
Twin Correlations for Differences in Social Responding to Mother and
Stranger (from Plomin & Rowe, 1979)[a]

	Twin correlation	
	Identical	Fraternal
Approach	.20	− .18
Proximity	.13	.12
Positive Vocalizations	.58	− .22
Smiling	.38	.18
Looking	.65	.00

[a] 21 pairs of identical twins and 25 pairs of fraternal twins

Some children might not look much at either the stranger or the mother, but their differential looking toward the stranger versus the mother offers another measure of attachment. Table 9.10 presents the twin correlations for difference scores in responding to mother versus stranger during the warm-up situation. As in the previous table, the identical twin correlations are larger than the fraternal twin correlations (except for proximity), again suggesting genetic influence only in behavior involving the stranger.

MEASURES OTHER THAN RATINGS

Few behavioral genetic studies of temperament use measures other than ratings. It would be unethical to frighten children in order to measure fearfulness, and young children often do not have the options that would reveal their gregariousness, but shyness in reaction to strangers is relatively easy to study. Only two twin studies involving children have used measures other than ratings. One study (Scarr, 1966) included measures only tangentially related to the EAS temperaments, such as preferred reaction time as a measure of activity. Another twin study demonstrates the difficulty of obtaining adequate test-retest reliability for measures other than ratings and also suggests problems that are encountered in using measures such as pedometers to measure activity (Plomin & Foch, 1980).

CONCLUSIONS

The major conclusion to emerge from the research reviewed in this chapter is that support for the heritability of the EAS traits has broadened since the publication of our 1975 book. There are now twin and family studies using a diverse array of measures, all converging on the conclusion that the EAS traits are heritable. In addition to adding evidence for genetic influence, these studies have pointed out issues important to the study of temperament in childhood, even if one were not interested in behavioral genetics. These issues emerge from comparisons of the twin method with other behavioral genetic methods, parental ratings with non-parental ratings, and global ratings with ratings of more specific behaviors. Thus ratings, particularly global ratings, appear to be sensitive to contrast effects in twins, especially fraternal twins, which accentuate differences between members of a pair. The greatest contrast effects occur for activity; parents might rate one twin as the "active" one and the other as the "inactive" one even though the twins actually differ only slightly.

Contrast effects in twins can explain why twin studies yield unreasonably high estimates of heritability, why these estimates are higher than those using other behavioral genetic methods, and why global ratings yield patterns of twin results different from ratings of more specific behaviors. With the testable assumption that contrast effects operate more strongly for fraternal twins (who differ genetically) than for identical twins, contrast effects can also explain the typical pattern of unexpectedly low fraternal twin correlations. For global ratings, fraternal twin correlations are often near zero and even significantly negative for activity level, as compared to identical twin correlations of about .50. Other behavioral genetic designs, especially the parent-offspring designs, should be less subject to contrast effects. Parent-offspring family studies suggest lower heritability than twin studies and greater resemblance for first-degree relatives than for fraternal twins. Both results are compatible with the hypothesis that contrast effects are more severe in twin studies. Parent-offspring studies are less useful for comparison purposes because parents and offspring differ greatly in age; studies of nontwin siblings are needed. However, any differences between parent-offspring comparisons and twin comparisons (whether genetic or environmental differences) should produce fraternal twin correlations that are higher than the parent-offspring twin correlations.

We also suggest that ratings of specific behaviors are less sensitive to contrast effects. The twin correlations for ratings of specific behaviors are higher than for global ratings—about .75 for identical and .40 for fraternals. This pattern of correlations fits genetic models better than the twin correlations based on global ratings, but there is still room for contrast effects. Thus, if there were no contrast effects involved in these twin correlations, heritabilities would be 70% or greater, which would be unprecedented for complex behavioral characters. The reason for the lower twin correlations when global ratings are used cannot be greater error because global ratings are more reliable than ratings of specific behaviors. Furthermore, contrast effects cannot be brushed off as merely due to some kind of biased rating. We propose two hypotheses concerning contrast effects: They might be in the eye of the beholder, or they might be in the behavior of the children. The latter possibility has not been considered previously, but there is evidence to support it. The contrast effect is not limited to the usual case in which one parent rates both twins but also occurs when midparent ratings are used and when each twin partner is rated by a different parent. Though parents may share their biases about their twin children, the contrast effect also occurs when trained observers rate the twins and even when different observers rate each member of the twin pair! This suggests that twins are contrasted both by themselves and by others, the outcome being exaggerated behavioral differences within pairs.

We need to learn more about such contrast effects in the study of temperament. Beyond studies of twins or siblings, the effect is sufficiently powerful—perhaps accounting for 20%–40% of the variance—that it could affect studies of one child per family. Even if parents or observers are not explicitly contrasting a pair of children in a family, they make such distinctions implicitly—for example, a parent contrasting the child with another child or a tester setting off the child from the preceding one—thus introducing error variance into the study of temperament. Contrast effects can be studied with methods such as that of Plomin (1974) and Matheny and Dolan (1975), in which twins are rated either by a single observer or by two different observers. Comparisons with measures other than ratings might also prove to be useful.

Three other conclusions remain to be drawn. First, the diversity of measures of temperament in recent years is a welcome trend. Temperament research will profit from the trend toward multimethod approaches that include molar and molecular ratings by parents, teachers, and trained observers, as well as observations of specific behaviors and other measures in addition to ratings. Second, investigators need to be more specific than generalizing about the "genetics of personality." At the least, we need to consider emotionality, activity, and sociability separately from other personality traits. Even with the EAS traits, we need to be aware of differences among them; for example, contrast effects appear to be especially powerful for activity level.

The third conclusion concerns differential heritability. Self-report questionnaires show overwhelming evidence for genetic influence, at least in twin studies. Despite possible artifact here, the lack of differential heritability is more likely caused by the infusion of extraversion and neuroticism in self-report questionnaires. Both of these super-traits show substantial genetic influence (Loehlin, 1982). Similarly, for rating studies of childhood temperament, evidence for genetic influence is widespread. However, nonheritable traits emerge in all of this research, especially the newer studies that involve observations of specific behaviors and other nonrating measures of temperament, for which genetic influences are by no means ubiquitous. Nonetheless, following Loehlin's (1982) suggestion for adult self-report data on personality, we might posit that childhood analogs of extraversion and neuroticism permeate measures of temperament in children, as they do for self-report questionnaires for adolescents and adults. In infancy, extraversion-like items are not so heavily loaded with such complexities of adult items as liking lively parties. Neuroticism-like items early in life would emphasize emotional arousal and reactivity without the anxiety typical of adult neuroticism items. Thus, the super-factors that seem to pervade temperament measures in infancy and early childhood may consist mainly of the traits of emotionality and sociability.

10
Continuity, Environment, and the EAS

The previous chapter documents genetic influence on the EAS but does not imply that the EAS necessarily will be stable throughout development or that the environment is unimportant. In fact, the behavioral genetic data provide the best evidence we have of the environment's importance. The purpose of this chapter is to examine continuity and environment.

CONTINUITY

Developmentalists' views on continuity have shifted sharply during the past decade. Personality was once thought to be stable from infancy onward, if it could only be measured properly. Now it is generally recognized that behavioral continuities from infancy to later childhood are rare:

> There is little firm evidence for the idea that individual differences in psychological qualities displayed during the first two years of life are predictive of similar or theoretically related behaviors a decade hence. . . . But stability . . . emerges rather clearly after 6 years of age. Almost all investigators find some theoretically reasonable relations between variation in behavior during the years prior to adolescence and variation a decade later. (Kagan, 1980, p. 63)

Temperament might prove to be an exception to the rule that individual differences early in life are not predictive of variation later in development.

Temperaments are likely to be more stable than other traits because temperaments are heritable. There appears to be a developmental relationship between stability and heritability for the few traits for which we have information on both topics, such as height, weight, and IQ (Plomin & DeFries, 1981). For IQ, there is only marginal long-term stability and only modest heritability in infancy. Both stability and heritability increase dramatically during early childhood until school age, when both stability and heritability attain levels comparable to those for adults. Before summarizing data on the stability of the EAS temperaments, we need to discuss the conceptual relationship between heritability and stability.

HERITABILITY AND STABILITY

Neither the biological origin nor the early appearance of temperament implies that temperament will necessarily be stable. Genes are a source of change as well as continuity in development, turning on and off with small changes in DNA transcription altering arrangements of entire systems of hierarchically organized genes. Thus, heritable traits need not be stable. A highly heritable trait might be unstable if different sets of genes affect the trait during successive phases of development. The many genes that feed into temperament variations—for example, in activity among toddlers—might overlap only slightly with the set of genes that affect activity in older children. On the other side of the coin, a trait low in heritability could be high in stability if environmental factors were stable.

The issue is one of genetic correlations and environmental correlations in development, as illustrated in Fig. 10.1, which depicts a measure of temperament in childhood and adulthood. At each age, the relative importance of genetic and environmental variation can be determined, which is the usual enterprise of behavioral genetics. Regardless of the relative importance of genetic variance at each age, we can determine the extent to which genes affecting childhood temperament correlate with genes affecting adult temperament. This is called a *genetic correlation,* which can be assessed if longitudinal behavioral genetic data are available (Plomin & DeFries, 1981). If the genes that affect temperament in childhood differ from those that affect temperament in adulthood, this difference obviously contributes to instability of temperament.

Though this approach has not yet been applied to the study of temperament, the research of Matheny (1983) is relevant. Using the twin design, he found evidence that heredity affects longitudinal profiles of temperament at 6, 12, 18, and 24 months of age. This finding implies that the genes that influence temperament at different ages do not overlap completely.

However, the set of genes affecting temperament in early childhood are unlikely to be completely independent of the set of genes affecting temperament in adulthood. If the two sets of genes overlapped, there would be at least some stability from childhood through adulthood. Therefore, we suspect that heritability and stability are related to some extent for temperament, as they are for height and IQ.

STABILITY OF THE EAS TEMPERAMENTS

An issue of current interest in personality research involves the need to aggregate over measures and occasions in order to obtain a composite that would yield consistency needed to infer traits (Epstein, 1980; Rush-

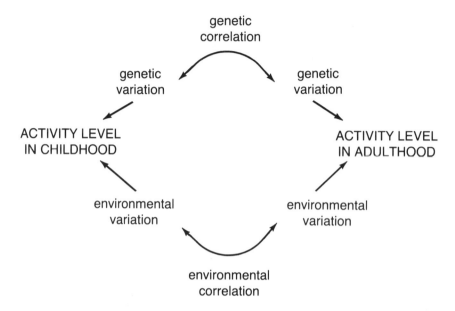

FIG. 10.1   Genetic and environmental correlations in development.

ton, Brainerd, & Pressley, 1983). The issue is just as relevant to the study of consistency over time (Block, 1981). When single measures of behavior in a single situation at a single time are used—as in most laboratory assessments—stability is less likely to be found. When measures are aggregated as in Block's (1971, 1981) study of personality over 30 years from adolescence through middle age, substantial stability can be found. The EAS data to be reviewed were collected and analyzed in most cases without consideration of the need to aggregate and thus probably represent underestimates of stability. Also the correlations are uncorrected for unreliability of measurement and are therefore underestimates (Conley, 1983).

There is surprisingly little long-term longitudinal research on personality, and few of these studies address traits related to the EAS temperaments (Moss & Susman, 1980). The NYLS median stability during the first 5 years of life was only .10 for the nine NYLS dimensions, and the median year-to-year correlation was .30 (Thomas & Chess, 1977). However, the greatest stability was found for the two NYLS traits most similar to the EAS: activity and adaptability (related to sociability/shyness). Similarly, McDevitt and Carey (1978), using their parental report measure of the NYLS dimensions, also found that activity alone showed moderate stability from infancy to 5–7 years of age. The NYLS traits appear to show greater stability later in childhood: Over an average 4.4-year span from 3–7 years to 8–12 years, a median correlation of .42 was found (Hegvik, McDevitt, & Carey, 1981).

In our earlier book (1975), we summarized longitudinal research related to the EAS temperaments, and little has happened since then to change our conclusions. The only major longitudinal research conducted during the past decade has recently been completed at the National Institute of Mental Health (Moss & Susman, 1980). Only scattered reports of the project, which studied children from infancy to early childhood, have been published. One report (Halverson & Waldrop, 1976) found substantial stability for activity level using observations in nursery school at 2½ years of age and observations during free play 5 years later. We look forward to a complete report of this project because it includes measures related to each of the EAS temperaments.

We shall briefly review our earlier conclusions, emphasizing the most important studies. Concerning emotionality, we said that "studies during the first year show weak to moderate stability of emotional reactivity; research on older children also demonstrates moderate stability for a number of variables related to emotionality" (Buss & Plomin, 1975, pp. 80–81). Aside from studies of crying in infancy, there were only the ratings of the Berkeley Growth Study (Schaefer & Bayley, 1963), which reported a correlation of .38 for ratings of irritability (excitable-calm) from 11 to 32 months of age; from 21 to 32 months, the correlation was .66. The Berkeley Guidance Study (Bronson, 1966) suggests that stability is higher in middle childhood. Between 6 and 9 years of age, the correlation for emotional stability was .59; for reactivity, .51; for tantrums, .42; however, for fearfulness, the correlation was only .14. Between 9 and 12 years, the correlations for these four traits were similar, though the correlation for fearfulness was higher than before. The correlations were .44, .58, .51, and .38, respectively. From 12 to 15 years, the correlations were about the same: .42, .54, .34, and .33. For the 9-year period from 6 to 15 years, however, the correlations are modest: .15, .26, .12, .44.

Concerning activity level, "beyond the first year of life, activity shows at least a moderate degree of continuity" (p. 52). This conclusion was based primarily on the results of the Berkeley Growth Study (Schaefer & Bayley, 1963), which yielded correlations of .48 for tester ratings of activity from 1 to 3 years of age. In the Fels longitudinal study (Battle & Lacey, 1972) activity correlated .52 from 2 years of age to 5–7 years; from 4 years to 14–16 years, the correlation was .45. However, other studies, especially those using laboratory measures such as locomotion, tend to find little support for the hypothesis of stability (Feiring & Lewis, 1980; Kagan, 1971).

Concerning sociability, we summarized, "Admittedly, there are variations in the amount of stability from one study to the next and between boys and girls. But the pattern of studies reveals adequate stability of sociability during the developmental sequence. In fact, sociability appears to be the most stable of the temperaments" (1975, p. 118).

This conclusion was also based primarily on ratings from the Berkeley Growth Study (Schaefer & Bayley, 1963), which found moderate stability for ratings of responsiveness to persons (r = .45) and shyness (r = .35) from 1 to 3 years of age. From 2 to 4 years, a rating of friendliness yielded a stability correlation of .42, similar to other 2-year periods from 4 to 6 years (.50) and 6 to 8 years (.49). From 4 to 8 years, the correlation was a moderate .45, but for the 6-year period from 2 to 8 years (infancy and middle childhood) the correlation was a negligible .04. Sociability appears to stabilize increasingly during childhood. For example, a rating of friendliness yielded a correlation of .63 from 9 to 12 years. Similarly, in the Berkeley Guidance Study (Bronson, 1966), a rating of "shy vs. socially easy" yielded a correlation of .53 from 6 to 15 years. Sociability also abides in adolescence and adulthood: A follow-up report of the Berkeley Guidance Study subjects when they were about 30 years old indicated that sociability endured through adulthood (Bronson, 1967). In the Fels study, "withdrawal from social interaction," rated from interviews, correlated .61 from 12 years of age to adulthood (Kagan & Moss, 1962). Kelly (1955) reported a correlation of .46 for a self-report sociability scale for adults over a 20-year period.

These longitudinal studies and others have recently been reviewed by Beckwith (1979) with a focus on long-term stability from infancy and early childhood. The most steadfast aspects of personality appear to be those that involve the EAS traits. Concerning irritability (one aspect of emotionality), she concludes that "the evidence presented here suggests the significance of irritability as a temperamental disposition that appears early in infancy and persists" (p. 693). Beckwith emphasizes heterotypic continuity for activity: "Infant activity intensity has been connected subsequently to peer interaction and assertive coping in nursery school, and to task orientation during the early elementary school years" (p. 691). The case for sociability is clear, at least after infancy: "Sociability, per se, appears to be a pervasive and enduring characteristic, whose origins in infancy need to be examined further" (p. 698). In summary, though heritable personality traits present in early childhood need not be stable, the EAS temperaments appear to be among the most stable personality traits in childhood.

ENVIRONMENT

Our definition of temperaments does not imply that they are unmodifiable, and the behavioral genetic research reviewed in Chapter 9 provides evidence for the importance of environmental variation. Even if all the variance of temperament were due to genetic differences among children, understanding the developmental course of temperament would require that we consider the environments in which temperaments are manifested. Another reason for considering environmental correlates of temperament is that they represent a major direction for future temperament research. In a recent review of early experience in human development, Wachs and Gruen (1982) conclude that the highest priority for environmental research involves:

> The question of the interface between individual differences and reactivity to environmental stimulation. Both from basic and applied data it has become increasingly clear that the relationship of early experience to development will be mediated by the nature of the organism on which the experience impinges. Unfortunately, virtually nothing is known about the specific organismic characteristics which mediate differential reactivity to the early environment. One hopes that future research and theory will begin to delineate the specific organismic characteristics which are relevant to this process. (p. 247)

In our view, emotionality, activity, and sociability are among the "organismic characteristics" being sought.

Early Research

The documentation for the influence of experience on personality development is usually the 1940s studies of traumatic deprivation, mainly institutionalization. This research is summarized by the Clarkes (1976) in their book, *Early Experience: Myth and Evidence,* which marks a turning point in thinking about the importance of early experience. The deprivation work focused less on personality per se than on the child's relationship with its mother, perhaps because the research had its roots in the psychoanalytic tradition. However, most researchers now acknowledge the shortcomings of this body of research, question its relevance to the normal range of environmental variation, and conclude that the importance attributed to a continuous one-to-one relationship between infant and mother was exaggerated.

The only other research relevant to environmental influences on personality development is a set of studies in the late 1950s and early 1960s, which related self-reported childrearing attitudes and practices to personality development (Kagan & Moss, 1962; Schaefer, 1961; Sears, Maccoby, & Levin, 1957). Two major dimensions accounted for much of the variance of parental behavior: love versus hostility and permissiveness versus restrictiveness (Becker, 1964). It was found, for example, that parental hostility was moderately correlated with the child's hostility, a fact that was interpreted to mean that the parent's attitude caused the child's behavior. It is just as reasonable to conclude, however, that the child's hostility caused the parent's negative attitude.

The Fels Longitudinal Study (Kagan & Moss, 1962) did not include measures of personality relevant to the EAS traits. The Berkeley Growth Study (Schaefer & Bayley, 1963) included activity and emotionality only during the first year of life; however, sociability was measured longitudinally and correlated with childrearing, especially the love dimension, at each age. The basic finding of these studies is that correlations between personality and childrearing are rare and weak. Concerning the few relationships that do emerge, parents may reflect rather than affect their children's personality. Thus, the correlation between warm, permissive parenting and children's sociability could reasonably be interpreted as a child effect rather than a parent effect: Parents find it easier to be warm and permissive with children who are sociable and warm.

New Research

Almost nothing new has been reported concerning environmental correlates of temperament. This is surprising because one of the justifications often given for the study of temperament is that it provides the child input to parent-child interaction: "In many instances it is the baby who shows initiative and the parent who responds by following . . . Even in the early months of life there are striking temperamental differences between infants which influence both their response to the environment and also how other people react to them" (Rutter, 1975, p. 208). This statement implies that relationships should be found between children's temperament and their parents' behavior.

Like the early work on the environmental correlates of mental development, the only information concerning the environmental correlates of temperament comes from nonspecific distal factors such as socioeconomic class. There is some evidence that class and race affect parental ratings of temperament (Thomas & Chess, 1977, pp. 146–151). These data involve parental ratings, however, and parental expectations for children's behavior might differ across cultural groups.

The EAS temperaments have been studied in the Colorado Adoption Project (Plomin & DeFries, 1983), for which there are preliminary data for 1-year-old infants. The Colorado Adoption Project includes two major measures of the home environment. The first is the Home Observation for Measurement of the Environment inventory (HOME; Caldwell & Bradley, 1978), a 45-minute observation and interview measure of physical and social aspects of the infant's environment. The second is the Family Environment Scale (FES; Moos, 1974), a 90-item self-report questionnaire concerning the family attitudinal and relationship climate which is

TABLE 10.1
Correlations Between Environmental Measures and Measures of
12-month-old EAS in Adoptive and Nonadoptive Homes

Measure		*Adoptive Families*		*Control families*	
Infant Temperament	*Home Environment*	*r*	*N*	*r*	*N*
CCTI Emotionality	HOME Responsivity	.02	80	− .05	67
	HOME Total	.12	80	− .04	52
	FES "Personal Growth"	− .02	97	− .23*	75
	FES "Traditional Organization"	− .28*	97	− .12	75
CCTI Activity	HOME Responsivity	.16	80	.11	67
	HOME Total	.10	63	− .07	52
	FES "Personal Growth"	.16	97	.17	75
	FES "Traditional Organization"	.05	97	.00	75
CCTI Sociability/ Shyness	HOME Responsivity	.13	80	.13	67
	HOME Total	− .10	63	.04	52
	FES "Personal Growth"	.02	97	.33*	75
	FES "Traditional Organization"	.08	97	.11	75

completed by both parents. The EAS of the adopted and nonadopted infants at 12 months of age was assessed by midparent ratings on the Colorado Childhood Temperament Inventory (Rowe & Plomin, 1977). Table 10.1 presents correlations between the infants' EAS and the environmental measures, specifically the HOME total score and the HOME responsivity scale (the two HOME measures with adequate psychometric properties) and two second-order factors derived from the 10 scales of the FES. For details concerning the measures, see the description by De-Fries, Plomin, Vandenberg, and Kuse (1981).

Few significant relationships emerged. In the control (nonadoptive) homes, FES Personal Growth was significantly related to low emotionality and high sociability of the children. Personal growth is a second-order factor of the FES with loadings above .50 on four FES scales: Intellectual-cultural orientation, Active-recreational orientation, Expressiveness, and Conflict (loading negatively). Families high on this dimension are thus intellectual and expressive, like active recreational activities, and have little conflict among family members. It seems reasonable that children in such families would be low in emotionality and high in sociability for environmental reasons but also, as we shall see, for genetic reasons. None of the HOME measures related significantly to the children's EAS.

An important feature of the Colorado Adoption Project design for environmental analysis is its ability to assess the influence of heredity in ostensibly environmental relationships such as these. In control families, in which parents share heredity as well as family environment with their children, relationships between parental attitudes and children's temperament could be mediated indirectly via heredity. For example, parents high on the FES personal growth factor might have sociable children for hereditary rather than environmental reasons. This hypothesis can be tested in adoptive families, in which parents share family environment but not heredity with their children. In Table 10.1 it may be seen that both environmental relationships disappear when the hereditary resemblance between parents and their offspring is controlled in the adoptive families. In the control homes, the correlations between FES personal growth and children's emotionality and sociability were $-.23$ and $.33$, respectively. The difference in correlations reaches statistical significance for the relationship between FES personal growth and CCTI sociability. Thus, these results suggest that the few obtained environmental relationships may be mediated genetically, not environmentally.

In summary, these first attempts to identify environmental correlates of temperament have yielded only a few modest relationships. Perhaps the wrong environmental variables were investigated, though parental correlates would seem to be a reasonable place to start the search. Another possibility is that the underlying models have been too simple. The search so far has been limited to main effects of environment: environmental correlates that affect all children. It has also been assumed that environmental influences primarily operate across families, making children in the same family similar to one another. The evidence suggests that investigators should now abandon this assumption and adopt more complex models of environmental influence.

Hierarchical multiple regression analyses of temperament interactions in infancy—including the EAS—have recently been reported (Plomin & Daniels, 1984). Temperament was treated as an independent variable, and 23 interactions were studied. Parental ratings of infant temperament and environmental measures including parental temperament, Caldwell and Bradley's (1978) Home Observation for Measurement of the Environment inventory, and Moos' (1974) Family Environment Scale were used to predict behavioral problems at 4 years of age as assessed by parental ratings on Achenbach and Edelbrock's (1981) Child Behavior Checklist. Though many main effects of temperament and environment were observed, only a chance number of significant interactions emerged.

Over 50 interactions of the second category, temperament as a dependent variable, were also examined. These analyses included parental personality and the HOME and FES environmental measures to predict children's temperament. Also analyzed were genotype-environment interactions in which characteristics of biological mothers who relinquished their children for adoption were used to estimate genotype of the adopted-away infants. Among the environmental measures were characteristics of the adoptees' adoptive mother and HOME and FES scores of the adoptive home. The power of these analyses permitted detection of interactions that accounted for as little as 5% of the variance, but *no significant interactions were detected.* So far, then, the environment has been shown to have little significant impact either as a main effect or as an interaction, but perhaps the wrong class of environmental variables has been examined.

INDIVIDUAL EXPERIENCES

We mentioned in Chapter 8 that behavioral geneticists can divide environmental variance into two components, *family-similar* and *individual experience.* Family-similar environmental variance, also called shared or common environment, makes members of a family similar to one another. Individual experience, also called nonshared, involves the environment peculiar to the individual, thus making family members as different from one another as are members of different families. In the past, resemblance among family members may have beguiled investigators into thinking that family-similar experiences are responsible for this similarity. However, behavioral genetic studies suggest that heredity accounts for the personality resemblance observed among family members. Environmental factors relevant to personality development seem to consist almost exclusively of individual experiences that make members of the same family as different from one another as are members of different families (Rowe & Plomin, 1981).

The importance of individual experiences was first highlighted by Loehlin and Nichols (1976):

> Thus, a consistent—though perplexing—pattern is emerging from the data (and it is not purely idiosyncratic to our study). Environment carries substantial weight in determining personality—it appears to account for at least half the variance—but that environment is one for which twin pairs are correlated close to zero . . . In short, in the personality domain we seem to see environmental effects that operate almost randomly with respect to the sorts of variables that psychologists (and other people) have traditionally deemed important in personality development. (p. 92)

Their conclusion was based primarily on self-report data for adolescents and adults, but parental rating studies of temperament yield similar results (Plomin, 1981). Though only a few studies used measures other than self-report or parental ratings, they suggest that family-similar environmental factors count for more than the other studies suggest (Plomin & Foch, 1980).

The conclusion that environmental influences operate as individual experience not shared by members of the same family has far-reaching implications for the study of environmental influences on temperament. The environmental factors typically studied, including those reported earlier in this chapter, have been conceptualized as family-similar factors. Nearly all this research focused on only one child per family, on the assumption that other children in the same family experience a similar environment. In this research, a single environmental assessment in each home and a measure of one child were correlated for environment-child pairs *across* families.

If the conclusion from behavioral genetic research is correct, both the approach to environment and measures of it need to be altered. In retrospect, any environmental factor can be viewed in terms of its contribution to individual experiences rather than to experiences shared by a family. For example, parental love could easily be construed as a source of differences among children in the same family, for most parents love one child more than another. Moreover, children may perceive differences in their parental affection toward siblings even when such differences do not exist.

One might counter that if such factors are important *within* families, why are they not also important *between* families? However, an environmental factor that causes differences within families might be unrelated to a factor that causes differences between families, even when the same factor is involved—parental love, for example. A child really knows only its own parents; it does not know if its parents love it more or less than other parents love their children. However, a child is likely to be painfully aware that parental affection toward it is less than toward siblings. Thus, individual experiences within families may be unrelated to family-similar factors across families.

To identify such influences, researchers need to study more than one child per family. The environmental factors that make children in the same family different from one another might include systematic experiences such as differential parental or sibling treatment, or extrafamilial experiences such as peer influences. Individual experience can also include idiosyncratic or chance events. Once such relationships are identified, the question of direction of effects arises. For example, if differential parental affection relates to differences in siblings' sociability, it might be because differences in the siblings' sociability *elicits* differences in the parents' affection toward them. One way of discovering the direction of effects is the use of identical twins for whom personality differences within pairs cannot be caused by genetic factors. Nonetheless, personality differences within pairs could still be caused by prior environmental influences rather than the particular environmental factor studied as a source of individual experience.

The importance of this class of environmental influence offers an exciting new approach to the study of the environmental correlates of the EAS. How similarly are two children in the same family treated by their parents, by each other, and outside the family, by peers? Do these individual experiences relate to temperamental differences within families? Research on these questions has begun with the construction of the *Sibling Inventory of Differential Experience* (SIDE) (Daniels & Plomin, 1983) which asks siblings to rate their perceptions of experiential differences in terms of parents, siblings, and peers. The SIDE and the EAS self-report questionnaire are being administered to several hundred pairs of adoptees and nonadopted sibling pairs as part of a design to distinguish genetic from environmental sources of temperament differences within pairs of siblings. Perhaps this research will yield stronger and more systematic relationships than previous studies.

TEMPERAMENT AND ENVIRONMENT

We have reviewed what is known about the relationship between postnatal environment, and temperament and the answer is Not Much. Our new data show that the major dimensions of childrearing and the home environment are generally unrelated to the development of temperament in infancy. We suggest that some ostensibly environmental relationships between parents' childrearing and children's temperament might be surreptitiously mediated by heredity. Nonetheless, behavioral genetic studies consistently point to a role for environmental influences in temperament development. Temperament-environment interactions would be a reasonable place to look for the missing variance, but research to date has uncovered few interactions. The behavioral genetic research described in the previous chapter points to previously unexplored environmental variance that affects the EAS: individual experiences within the family that make children in the same family as different from one another as are children in other families.

Even changes that involve the entire family may affect one child more than others in the family. Suppose there is a divorce, and the children now live with only the mother. One child might have been closer to the father, and therefore the loss would be worse for this child than for its siblings. Or one child might have had an especially bad relationship with the father, and the father's absence from the home would be beneficial to this child but not to its siblings. When a baby is born, the previously youngest child in the family is more likely to suffer from jealousy and a feeling of displacement than are older siblings.

Aside from familial changes, investigators should also consider the modifications that occur as each child matures. As the child's body and psychological capabilities grow, members of the family and other socializing agents expect more of the child, and these expectations tend to vary from one child to the next even in the same family. As the child matures, individual tendencies (including temperaments) that were previously ignored or condoned may suddenly come under pressure for change. Thus a child who has frequent temper tantrums which previously were tolerated may discover that they are no longer tolerated. Bjorn Borg, the tennis player, had violent displays of temper on the court until he was 10 years old, when his parents threatened to prevent his playing for a month if he did not stop the childish behavior. They made good their threat, and thereafter he was a model of good behavior on the tennis court.

There are also traits, including temperaments, that parents may attempt to change for years, but as the child matures and shows no change, the parents surrender and stop pressuring the child. By this time, the older child or adolescent may attempt to modify his or her own personality tendencies. Even within the same family, one child might strive for mature behavior while another attempts to remain childish for as long as possible. Models of personality may have to change to adapt to the fact of these various individual experiences.

11 Concluding Comments

Let us review our approach to temperament, which has been described in the last six chapters. In discussing emotionality (Chapter 5) we distinguished between high-arousal and low-arousal emotions and then restricted emotionality as a temperament to two of the high-arousal emotions, fear and anger, as well as their developmental precursor, distress. We tried to show that there are essentially no physiological differences between fear and anger, and we traced the developmental path of these temperaments, including the socialization of gender differences.

The temperament of sociability (Chapter 6) required an analysis of social rewards, and we linked sociability to the class of rewards that includes sharing of activities and responsivity from others. The development of sociability was outlined, and shyness was distinguished from sociability. And we suggested that extraversion represents a combination of sociability and (un)shyness.

We defined temperament in Chapter 7 and listed two criteria: inheritance and early appearance. We suggested that temperaments might influence the environment by choice of environments, contributing to social contexts, and modifying the impact of environments. A variety of measures of our three temperaments were offered, including objective measures, ratings, and questionnaires, and psychometric data were presented for the latest questionnaires.

Some recent developments in behavioral genetics (Chapter 8) were followed by data on the inheritance of emotionality, activity, and sociability (Chapter 9). Behavioral genetics research on personality traits inevitably reveals the important role that environment plays, and in Chapter 10 we discussed environment in relation to continuity throughout childhood. There is evidence that our three temperaments are at least moderately stable, but we have not yet discovered their environmental influences.

In describing our theory, we have tried to be specific and to outline ways of testing it. We propose that emotionality, activity, and sociability are the major dimensions of personality in infancy and early childhood; if not, the theory is wrong. We propose that these three traits are heritable; if not, the theory is wrong. If other early-appearing personality traits are shown to be heritable and not derivable from our three temperaments, the theory must be amended. If there are better ways to slice the personality pie early in life, the theory may have to be discarded.

Our theory also leads to several predictions less critical as tests of the theory. For example, we assume that the primordial component of emotionality is distress, which differentiates primarily into either fear or into anger, not both. We submit that in infancy and early childhood, the primary component of neuroticism is emotionality. Other examples of specific predictions involve sociability: Sociability involves interaction rewards (such as the mere presence of others, their attention, responsivity, and stimulation) rather than content rewards (such as respect, praise, sympathy, and affection); shyness is distinct from sociability; in infancy and early childhood, the primary component of extraversion is sociability and high fearfulness.

Our theory also emphasizes matches and mismatches between the child and its environment, especially between the child and its parents. For example, matches in activity between parent and child tend to promote harmony. The inactive parent expects little energy expenditure from the child, so the child's low activity poses no problems for the parent. Similarly, the expectations of an active parent tend to be met by an active child, and this match also promotes harmony. A mismatch, however, may cause problems. An inactive mother may have trouble in keeping up with her energetic child and might even suspect that the child is abnormally overactive; at the least, she might tend to tire easily and therefore be irritable. An active mother is likely to expect considerable energy from her child and be disappointed at the relative lack of energy if her child is inactive. She may regard the child as lazy or perhaps even ill. Inactive children are less of a problem than active ones, and therefore the mismatch is worse when it is the child who is active and the mother, inactive. Thus the interaction of the child's temperament with that of a parent is a source of harmony or disturbance in the relationship. Matches are best for activity and sociability (discussed earlier), and the only bad match appears to occur when both child and parent are emotional.

A major distinction between our theory and other approaches to temperament is that we specify a genetic origin, whereas other theorists tend to be vague about the origins of temperament. We have been impressed during the past decade with the extent to which behavioral genetic data—often obtained by researchers with perspectives quite different from ours—support our major contention that emotionality, activity, and sociability are among the most heritable aspects of personality in early childhood. These data were presented in Chapter 9, but as emphasized in Chapter 10, ours is not a simple theory of genetic determinism. The behavioral genetic methodologies provide the best available evidence for the importance of environmental variance and may offer the best hope for advancing our knowledge of environmental influences.

Another major distinction is that we take a personality perspective, regarding temperaments as a class of personality traits. This perspective can contribute to the study of temperament because personality researchers have already faced many of the conceptual and methodological problems common to the study of temperament. Consider, for instance, the conceptual and measurement issues involved in deciding on how broad a temperament should be.

BROAD VERSUS NARROW TEMPERAMENTS

Let us assume for the moment that temperaments are a special class of personality traits. How inclusive should a trait be? The answer would appear to depend on the focus of the investigator. To make the issue concrete, let us consider examples of how traits vary in breadth. Our temperament of emotionality is a broad trait in that it includes any kind of distress (see Chapter 5). It is clearly broader than one of its differentiated components, fearfulness. When fearfulness is restricted to social situations, the trait shrinks to (fearful) shyness. If social fearfulness is restricted to the smaller class of situations involving an audience, the result is the narrow trait of audience anxiety.

Broad traits have their advantages. They are sufficiently inclusive, so that even if some individual members of the response class disappear during development, other members will remain, and the trait might display developmental consistency. Furthermore, when broad traits are employed, only a small number of them will be required to account for an individual's personality. The most serious disadvantage of broad traits is also their inclusiveness: They may include several subtraits which are sufficiently different that they should be regarded as separate traits. Thus in older children and adults, fearfulness and anger may become so distinct behaviorally that they should no longer be in the same category (emotionality). This disadvantage of broad traits is precisely the advantage of narrow traits: They tend to be homogeneous and do not include subtraits that need to be differentiated.

In the study of adult personality, most theorists have relied on broad traits. We still know little about adult personality, and one explanation for this ignorance may lie in the excessive use of broad traits, though this surely is not the only explanation. When the focus is on temperament, however, there appear to be two reasons for preferring broad traits. First, temperaments are regarded as early developing personality traits. The behavior seen in infants and young children is often diffuse and generalized, and only later does more specific and differentiated behavior begin to appear. Given the generalized nature of such early behavior, it would seem best to employ broader traits in attempting to explain individual differences. Second, inclusive traits are more likely to contain individual responses that might persevere throughout development. Thus, the temperaments seen early in life would also appear in later childhood and adulthood, or at least leave behind residuals. In brief, other things equal, a focus on early-developing personality traits would seem to suggest that broad traits be preferred as temperaments.

Responses and Traits

Should we regard temperaments as personality traits or as individual responses, bearing in mind that the focus must be on *person variance,* the tendencies that contribute to individual differences? The advantages of single responses have been demonstrated many times in the laboratory study of behavior. A single response is convenient to observe, easy to delineate, and therefore susceptible to reliable measurement. If we were willing to call the response of smiling a temperament, our task would be simplified. No observer is likely to misidentify a smile, and the measure of the strength of this temperament would simply be the number of smiles that occurred during any brief period under study. Two observers might be necessary to obtain an estimate of the reliability of the observations, but surely their agreement would be high. Thus, in the study of temperament, precision of measurement is enhanced when the response is narrowly defined, and it is studied in a single situation during a limited, brief period of time. There are temperament researchers who believe that the advantage of precision is a sufficient reason for studying temperaments as single responses, such as behavior is studied by experimental psychologists.

Whatever one's specific definition of temperament, it must be considered as a personality trait. The concept of a personality trait involves the disposition to make one or more of a *class* of responses in at least several situations, and there must be some stability to the disposition over time (days, weeks, months). In measuring temperament, researchers average across situations and over time; if they did not, transient and situational variables would almost completely determine the nature of the response. Consider baseball hitting, for example. The difference between a .300 hitter and a .200 hitter involves a considerable gap in whatever ability it takes to generate hits. Suppose we allowed the hitter only one chance to bat or only one swing at the ball. If our measure of hitting were so constricted, we would never discover the trait of hitting ability, for most of the determinants of whether a hit occurred would be transitory, and the contribution of hitting ability would be trivial. If we were to average the number of hits over a baseball season, however, the various transitory determinants of obtaining hits would cancel out, and the trait (ability) would be revealed as a major determinant. A similar procedure is used in the Average Evoked Potential or the Computer of Average Transients (CAT), which cumulates the second-by-second records in such a way that momentary variations gradually cancel out over time.

Another problem with regarding a single response as a temperament is that it may occur too seldom or too unsystematically in relation to the situations or stimuli that normally elicit the response. Consider the response of an infant to a large, loud, intruding stranger. If the particular temperament in question is defined solely as crying, all will be well for science if the infant cries. The infant may not cry, however, but hide, shrink, reach for its mother, or merely make a cry face. It is well known that any of these responses indicates stranger anxiety, but if crying were the sole measure of the temperament and the infant made one of these other responses, we would not discover the association between the temperament and a threatening stranger.

The need for multiple responses grouped into a class (which defines the trait) is also acute when development is considered. If crying is a temperament, it tends to wane and perhaps even disappear as infants mature into adolescents. Instead, if the temperament is fearfulness, though one member of the response class (crying) may disappear during development, other members of the response class persist, allowing us to measure the trait in adolescence: wariness, phobias, certain kinds of behavioral inhibition, and several aspects of arousal of the sympathetic nervous system. Our point here is that unless temperaments are defined in terms of response classes, there may be nothing to study developmentally, the single response having dropped out of the repertoire of the older child or adolescent.

Finally, there are conceptual problems linked with defining a trait as a single response. If that were done, the number of traits would be so large that it would be difficult to make sense of them. Presumably, the unit of measurement would be so small that it would be difficult for any systematic patterns to emerge. It would be like trying to observe a shoreline from the ground, inch by inch, instead of from an airplane thousands of feet above; or like getting too close to an impressionist painting and seeing blobs of paint instead of a scene.

Aggregation

These conceptual issues have immediate empirical consequences. If single responses are measured once, it may be difficult to accumulate evidence for personality traits (and therefore for temperaments, by implication). This is not the place to review the literature (see Epstein, 1980, 1983, and Rushton et al., 1983), and we shall cite only three examples.

Moskowitz and Schwarz (1982) observed individual children of 3 to 5 years of age in a nursery school. There were many 4-minute periods of observation, each divided into 10-second intervals, during which dominance was counted (no more than once per 10-second period). In addition to these behavior counts, the head teacher and other observers, who watched the children during the 8 weeks of the study, rated the children for dominance. The behavior counts were correlated with the ratings of dominance. Adding raters had a small beneficial effect on the correlations, elevating them from five to eight points, but cumulating across weeks of observation had a much larger effect. Thus when there was a single rater, the correlations between ratings and behavior counts were as follows: 1 week of observations, .33; 4 weeks, .46; and 8 weeks, .51. When there were four raters, the correlations were: 1 week, .38; 4 weeks, .54; and 8 weeks, .59. Thus, a week's worth of observations yielded modest correlations (in the thirties) between behavior counts and ratings, but when the observations of all 8 weeks were cumulated, these correlations went up to the fifties. Moskowitz and Schwarz (1982) asked why so many weeks of observation were necessary to obtain the high correlations and then suggested two reasons:

> The base rate for the behavior is undoubtedly a major factor. The less frequently a behavior is manifested by individuals in a given setting, the longer it takes to establish reliable indexes of the rates of occurrence for each individual in the group. Furthermore, while a knowledgeable informant can take the context into consideration when forming opinions, an observer who is restricted to counting must treat variation due to context as error that will average out over many instances of the target behavior. (pp. 527–528)

When people who know the subject are used as raters, it may be important to aggregate both their ratings and the different behaviors being rated. Cheek (1982) had fraternity men rate themselves and three other members of the fraternity on several personality variables, but we shall concentrate on the one most closely linked to temperament, extraversion. Three individual extraversion items were graded: talkative-silent, sociable-reclusive, and adventurous-cautious. When both raters and items were combined, the correlations between self-reports and ratings by peers rose considerably. Thus for one item and a single rater, the correlation for extraversion was .43; for two items and two raters, the correlation was .53; and for three items and three raters, the correlation was .59. For present purposes, Cheeks' failure to separate aggregation of items from aggregation of the ratings from different raters is unfortunate, but it takes nothing away from the conclusion that must be drawn from his data: Combining ratings from different raters and aggregating individual items of behavior lead to greater validity (higher correlation between self-report and peer ratings).

The importance of summing across behaviors within a response class has also been demonstrated for energetic behavior, which is identical to our temperament of activity. Gormley and Champagne (1974) had college men come to the laboratory, where they not only answered questions about themselves (self-report) but also engaged in a series of tasks involving energy expenditure. When each task was correlated separately with the self-report, the average of these correlations was .22. When subjects' average performance across tasks was correlated with the self-report, the correlation rose to .78. A subsequent study yielded a correlation of .70 between peer ratings and the average of several observed measures of energetic activity (McGowan & Gormley, 1976).

These studies are only a sample of recent research that demonstrates the conditions under which evidence for personality traits is likely to be discovered. Different members of a response class (trait) should be assessed and then cumulated. Behavior should be assessed over time, so that momentary, nonpersonality determinants of behavior tend to cancel out. And when those who know the subjects well are used as sources of information, it is best to average the assessments of several raters. When these conditions are met, the impact of traits on behavior is likely to be documented.

FUTURE DIRECTIONS

Any crystal ball will predict that one major direction for research will be methodological, for measurement is usually the hardest problem in behavioral research. We will see studies using a variety of measures—laboratory measures, mechanical measures, naturalistic observations, structured observations, and teacher ratings in addition to the ubiquitous parental rating questionnaire. Aggregation of measures across sources of information, across situations, and across time will be a major advance in the measurement of temperament, bringing with it the realization that no quickly assembled, one-shot assessment is enough to paint a detailed meaningful picture of a child's temperament. These methodological advances should proceed more quickly if researchers do not haphazardly pick personality traits, for there simply are too many.

The future also undoubtedly holds more behavioral genetic research: applying quantitative genetic theory and methodology to the study of temperament, using the diverse measures mentioned above as well as designs other than the classical twin design. This research should resolve issues such as the contrast effect, which may reside in the behavior of fraternal twins rather than in the mind of the rater; the higher familial correlations for ratings of specific behaviors as compared to more global ratings; and the better case for differential heritability when methods other than ratings are employed. When this research is concluded, we predict that the personality traits left standing as heritable in early childhood will include emotionality, activity, and sociability.

A third direction of temperament research is likely to be in the application of recent advances in the study of environmental influences. For example, the Lerners' work on temperament-environment interactions testing the concept of goodness-of-fit will spawn research on such interactions and, especially, longitudinal research that examines such interactions developmentally. Research on environmental main effects is also needed, though the meager data currently available do not make this a blue-chip stock in the temperament futures market. Individual environment appears to be more important than family-similar environment, which means that researchers should study the environmental causes of temperamental differences among children in the same family.

What about clinical and other applications of temperament research in the future? We predict that the global construct of "difficult temperament" will lose its promise as a predictor of later problems of adjustment. However, new advances in the measurement of temperament, including multimethod and multivariate approaches and the study of temperament-environment interactions, will keep clinicians interested in temperament.

We should not expect too much too soon. Temperament is a difficult and complex field—perhaps as difficult as several "intelligences." Research on temperament and research on intelligence can be usefully compared. Intelligence research began well over 50 years ago and has been studied continuously and often intensively during this time. However, all that is known about origins is that genetics plays an important role after infancy, and little is known about the locus of environmental sources of variance. Intelligence includes many diverse abilities in addition to g, none well understood etiologically or developmentally. In contrast, the systematic study of temperament began only a little more than two decades ago, and it has been investigated in earnest by many researchers only during the past decade. There will be no general factor for temperament because it includes such diverse aspects of behavior. There is already evidence of genetic influence for some temperament traits, as well as some new ways of approaching environmental sources of variance. Unlike students of intelligence, temperament researchers have no standard measure such as the IQ test, which would produce comparable data.

Temperament research therefore suffers from the lack of comparability among studies, but the absence of a single method of measurement may benefit temperament research because multimethod, multivariate eclecticism should lead to generalizability.

Finally, we cannot resist saying, tongue in cheek, that we hope that researchers will be sociable in coming together from their diverse backgrounds, unemotional in their attempts to understand the multidisciplinary perspectives on temperament, and active in their efforts, so that progress is made EAS-ily.

References

Achenbach, T. M., & Edelbrock, C. S. Behavior problems and competencies reported by parents of normal and disturbed children aged four through sixteen. *Monographs of the Society for Research in Child Development*, 1981, *46* (whole no. 1).

Ainsworth, M. The development of infant-mother attachment. In B. Caldwell & H. Ricciutti (Eds.), *Review of child development research* (Vol. 3). Chicago: University of Chicago Press, 1973.

Ainsworth, M. Infant-mother attachment. *American Psychologist*, 1979, *34*, 932–937.

Ainsworth, M., Blehar, M., Waters, E., & Wall, S. *Patterns of attachment.* Hillsdale, N.J.: Lawrence Erlbaum Associates, 1978.

Allen, G. Within and between group variation expected in human behavioral characters. *Behavior Genetics*, 1970, *1*, 175–194.

Allport, G. W. *Pattern and growth in personality.* New York: Holt, Rinehart & Winston, 1961.

Altman, T. *The environment and social behavior.* Monterey, CA: Brooks/Cole, 1975.

Andreassi, J. L. *Psychophysiology.* New York: Oxford University Press, 1980.

Ax, A. F. The physiological differentiation between fear and anger in humans. *Psychosomatic Medicine*, 1953, *15*, 433–442.

Bates, J. E. The concept of difficult temperament. *Merrill-Palmer-Quarterly*, 1980, *26*, 299–319.

Bates, J. E., Freeland, C. B., & Lounsbury, M. L. Measurement of infant difficulty. *Child Development*, 1979, *50*, 794–803.

Battle, E., & Lacey, B. A context for hyperactivity in children over time. *Child Development*, 1972, *43*, 757–773.

Bayley, N. *Manual for the Bayley Scales of Infant Development.* New York: Psychological Corporation, 1969.

Becker, W. Consequences of different kinds of parental discipline. In M. Hoffman & C. B. Hoffman (Eds.), *Review of child development research* (Vol. 1). New York: Russell Sage Foundation, 1964.

Beckwith, L. Prediction of emotional and social behavior. In J. D. Osofsky (Ed.), *Handbook of infant development.* New York: Wiley-Interscience, 1979, 671–706.

Berberian, K. E., & Snyder, S. S. The relationship of temperament and stranger reaction for younger and older infants. *Merrill-Palmer Quarterly*, 1982, *28*, 79–94.

Block, J. *Lives through time.* Berkeley, CA: Bancroft Books, 1971.

Block, J. Some enduring and consequential structures of personality. In. A. I. Rabin, J. Arnonoff, A. M. Barclay & R. A. Zucker (Eds.), *Further explorations in personality.* New York: Wiley, 1981.

Bohlin, G., Hagekull, B., & Lindhagen, K. Dimensions of infant behavior. *Infant Behavior and Development*, 1981, *4*, 83–96.

Brady, J. V. Emotion: Some conceptual problems and psychological experiments. In M. B. Arnold (Ed.), *Feelings and emotions.* New York: Academic Press, 1970, 69–100.

Brazelton, T. B. Neonatal Behavior Assessment Scale. *Little Club Clinics in Developmental Medicine*, no. 50. London: William Heinemann Medical Books, 1973; Lippin, 1973.

Bretherton, I., O'Connell, B., & Tracy, R. *Styles of mother-infant and stranger-infant interaction: Consistencies and contrasts.* Paper presented at the International Conference on Infant Studies, New Haven, CT, 1980.

Bridges, K. Emotional development in early infancy, *Child Development,* 1932, *2,* 324–341.

Broadhurst, P. L. Determinants of emotionality in the rat. III Strain differences. *Journal of Comparative Physiology and Psychology,* 1958, *51,* 55–59.

Broadhurst, P. L. Experiments in psychogenetics: Application of biometrical genetics to the inheritance of behavior. In H. J. Eysenck (Ed.), *Experiments in personality* (Vol. 1). Psychogenetics and psychopharmacology. London: Routledge & Kegan Paul, 1960.

Broadhurst, P. L. The Maudsley reactive and nonreactive strains of rats: A survey. *Behavior Genetics,* 1975, *5,* 299–319.

Broman, S. H., Nichols, P. L., & Kennedy, W. A. *Preschool IQ: Prenatal and early development correlates.* Hillsdale, NJ: Lawrence Erlbaum Associates, 1975.

Bronson, G. W., & Pankey, W. B. On the distinction between fear and wariness. *Child Development,* 1977, *48,* 1167–1183.

Bronson, W. C. Central orientations: A study of behavior organization from childhood to adolescence. *Child Development,* 1966, *37,* 125–155.

Bronson, W. C. Adult derivatives of emotional expressiveness and reactivity control: Developmental continuities from childhood to adulthood. *Child Development,* 1967, *38,* 801–817.

Buss, A. H. *The psychology of aggression.* New York: Wiley, 1961.

Buss, A. H. The effect of harm on subsequent aggression. *Journal of Experimental Research in Personality,* 1966, *1,* 249–255.

Buss, A. H. *Self-consciousness and social anxiety.* San Francisco: Freeman, 1980.

Buss, A. H. Social rewards and personality. *Journal of Personality and Social Psychology,* 1983, *44,* 553–563.

Buss, A. H. Two kinds of shyness. In R. Schwarzer (Ed.) *Self-related cognitions in anxiety and motivation.* Hillsdale, N.J.: Lawrence Erlbaum Associates, in press.

Buss, A. H., & Plomin, R. *A temperament theory of personality development.* New York: Wiley-Interscience, 1975.

Buss, A., Plomin, R., & Willerman, L. The inheritance of temperaments. *Journal of Personality,* 1973, *41,* 513–524.

Caldwell, B. M., & Bradley, R. H. *Home observation for measurement of the environment.* Little Rock, AR: University of Arkansas at Little Rock, 1979.

Caldwell, B. M., & Herscher, L. Mother-infant interaction during the first year of life. *Merrill-Palmer Quarterly,* 1964, *10,* 119–128.

Carey, G., Goldsmith, H. H., Tellegen, A., & Gottesman, I. I. Genetics and personality inventories: The limits of replication with twin data. *Behavior Genetics,* 1978, *8,* 299–314.

Carey, W. B. A simplified method for measuring infant temperament. *Journal of Pediatrics,* 1970, *77,* 188–194.

Carey, W. B., Fox, M., & McDevitt, S. C. Temperament as a factor in early school adjustment. *Pediatrics,* 1977, *60,* 621–624.

Carey, W. B., Lipton, W. L., & Meyers, R. A. Temperament in adopted and foster babies. *Child Welfare,* 1974, *53,* 352–359.

Carey, W. B., & McDevitt, S. C. Revision of the infant temperament questionnaire. *Pediatrics,* 1978, *61,* 735–739.

Cattell, R. B., Eber, H. W., & Tatsuoka, M. M. *Handbook for the sixteen personality factor questionnaire.* Champaign, IL: IPAT, 1970.

Chamove, A. S., Eysenck, H. J., & Harlow, H. Factor analysis of rhesus social behavior. *Quarterly Journal of Experimental Psychology,* 1972, *24,* 496–504.

Cheek, J. M. Aggregation, moderator variables, and the validity of personality tests: A peer-rating study, *Journal of Personality and Social Psychology,* 1982, *43,* 1254–1269.

Cheek, J. M., & Buss, A. H. Shyness and sociability. *Journal of Personality and Social Psychology,* 1981, *41,* 330–339.

Chess, S., & Thomas, A. Infant bonding: Mystique and reality. *American Journal of Orthopsychiatry,* 1982, *52,* 211–222.

Clarke, A. M., & Clarke, A. D. B. *Early experience: Myth and evidence.* New York: The Free Press, 1976.

Clements, P., Hafer, M., & Vermillion, M. E. Psychometric, diurnal, and electrophysiological correlates of activation. *Journal of Personality and Social Psychology,* 1976, *33,* 387–394.

Cohen, D. J., Dibble, E., & Grawe, J. M. Fathers' and mothers' perceptions of children's personality. *Archives of General Psychiatry,* 1977, *34,* 480–487.

Cohen, J. *Statistical power analysis for the behavioral sciences.* New York: Academic Press, 1977.

Cohen, J., & Cohen, P. *Applied multiple regression/correlation analysis for the behavioral sciences.* New York: Halstead Press, 1975.

Conley, J. J. The hierarchy of consistency: A review and model of longitudinal findings on adult individual differences in intelligence, personality, and self-opinion. *Personality and Individual Differences,* in press.

Conners, C. K. Symptom patterns in hyperkinetic, neurotic and normal children. *Child Development,* 1970, *41,* 667–682.

Daniels, D., & Plomin, R. Origins of individual differences in infant shyness. *Developmental Psychology,* 1984, in press.

Daniels, D., & Plomin, R. *The Sibling Inventory of Differential Experience* (SIDE). University of Colorado, Boulder, 1983.

Daniels, D., Plomin, R., & Greenhalgh, J. Correlates of difficult temperament in infancy. *Child Development,* 1984, in press.

DeFries, J. C., Gervais, M. C., & Thomas, E. A. Response to 30 generations of selection for open-field activity in laboratory mice. *Behavior Genetics,* 1978, *8,* 3–13.

DeFries, J. C., Plomin, R., Vandenberg, S. G., & Kuse, A. R. Parent-offspring resemblance for cognitive abilities in the Colorado Adoption Project: Biological, adoptive and control parents and one-year-old children. *Intelligence,* 1981, *5,* 245–277.

Diamond, S. *Personality and temperament.* New York: Harper, 1957.

Dibble, E., & Cohen, D. J. Companion instruments for measuring children's competence and parental style. *Archives of General Psychiatry,* 1974, *30,* 805–815.

Dixon, L. K., & Johnson, R. C. *The roots of individuality: A survey of human behavior genetics.* Belmont, CA: Wadsworth, 1980.

Eason, R. G., & Dudley, L. M. Physiological and behavioral indicants of activation. *Psychophysiology,* 1971, *7,* 223–232.

Easterbrooks, M. A., & Lamb, M. E. The relationship between quality of mother-infant attachment and infant competence in initial encounters with peers. *Child Development,* 1979, *50,* 380–387.

Eaton, W. O. Measuring activity level with actometers: Reliability, validity, and arm length. *Child Development,* 1983, *54,* 720–726.

Ekman, R., & Friesen, W. V. *Unmasking the face.* Englewood Cliffs, NJ: Prentice-Hall, 1975.

Epstein, S. The stability of behavior II. Implications for psychological research. *American Psychologist,* 1980, *35,* 790–806.

Epstein, S. Aggregation and beyond: Some basic issues in the prediction of behavior. *Journal of Personality,* 1983, *51,* 360–392.

Eysenck, H. J. *Dimensions of personality*. London: Kegan, Trench, & Trubner, 1947.

Eysenck, H. J. *The Maudsley Personality Inventory*. London: University of London Press, 1959.

Eysenck, H. J. *The biological basis of personality*, Springfield, IL: Charles C. Thomas, 1967.

Eysenck, H. J. A biometrical-genetical analysis of impulsive and sensation seeking behavior. In M. Zuckerman (Ed.), *Biological bases of sensation seeking, impulsivity, and anxiety*. Hillsdale, NJ: Lawrence Erlbaum Associates, 1983.

Falconer, D. S. *Quantitative genetics*. New York: Ronald Press, 1960.

Feiring, C., & Lewis, M. Temperament: Sex differences and stability in vigor, activity, and persistence in the first three years of life. *Journal of Genetic Psychology*, 1980, *136*, 65–75.

Fiske, D. W., & Maddi, S. R. (Eds.). *Functions of varied experience* (Rev. ed.). Homewood, IL: Dorsey, 1961.

Floderus-Myrhed, B., Pederson, N., & Rasmuson, I. Assessment of heritability for personality, based on a short form of the Eysenck Personality Inventory: A study of 12,898 twin pairs. *Behavior Genetics*, 1980, *10*, 153–162.

Foa, U. G., & Foa, E. B. *Societal structures of the mind*. Springfield, IL: Charles C. Thomas, 1974.

Frankenhaeuser, M. Behavior and circulating catecholamines. *Brain Research*, 1971, *31*, 241–262.

Freedman, D. G. *Human infancy: An evolutionary perspective*. Hillsdale, NJ: Lawrence Erlbaum Associates, 1974.

Freedman, D. G., & Freedman, N. A. Differences in behavior between Chinese-American and European-American newborns. *Nature*, 1969, *224*, 1227.

Freedman, J. L. *Crowding and behavior*. San Francisco: Freeman, 1975.

Freeman, D. *Margaret Mead and Samoa: The making and unmaking of an anthropological myth*. Cambridge, MA: Harvard University Press, 1983.

Fulker, D. W., Eysenck, H. J., & Zuckerman, M. A genetic and environmental analysis of sensation seeking. *Journal of Research in Personality*, 1980, *14*, 261–281.

Fullard, W., McDevitt, S. C., & Carey, W. B. *Toddler Temperament Scale*. Unpublished Scale, Temple University, 1978.

Fuller, J. L., & Thompson, W. R. *Behavior genetics*. New York: John Wiley, 1960.

Fuller, J. L., & Thompson, W. R. *Foundations of behavior genetics*. St. Louis, MO: C. V. Mosby, 1978.

Garcia Coll, C., Kagan, J., & Reznick, J. S. Behavior inhibition in young children. *Child Development*, in press.

Gardner, R. A., & Gardner, B. T. Teaching sign language to a chimpanzee. *Science*, 1969, *165*, 664–672.

Goldsmith, H. H. *The objective measurement of infants*. Unpublished paper. University of Texas, 1982.

Goldsmith, H. H. Emotionality in infant twins: Longitudinal results. Abstracts of the Fourth International Congress on Twin Studies, June 28–July 1, 1983, London.

Goldsmith, H. H., & Campos, J. J. Toward a theory of infant temperament. In R. N. Emde & R. Harmon (Eds.), *The development of attachment and affiliative systems*. New York: Plenum, 1982, 161–193.(a)

Goldsmith, H. H., & Campos, J. J. Genetic influence on individual differences in emotionality. *Infant Behavior and Development*, 1982, *5*, 99.(b)

Goldsmith, H. H., & Gottesman, I. I. Origins of variation in behavioral style: A longitudinal study of temperament in young twins. *Child Development*, 1981, *52*, 91–103.

Goodall, J. *In the shadow of man*. Boston: Houghton-Mifflin, 1971.

Gormley, J. Predicting behavior from personality trait scores. *Personality and Social Psychology Bulletin*, 1983, *9*, 267–270.

Gormley, J., & Champagne, B. *Validity in personality trait ratings: A multicriteria approach*. Paper presented at Eastern Psychological Association meetings, 1974.

Graham, P., Rutter, M., & George, S. Temperamental characteristics as predictors of behavioral disorders in children. *American Journal of Orthopsychiatry*, 1973, *43*, 328–339.

Gray, J. A. Strength of the nervous system and levels of arousal: A reinterpretation. In J. A. Gray (Ed.), *Pavlov's typology*. New York: Macmillan, 1964.

Gray, J. A. *The psychology of fear and stress*. New York: McGraw-Hill, 1971.

Gray, J. A. The psychophysiological nature of introversion-extraversion: A modification of Eysenck's theory. In V. Nebylitsyn & J. A. Gray (Eds.), *Biological bases of individual behavior*. New York: Academic Press, 1972.

Gray, J. A. *The neuropsychology of anxiety and impulsivity*. Paper presented at the Meeting of the International Society for the Study of Individual Differences. London, July 7, 1983.

Guilford, J. P. *Personality*. New York: McGraw-Hill, 1959.

Guilford, J. P., & Fruchter, B. *Fundamental statistics in psychology and education* (5th ed.). New York: McGraw-Hill, 1973.

Hall, C. S. The inheritance of emotionality. *Sigma Xi Quarterly*, 1938, *26*, 17–27.

Halverson, C. F., Jr., & Post-Gordon, J. C. *The measurement of open-field activity in children: A critical analysis*. Unpublished paper, University of Georgia, 1983.

Halverson, C. F. & Waldrop, M. F. Relations between preschool activity and aspects of intellectual and social behavior at age 7½. *Journal of Developmental Psychology*, 1976, *12*, 107–112.

Hebb, D. O. Drives and the CNS (conceptual nervous system). *Psychological Review*, 1955, *62*, 243–254.

Hegvik, R. L., McDevitt, S. C., & Carey, W. B. *Longitudinal stability of temperament characteristics in the elementary school period*. Paper presented at the meeting of the International Society for the Study of Behavioral Development, Toronto, August, 1981.

Hegvik, R. L., McDevitt, S. C., & Carey, W. B. The Middle Childhood Temperament Questionnaire. *Developmental and Behavioral Pediatrics*, 1982, *3*, 197–200.

Hendrick, C., & Brown, S. R. Introversion, extraversion, and interpersonal attraction. *Journal of Personality and Social Psychology*, 1971, *20*, 31–36.

Hertzig, M. Neurologic findings in prematurely born children at school age. In D. Ricks, A. Thomas, & M. Roff (Eds.), *Life history research in psychopathology* (Vol. 3). Minneapolis: University of Minnesota Press, 1974.

Hertzog, C. Confirmatory factor analysis. In D. K. Detterman (Ed.), *Current topics in human intelligence: Research methodology*. Norwood, NJ: Ablex, 1984.

Ho, H-Z, Foch, T. T., & Plomin, R. Developmental stability of the relative influence of genes and environment on specific cognitive abilities during childhood. *Developmental Psychology*, 1980, *16*, 340–346.

Horn, J., Plomin, R., & Rosenman, R. Heritability of personality traits in adult male twins. *Behavior Genetics*, 1976, *6*, 17–30.

Hsu, C., Stigler, J., Hong, C., Soong, W., & Liang, C. The temperamental characteristics of Chinese babies. *Child Development*, in press.

Huttunen, M. O., & Nyman, G. On the continuity, change and clinical value of infant temperament in a prospective epidemiological study. In R. Porter & G. M. Collins (Eds.), *Temperamental differences in infants and young children*. London: Pitman, 1982.

Izard, C. E. (Ed.). *Measuring emotions in infants and children*. New York: Cambridge University Press, 1982.

James, W. T. Morphologic form and its relation to behavior. In C. R. Stockard (Ed.), *The *genetic and endocrine basis for differences in form and behavior.* Philadelphia: Ulster Institute, 1941, 525–643.

Jost, H., & Sontag, L. W. The genetic factor in autonomic nervous system function, *Psychosomatic Medicine,* 1944, *6,* 308–310.

Kagan, J. *Change and continuity in infancy.* New York: Wiley, 1971.

Kagan, J. Perspectives on continuity. In O. G. Brim, Jr., & J. Kagan (Eds.), *Constancy and change in human development.* Cambridge, MA: 1980.

Kagan, J. Comments on the construct of difficult temperament. *Merrill-Palmer Quarterly,* 1982, *28,* 21–24. (a)

Kagan. J. *Psychological research on the human infant: An evaluative summary.* New York: William T. Grant Foundation, 1982. (b)

Kagan, J., & Moss, H. *Birth to maturity: A study in psychological development.* New York: John Wiley & Sons, 1962.

Kaye, K. Discriminating among infants by multivariate analysis of Brazelton scores: lumping and smoothing. A. J. Sameroff (Ed.), *Organization and stability of newborn behavior: A commentary on the Brazelton Neonatal Behavior Assessment Scale.* Monographs of the Society for Research in Child Development, 1978, *43,* Nos. 5–6, pp. 60–80.

Kaufman, I. C., & Rosenblum, L. A. Depression in infant monkeys separated from their mothers. *Science,* 1967, *155,* 1030–1031.

Kellogg, W. N., & Kellogg, L. A. *The ape and the child.* New York: McGraw-Hill, 1933.

Kelly, E. L. Consistency of the adult personality. *American Psychologist,* 1955, *10,* 659–681.

Keogh, B. K. Children's temperament and teachers' decisions. In R. Porter & G. M. Collins (Eds.), *Temperamental differences in infants and young children.* London: Pitman, 1982.

Klaus, M., & Kennell, J. *Maternal-infant bonding.* St. Louis: C. V. Mosby, 1977.

Kopp, C. B., & Parmelee, A. H. Prenatal and perinatal influences on infant behavior. In J. D. Osofsky (Ed.), *Handbook of infant development.* New York: Wiley, 1979.

Korner, A. F., Hutchinson, C. A., Koperski, J. A., Kraemer, H. C., & Schneider, P. A. Stability of individual differences of neonatal motor and crying patterns. *Child Development,* 1981, *52,* 83–90.

Lacey, J. I. The evaluation of autonomic responses: Toward a general solution. *Annals of the New York Academy of Science,* 1956, *67,* 123–163.

Lacey, J. I. Somatic response patterning and stress: Some revisions of activation theory. In M. H. Appley & R. Trumbull (Eds.), *Psychological Stress.* New York: Appleton-Century-Crofts, 1967, pp. 15–37.

Leenders, F. H. R. *Maternal instruction styles with 3- and 4-year old children as a function of maternal attitudinal variables and child characteristics as behavioral style and cognitive variables.* Paper presented at the Sixth Biennial Meeting of the International Society for the Study of Behavioral Development, Toronto, August 17–21, 1981.

Lerner, J. V. The import of temperament for psychosocial functioning: Tests of a "goodness of fit" model. *Merrill-Palmer,* in press.

Lerner, J. V., & Lerner, R. M. *Inventory of the New York Longitudinal Study.* Unpublished document, Pennsylvania State University, 1983.

Lerner, J. V., & Lerner, R. M. Temperament and adaptation across life: Theoretical and empirical issues. In P. B. Baltes, & O. G. Brim, (Eds.), *Life-span development and behavior* (Vol. 5). New York: Academic Press, 1983.

Lerner, J. V., Lerner, R. M., & Zabski, S. Temperament and elementary school children's actual and rated academic abilities: A test of a "goodness of fit" model. *Journal of Child Psychology and Psychiatry and Applied Disciplines,* in press.

Lerner, R. M., Palermo, M., Spiro, A., & Nesselroade, J. R. Assessing the dimensions of temperamental individuality across the life-span: The Dimensions of Temperament Survey (DOTS). *Child Development*, 1982, *53*, 149–159.

Lieberman, A. F. Preschoolers' competence with a peer: Relations with attachment and peer experience. *Child Development*, 1977, *48*, 1277–1287.

Lindsley, D. B. Psychophysiology and motivation. In M. R. Jones (Ed.), *Nebraska Symposium on Motivation* (Vol. 5). Lincoln: University of Nebraska Press, 1957.

Lindsley, D. B. Common factors in sensory deprivation, sensory distortion and sensory overload. In P. Solomon, P. E. Kubzanski, P. H. Leiderman, J. H. Trumball, & D. Wexler (Eds.), *Sensory deprivation*. Cambridge, MA.: Harvard University Press, 1961.

Lipton, E. L., & Steinschneider, A. Studies on the psychophysiology of infancy. *Merrill-Palmer Quarterly*, 1964, *10*, 102–117.

Lipton, E. L., Steinschneider, A., & Richmond, J. B. Autonomic function in the neonate: 4. Individual differences in cardiac reactivity. *Psychosomatic Medicine*, 1961, *23*, 472–484.

Loehlin, J. C. Are CPI scales differentially heritable: How good is the evidence? *Behavior Genetics*, 1978, *8*, 381–382.

Loehlin, J. C. Are personality traits differentially heritable? *Behavior Genetics*, 1982, *12*, 417–428.

Loehlin, J. C., & Nichols, R. C. *Heredity, environment and personality*. Austin: University of Texas Press, 1976.

Lynn, R. *Attention, arousal, and the orientation reaction*. Oxford: Pergamon Press, 1966.

Lyon, M. E., & Plomin, R. The measurement of temperament using parental ratings. *Journal of Child Psychology and Psychiatry*, 1981, *22*, 47–53.

Lytton, H. Do parents create, or respond to, differences in twins? *Developmental Psychology*, 1977, *13*, 456–459.

Lytton, H., Martin, N. G., & Eaves, L. Environmental and genetical causes of variation in ethological aspects of behavior in two-year-old boys. *Social Biology*, 1977, *24*, 200–211.

Maccoby, E. E., & Jacklin, C. N. *The psychology of sex differences*. Stanford: Stanford University Press, 1974.

Maddi, S. R. *Personality theories* (Revised Ed.). Homewood, IL.: Dorsey, 1972.

Main, M. Exploration, play, and cognitive functioning as related to child-mother attachment. *Dissertation Abstracts International*, 1974, *34*, 5718B.

Main, M., & Weston, D. The quality of the toddler's relationship to mother and to father: Related to conflict behavior and readiness to establish new relationships. *Child Development*, 1981, *52*, 922–940.

Malhotra, S., Randhawa, A., & Malhotra, A. Children's temperament: Its relationship with emotional disorders of childhood and factorial validity. Submitted for publication, 1983.

Mangan, G. *The biology of human conduct: East-West models of temperament and personality*. Oxford: Pergamon Press, 1982.

Mason, W. A. Motivational factors in psychosocial development, In U. J. Arnold & M. M. Page (Eds.), *Nebraska Symposium on Motivation*. Lincoln: University of Nebraska Press, 1970, 35–67.

Masters, W. H., & Johnson, V. E. *Human sexual responses*. Boston: Little, Brown, 1966.

Matas, L., Arend, R. & Sroufe, L. Continuity of adaption in the second year: The relationship between quality of attachment and later competence. *Child Development*, 1978, *49*, 547–556.

Matheny, A. P. Bayley's Infant Behavior Record: Behavioral components and twin analyses. *Child Development*, 1980, *51*, 1157–1167.

Matheny, A. P. A longitudinal twin study of stability of components from Bayley's Infant Behavioral Record. *Child Development*, 1983, *54*. 356–360.

Matheny, A. P., Dolan, A. B. Persons, situations and time: A genetic view of behavioral change in children. *Journal of Personality and Social Psychology,* 1975, *32,* 1106–1110.

Matheny, A. P., & Dolan, A. B. A twin study of personality and temperament during middle childhood. *Journal of Research in Personality,* 1980, *14,* 224–234.

Matheny, A. P., Dolan, A. B., & Wilson, R. S. Within-pair similarity on Bayley's Infant Behavior Record. *Journal of Genetic Psychology,* 1976, *128,* 263–270.

Matheny, A. P., & Wilson, R. S. Developmental tasks and ratings scales for the laboratory assessment of infant temperament. *JSAS Catalog of Selected Documents in Psychology,* 1981, *11,* 81–82 (Ms. No. 2367).

Matheny, A. P., Wilson, R. S., Dolan, A. B., & Krantz, J. Z. Behavior contrasts in twinships: Stability and patterns of differences in childhood. *Child Development,* 1981, *52,* 579–588.

McDevitt, S. *A longitudinal assessment of continuity and stability in temperamental characteristics from infancy to early childhood.* Unpublished Doctoral Dissertation, Temple University, 1976.

McDevitt, S. C., & Carey, W. B. The measurement of temperament in 3–7 year old children. *Journal of Child Psychology and Psychiatry,* 1978, *19,* 245–253.

McDevitt, S. C., & Carey, W. B. Stability of ratings vs. perceptions of temperament from early infancy to 1–3 years. *American Journal of Orthopsychiatry,* 1981, *51,* 342–345.

McGowan, J., & Gormley, J. Validation of personality traits: A multicriteria approach. *Journal of Personality and Social Psychology,* 1976, *34,* 791–795.

McNeil, T. F., & Persson-Blennow, I. Temperament questionnaires in clinical research. In R. Porter & G. M. Collins (Eds.), *Temperamental differences in infants and young children.* London: Pitman, 1982.

Mead, M. *Coming of age in Samoa.* New York: Mentor Books, 1949.

Meshkova, T. A., & Ravich-Scherbo, I. V. In H. D. Schmidt & G. Tembrock (Eds.), *Evolution and determination of animal and human behavior.* Berlin: VEB Detuchen Verlag der Wissenschaften, 1981.

Moos, R. H. *Preliminary manual for Family Environment Scale, Work Environment Scale, and Group Environment Scale.* Palo Alto, CA: Consulting Psychologists, 1974.

Moskowitz, D. S., & Schwarz, J. C. Validity comparison of behavior counts and ratings by knowledgeable informants. *Journal of Personality and Social Psychology,* 1982, *42,* 518–528.

Moss, H. A., & Susman, E. J. Longitudinal study of personality development. In O. G. Brim, Jr. & J. Kagan (Eds.), *Constancy and change in human development.* Cambridge, MA: Harvard University Press, 1980.

Nebylitsyn, V. D. The relationship between sensitivity and strength of the nervous system. B. M. Teplov (Ed.), *Typological features of higher nervous activity in man* (Vol. 1). Moscow: Academy of Pedagogy, 1956.

Nebylitsyn, V. D. *Fundamental properties of the human nervous system.* Moscow: Proveschcheniye, 1966. English translation, G. L. Mangan (Ed.). New York: Plenum, 1972.

Nichols, R. C., & Schnell, R. R. Factor scales for the California Psychological Inventory. *Journal of Consulting Psychology,* 1963, *27,* 228–235.

O'Connor, M., Foch, T., Sherry, T., & Plomin, R. A twin study of specific behavioral problems of socialization as viewed by parents. *Journal of Abnormal Child Psychology,* 1980, *8,* 189–199.

Pastor, D. L. The quality of mother-infant attachment and its relationship to toddler's initial sociability with peers. *Developmental Psychology,* 1981, *17,* 326–335.

Pavlov, I. P. *Conditioned reflexes: An investigation of the physiological activity of the cerebral cortex.* Translated and edited by G. V. Anrep. Oxford: Oxford University Press, 1927.

Pavlov, I. P. *Lectures on conditioned reflexes* (Vol. 1) (W. H. Grant, Ed. and trans.) New York: International Publishers, 1928.

Persson-Blennow, I., & McNeil, T. F. Questionnaires for measurement of temperament in one- and two-year-old children: Development and standardization. *Journal of Child Psychology, Psychiatry, and Allied Disciplines,* 1980, *21,* 37–46.

Plomin, R. *A temperament theory of personality development: Parent-child interactions.* Unpublished doctoral dissertation, University of Texas, 1974.

Plomin, R. A twin and family study of personality in young children. *Journal of Psychology,* 1976, *94,* 233–235.(a)

Plomin, R. Extraversion: Sociability and impulsivity. *Journal of Personality Assessment,* 1976, *40,* 24–30. (b)

Plomin, R. Heredity and temperament: A comparison of twin data for self-report questionnaires, parental ratings, and objectively assessed behavior. In L. Gedda, P. Parisi, & W. E. Nance (Eds.), *Progress in clinical and biological research* (Vol. 69B). *Twin research 3, Part B, Intelligence, personality, and development.* New York: Alan R. Liss, 1981. (a)

Plomin, R. Ethnological behavioral genetics and development. In K. Immelman, G. W. Barlow, L. Petrinovich, & M. Main (Eds.), *Behavioral development: The Bielefeld Interdisciplinary Project.* Cambridge: Cambridge University Press, 1981. (b)

Plomin, R. Developmental behavioral genetics. *Child Development,* 1983, *54,* 253–259.

Plomin, R., & Daniels, D. Temperament interactions. *Merrill-Palmer Quarterly,* 1984, in press.

Plomin, R., & DeFries, J. C. Multivariate behavioral genetics and development: Twin studies. In L. Gedda, P. Parisi and W. E. Nance (Eds.), *Progress in clinical and biological research* (Vol. 69B), *Twin Research 3, Part B, Intelligence, personality and development.* New York: Alan R. Liss, 1981.

Plomin, R., & DeFries, J. C. The Colorado Adoption Project. *Child Development.* 1983, *54,* 276–289.

Plomin, R., DeFries, J. C., & Loehlin, J. C. Genotype-environment interaction and correlation in the analysis of human behavior. *Psychological Bulletin,* 1977, *84,* 309–322.

Plomin, R., DeFries, J. C. & McClearn, G. E. *Behavioral genetics: A primer.* San Francisco: Freeman, 1980.

Plomin, R., & Deitrich, R. A. Neuropharmacogenetics and behavioral genetics. *Behavior Genetics,* 1982, *12,* 111–112.

Plomin, R., & Foch, T. T. A twin study of objectively assessed personality in childhood. *Journal of Personality and Social Psychology,* 1980, *39,* 680–688.

Plomin, R., & Rowe, D. C. A twin study of temperament in young children. *Journal of Psychology,* 1977, *97,* 107–113.

Plomin, R., & Rowe, D. C. Genetic and environmental etiology of social behavior in infancy. *Developmental Psychology,* 1979, *15,* 62–72.

Plutchik, R. *Emotion: A psychoevolutionary synthesis.* New York: Harper & Row, 1980.

Reppucci, C. M. *Hereditary influences upon distribution of attention in infancy.* Unpublished doctoral dissertation, Harvard University, 1968.

Richards, T. W., & Simons, M. P. The Fels Child Behavior Scales. *Genetic Psychology Monographs,* 1941, *24,* 259–309.

Rose, R. J., Miller, J. Z., Pogue-Geile, M. F., & Cardwell, G. F. Twin-family studies of common fears and phobias. In L. Gedda, P. Parisi, & W. E. Nance (Eds.), *Twin research 3: Intelligence, personality and development.* New York: A. R. Liss, 1981.

Rothbart, M. K. Measurement of temperament in infancy. *Child Development,* 1981, *52,* 569–578.

Rothbart, M. K., & Derryberry, D. Development of individual differences in temperament.

In M. E. Lamb & A. L. Brown (Eds.), *Advances in Developmental Psychology* (Vol. 1). Hillsdale, NJ: Lawrence Erlbaum Associates, 1981.

Rowe, D. C. A biometrical analysis of perception of family environment: A study of twin and singleton sibling kinships. *Child Development*, 1983, *54*, 416–423.

Rowe, D. C., & Plomin, R. Temperament in early childhood. *Journal of Personality Assessment*, 1977, *41*, 150–156.

Rowe, D. C., & Plomin, R. The importance of nonshared (E1) environmental influences in behavioral development. *Developmental Psychology*, 1981, *17*, 517–531.

Royce, J. R. The conceptual framework for a multi-factor theory of individuality. In J. R. Royce (Ed.), *Multivariate analysis and psychological theory*. New York: Academic Press, 1973.

Rundquist, E. A. The inheritance of spontaneous activity in rats. *Journal of Comparative Psychology*, 1933, *16*, 415–438.

Rusalov, V. M. *Biological principles of individual differences in physiology*. Moscow: Hayka, 1979.

Rushton, J. P., Brainerd, C. J. & Pressley, M. Behavioral development and construct validity: The principle of aggregation. *Psychology Bulletin*, 1983, *94*, 18–38.

Rutter, M. A child's life. In R. Lewin (Ed.), *Child alive*. London: Temple Smith, 1975.

Sameroff, A. J. Summary and conclusions: the future of newborn assessment. In A. J. Sameroff (Ed.), Organization and stability of newborn behavior: A commentary on the Brazelton Neonatal Behavior Assessment Scale. *Monographs of the Society for Research in Child Development*, 1978, *43*, Nos. 5–6, pp. 102–117.

Sameroff, A., & Chandler, M. Reproductive risk and the continuum of caretaking casualty. In F. Horowitz (Ed.), *Review of child development research* IV. Chicago: University of Chicago Press, 1975.

Sameroff, A. J., Krafchuk, E. E., & Bakow, H. A. Issues in grouping items from the neonatal behavioral assessment scale. A. J. Sameroff (Ed.), Organization and stability of newborn behavior: A commentary on the Brazelton Neonatal Behavior Assessment Scale. *Monographs of the Society for Research in Child Development*, 1978, *43*, Nos. 5–6, pp. 46–59.

Scarr, S. The origins of individual differences in adjective check list scores. *Journal of Consulting Psychology*, 1966, *30*, 354–357.

Scarr, S. Environmental bias in twin studies. *Eugenics Quarterly*, 1968, *15*, 34–40.

Scarr, S. Social introversion-extraversion as a heritable response. *Child Development*, 1969, *40*, 823–832.

Scarr, S., & Carter-Saltzman, L. Twin method: Defense of a critical assumption. *Behavior Genetics*, 1979, *9*, 527–542.

Scarr, S., & McCartney, K. How people make their own environments: A theory of genotype-environment correlations. *Child Development*, 1983, *54*, 424–435.

Schachter, J. Pain, fear, and anger in hypertensives and normotensives. *Psychosomatic Medicine*, 1957, *19*, 17–19.

Schachter, S. *The psychology of affiliation*. Stanford: Stanford University Press, 1959.

Schaefer, E. S. Converging conceptual models for maternal behavior and for child behavior. In J. C. Glidewell, Ed., *Parental attitudes and child behavior*. Springfield, IL: Thomas, 1961.

Schaefer, E. S., & Bayley, N. Maternal behavior, child behavior, and their intercorrelations from infancy through adolescence. *Monographs of the Society for Research in Child Development*, 1963, *28*, whole number 3.

Scholom, A., Zucker, R. A., & Stollak, G. E. Relating early child adjustment to infant and parent temperament. *Journal of Abnormal Child Psychology*, 1979, *7*, 297–308.

Scott, J. P., & Fuller, J. L. *Genetics and the social behavior of the dog*. Chicago: University of Chicago Press, 1965.

Sears, R. R., Maccoby, E., & Levin, H. *Patterns of childrearing*. Evanston, IL: Row & Peterson, 1957.

Seifer, R. *The structure of infant temperament: An examination of the Infant Temperament Questionnaire*. Paper presented at the Fiftieth Biennial meeting of the Society for Research in Child Development, Detroit, April 22, 1983.

Sheldon, W. *The varieties of temperament: A psychology of constitutional differences*. New York: Harper, 1942.

Slivken, K. *Prior expectancies and introversion-extraversion*. Unpublished doctoral dissertation. University of Texas, 1983.

Sroufe, L. A. Socioemotional development. In J. D. Osofsky (Ed.), *Handbook of infant development*. New York: John Wiley, 1979.

Sroufe, L. A. Issues of temperament and attachment. *American Journal of Orthopsychiatry*, 1982, *52*, 743–746.

Sroufe, L. Infant-caregiver attachment and patterns of adaptation in the preschool: The roots of maladaption and competence. In M. Perlmutter (Ed.), *Minnesota Symposium in Child Psychology* (Vol. 16). Hillsdale, NJ: Lawrence Erlbaum Associates, in press.

Stevenson-Hinde, J., Stillwell-Barnes, R., & Zung, M. Subjective assessment of rhesus monkeys over four successive years. *Primates*, 1980, *21*, 66–82.

Strauss, M. E., & Rourke, D. L. VI. A multivariate analysis of the neonatal behavioral assessment scale in several samples. A. J. Sameroff (Ed.), Organization and stability of newborn behavior: A commentary on the Brazelton Neonatal Behavior Assessment Scale. *Monographs of the Society for Research in Child Development*, 1978, *43*, Nos. 5–6, pp. 81–91.

Strelau, J. *Problems and methods of investigation into types of nervous system in man*. Wroclaw-Warszawa: Ossolineum, 1965.

Strelau, J. Pavlov's nervous system typology and beyond. In A. Gale & J. A. Edwards (Eds.), *Physiological correlates of human behavior* (Vol. 3). New York: Academic Press, 1983. (a)

Strelau, J. *Temperament-personality-activity*. New York: Academic Press, 1983. (b)

Sullivan, J. W., Pannabecker, B. J., & Horowitz, F. D. *Continuity of infant temperament from birth to 6 months of age*. Paper presented at the Temperament Conference, Salem, MA, October 28, 1982.

Suomi, S. J. *Consequences of differences in reactivity to stress*. Paper given at Temperament Conference, Salem, Massachusetts, October 28, 1982.

Super, C. M., & Harkness, S. Figure, ground and Gestalt: The cultural context of the active individual. In R. M. Lerner & N. A. Busch-Rossnagel (Eds.) *Individuals as producers of their development*. New York: Academic Press, 1981.

Tennes, K., Downey, K., & Vernadakis, A. Urinary cortisol excretion rates and anxiety in normal one-year-old infants. *Psychosomatic Medicine*, 1977, *39, 3*, 178–187.

Teplov, B. M. Problems in the study of general types of higher nervous activity in man and animals. B. M. Teplov (Ed.), *Typological features of higher nervous activity in man* (Vol. 1). Moscow: Academy of Pedagogy, 1956.

Thayer, R. E. Measurement of activation through self-report. *Psychological Reports*, 1967, *20*, 663–678.

Thayer, R. E. Factor analytic and reliability studies on the activation-deactivation adjective check list. *Psychological Reports*, 1978, *42*, 747–756. (a)

Thayer, R. E. Toward a psychological theory of multidimensional activation (arousal). *Motivation and Emotion*, 1978, *2*, 1–34. (b)

Thomas, A., Birch, H. G., Chess, S., & Robbins, L. C. Individuality in responses of children to similar environmental situations. *American Journal of Psychiatry*, 1961, *2*, 236–245.

Thomas, A., & Chess, S. *Temperament and development*. New York: Bruner/Mazel, 1977.

Thomas, A., & Chess, S. *The dynamics of psychological development*. New York: Bruner/Mazel, 1980.

Thomas, A., & Chess, S. Temperament and follow-up to adulthood. In R. Porter & G. M. Collins (Eds.), *Temperamental differences in infants and young children*. London: Pitman, 1982.

Thomas, A., Chess, S., & Birch, H. *Temperament and behavior disorders in children*. New York: University Press, 1968.

Thomas, A., Chess, S., Birch, H., Hertzig, M., & Korn, S. *Behavioral individuality in early childhood*. New York: New York University Press, 1963.

Thompson, R. A., & Lamb, M. E. Security of attachment and stranger sociability in infancy. *Developmental Psychology*, 1983, *19*, 184–191.

Thompson, W. R. The inheritance of behavior: Behavioral differences in fifteen mouse strains. *Canadian Journal of Psychology*, 1953, *7*, 145–155.

Torgersen, A. M. *Temperamental differences in infants: Their cause as shown through twin studies*. Unpublished doctoral dissertation, University of Oslo, Norway, 1973.

Torgersen, A. M. Influence of genetic factors on temperament development in early childhood. In R. Porter & G. M. Collins (Eds.), *Temperamental differences in infants and young children*. London: Pitman, 1982.

Vale, J. R. *Genes, environment and behavior: An interactionist approach*. New York: Harper & Row, 1980.

Van den Daele, L. Infant reactivity to redundant proprioceptive and auditory stimulation: A twin study. *Journal of Psychology*, 1971, *78*, 269–276.

Van der Meulen, B. F., & Smrkovsy, M. *Factor analysis of Bayley's Infant Behavior Record*. Paper presented at the International Conference on Infant Studies, Austin, TX, 1982.

Vaughn, B., Deinard, A., & Egeland, B. Measuring temperament in pediatric practice. *Journal of Pediatrics*, 1980, *96*, 510–518.

de Waal, F. *Chimpanzee politics*. New York: Harper & Row, 1982.

Wachs, T. D., & Gruen, G. E. *Early experience and human development*. New York: Plenum, 1982.

Waters, E., Wippman, J., & Sroufe, L. A. Attachment, positive affect, and competence in the peer group: Two studies in construct validation. *Child Development*, 1979, *50*, 821–829.

Wenger, M. A. The measurement of individual differences in autonomic balance. *Psychosomatic Medicine*, 1941, *3*, 427–434.

Wenger, M. A. Studies of autonomic balance: A summary. *Psychophysiology*, 1966, *2*, 173–186.

Wenger, M. A., Engel, B. T., & Clem, T. L. Studies of autonomic response patterns: Rationale and methods. *Behavioral Science*, 1957, *2*, 216–221.

Wenger, M. A., Clemens, T. L., Coleman, D. R., Cullen, T., & Engel, B. T. Autonomic response specificity. *Psychosomatic Medicine*, 1961, *23*, 185–193.

Wenger, M. A., Jones, F. N., & Jones, M. *Physiological psychology*. New York: Holt, 1956.

Werry, J. S., & Sprague, R. L. Hyperactivity. In C. Costello, (Ed.), *Symptoms of psychopathology: A handbook*. New York: Wiley, 1970.

Willerman, L. Activity level and hyperactivity in twins. *Child Development*, 1973, *44*, 288–293.

Wilson, R. S. Sychronies in mental development: An epigenetic perspective. *Science*, 1978, *202*, 939–948.

Wilson, A., Brown, A., Matheny, A. Emergence and persistence of behavioral differences in twins. *Child Development*, 1971, *42*, 1381–1398.

Yerkes, R. M. *Chimpanzees*. New Haven, CT: Yale University Press, 1943.

Zajonc, R. B. Social facilitation. *Science*, 1965, *149*, 269–274.

Zonderman, A. B. Differential heritability and consistency: A reanalysis of the National Merit Scholarship Qualifying Test (NMSQT) California Psychological Inventory (CPI) data. *Behavior Genetics*, 1982, *12*, 193–208.

Zuckerman, M. Theoretical formulations. In J. P. Zubeck (Ed.), *Sensory deprivation: Fifteen years of research*. New York: Appleton-Century-Crofts, 1969.

Zuckerman, M. *Sensation seeking: Beyond the optimal level of arousal*. Hillsdale, NJ: Lawrence Erlbaum Associates, 1979.

Zuckerman, M., Ballenger, J. C., Jimerson, D. C., Murphy, D. L., & Post, R. M. A correlational test in humans of the biological models of sensation seeking, impulsivity, and anxiety. In M. Zuckerman (Ed.), *Biological bases of sensation seeking, impulsivity, & anxiety*. Hillsdale, NJ: Lawrence Erlbaum Associates, 1983.

Author Index

Subject Index